HTML5 Canvas

From Noob to Ninja

(edition numero first)

Copyright © 2016 Kirupa Chinnathambi

All rights reserved.

ISBN-13: 978-1523978090

ISBN-10: 1523978090

Dedicated to Meena – my awesome wife...

…who has tirelessly supported me in my childhood dream of one day writing a book about the canvas!

Table of Contents

CHAPTER 0: THE INTRODUCTION 6

CHAPTER 1: HELLO, WORLD! 10

CHAPTER 2: GETTING STARTED WITH THE CANVAS 16

PART I: DRAWING

CHAPTER 3: DRAWING LINES (AKA THE BASICS) 30

CHAPTER 4: DRAWING BEZIÉR CURVES 44

OUR STARTING POINT – SAVE FOR LATER! 52

CHAPTER 5: DRAWING MULTIPLE THINGS 54

CHAPTER 6: DRAWING RECTANGLES (AND SQUARES) 64

CHAPTER 7: DRAWING TRIANGLES 72

CHAPTER 8: DRAWING CIRCLES 82

CHAPTER 9: MODIFYING HOW CORNERS LOOK 92

CHAPTER 10: WORKING WITH COLORS 98

CHAPTER 11: DRAWING TEXT 120

CHAPTER 12: DRAWING IMAGES 130

CHAPTER 13: TRANSFORMATIONS 142

CHAPTER 14: STRUCTURING YOUR DRAWING CODE 156

PART II: ANIMATION

CHAPTER 15: CREATING ANIMATIONS 168

CHAPTER 16: ANIMATING WITH REQUESTANIMATIONFRAME 186

CHAPTER 16: ANIMATING MANY THINGS 194

CHAPTER 16: CREATING SPRITE ANIMATIONS 224

CHAPTER 18: CREATING MOTION TRAILS 238

PART III: INTERACTIVITY

CHAPTER 19: WORKING WITH THE MOUSE 258

CHAPTER 20: FOLLOW THE MOUSE CURSOR 268

CHAPTER 20: MOUSE FOLLOW WITH EASE 282

CHAPTER 21: WORKING WITH THE KEYBOARD 294

CHAPTER 22: USING THE ARROW KEYS TO MOVE THINGS AROUND 306

CHAPTER 23: CONCLUSION 320

Chapter 0: The Introduction

At one point, the web was made up documents, gray background colors, and lot of text styled in Times New Roman:

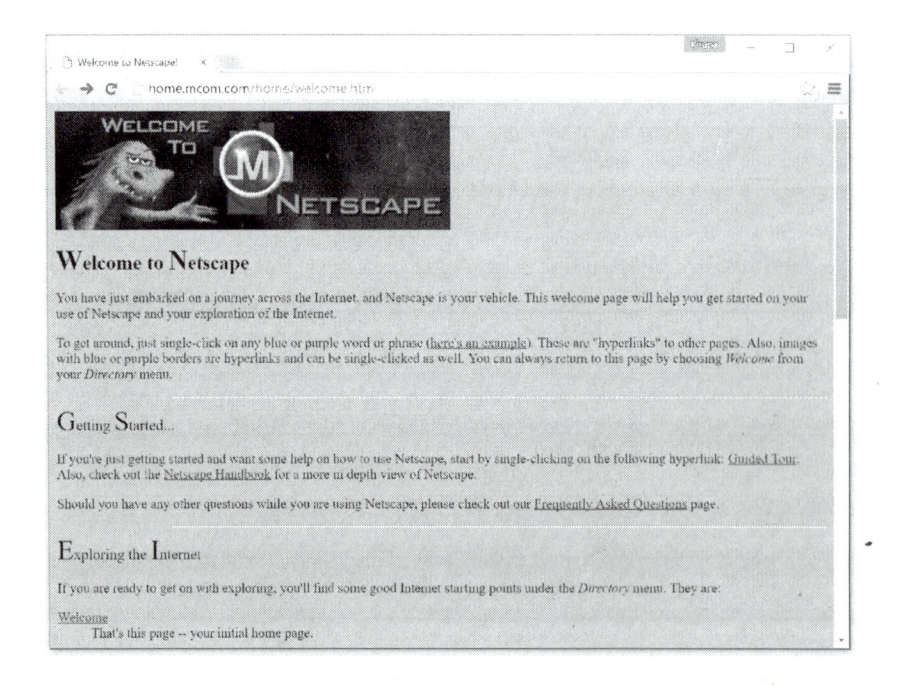

That was then. Things are different today. Nowadays, you have web applications that compete with the best apps on your desktop and mobile devices for how nice they look and feel. You have games that run smoothly in your browser without any hiccups. You can manipulate large amounts of data and visualize information like you never could before. You can do a whole lot more using your browser than you could back then, and all of this is possible thanks to some new and improved web technologies. One of those new technologies is the topic of this book, the **canvas**.

Before the `canvas` came in the picture, if you wanted to do anything visually complex and interactive in your browser, you only had two options. You could fiddle with the DOM and all of the memory and performance overhead involved. Or, you could rely on a 3rd party plug-in like Adobe Flash. Both of these options were great for a time, but to really push the boundaries (especially on your mobile devices), you needed a way to draw and manipulate pixels directly. That is where the `canvas` element comes in. On the surface, the `canvas` literally looks like a blank sheet of paper that you can directly draw into:

As you dig deeper, you'll find that your `canvas` is actually **so much more**:

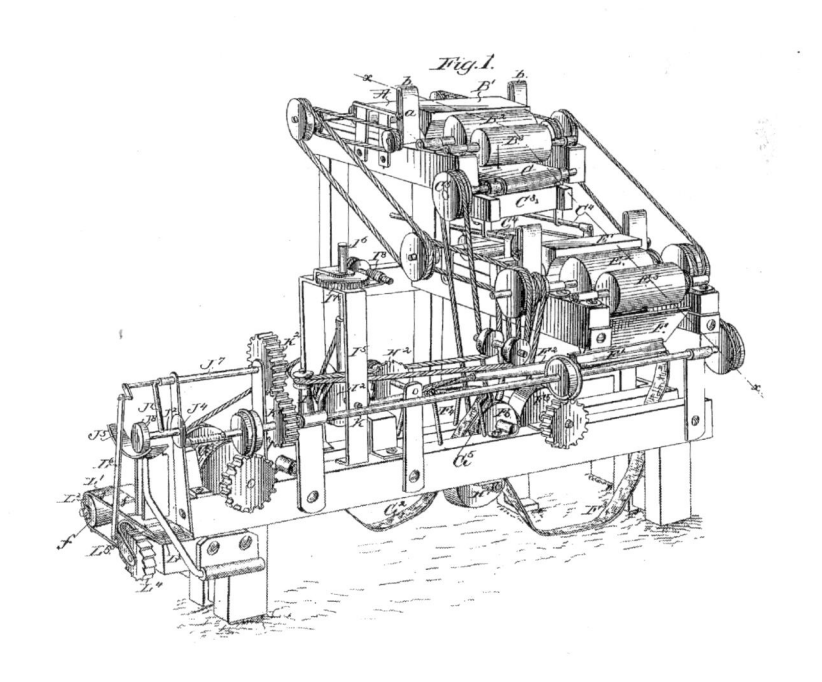

To make sense of all that the canvas offers, that's where this book comes in. We start from the very beginning and look at the canvas as if it were the first time any of us are seeing it. From there, we gradually go deeper into all the functionality the canvas provides for drawing, animation, and interactivity. Along the way, we will take many detours, scenic routes, heroic falls, and the (occasional) backtracking from a dead-end to ensure that we don't miss anything important.

Who is this book for?

This book is primarily aimed at those of us who think in terms of UI elements, pixels, and shapes...and less so in terms of numbers, graphs, trees, and code. You'll find that almost everything is explained visually with a great deal of time invested in explaining concepts using English before diving into the code. This doesn't mean that if you are a seasoned programmer, you should put this book down. It also doesn't mean that if you only know Photoshop and have no working knowledge of web development, you'll be successful in learning about the canvas.

To get the most out of this book, you need these two things:

1. A wicked sense of humor

2. Basic JavaScript knowledge

If you are not sure if this describes you, shuffle (or push / click / flick / scroll) through the pages in this book and see how you feel after glancing through some of the pages. I am fairly confident that everything you see should make sense, but if it doesn't, then I encourage you to take a short break and learn the basics of working in JavaScript first. There are a lot of great books and online tutorials out there (some even written by me!), so you should be up and running very quickly. After that, you will probably have a much better time with this book.

What Special Tools Do I Need?

Absolutely nothing! Everything we do will revolve around writing some HTML and JavaScript. A basic text editor like Notepad is totally fine, but if you were to invest in a more feature-filled code editor like Atom, Visual Studio Code, Sublime Text, etc., that's totally cool as well.

Thanks!

Before I wrap things up and send you off to Chapter 1, I just want to say "**THANK YOU!!!**" for giving this book a shot. I know you have a lot of options when it comes to learning how to work with the canvas, so I'm just happy that you chose to invest your time and money in this book.

And with that, it's time to get started!

Cheers,

[signature: Kirupa]

Kirupa ☺

Contacting Me / Getting Help

If you ever get stuck at any point, the easiest way to quickly get help is to post on the Forums: http://forum.kirupa.com.

If you would like to contact me for any reason, send e-mail to kirupa@kirupa.com, tweet to @kirupa, or message me on Facebook (facebook.com/kirupa). I love hearing from readers like you, and I make it a point to personally respond to every message I receive.

Chapter 1: Hello, World!

Did you know that you have a choice in how you can get things to display in your browser? Well...you do! The most common approach for getting content to display on your screen is by working with DOM elements. This is where you (and 99% of the entire world) create HTML, CSS, and JavaScript and have elements appear magically. The other approach uses the `canvas` element. With the `canvas`, you manually specify exactly what you want drawn and displayed on your screen. Both of these approaches have their uses. For the kinds of visually complex applications you will be creating, knowing when to use which is a good thing for you to be aware of.

To help you with this, let's take a step back. In fact, let's take many steps back and look at how our two approaches map to how your browser translates what you want into something that gets displayed. Core to this translation are two modes called **Retained Mode** and **Immediate Mode**. While it may not seem like it right now, understanding the details of both of these modes will help you know when to rely on the DOM APIs and when to use `canvas` to display visuals on the screen. This knowledge will also give you a good idea of what to expect with the `canvas` for the rest of this book!

Retained Mode (DOM)

In a retained mode system, the way you get things to display on the screen is by sending your hopes, dreams, and desires to your browser's Graphics API. This API, much like Santa Claus, gives you whatever you ask for.

The following diagram roughly describes the division of labor between you, the Graphics API, and your browser:

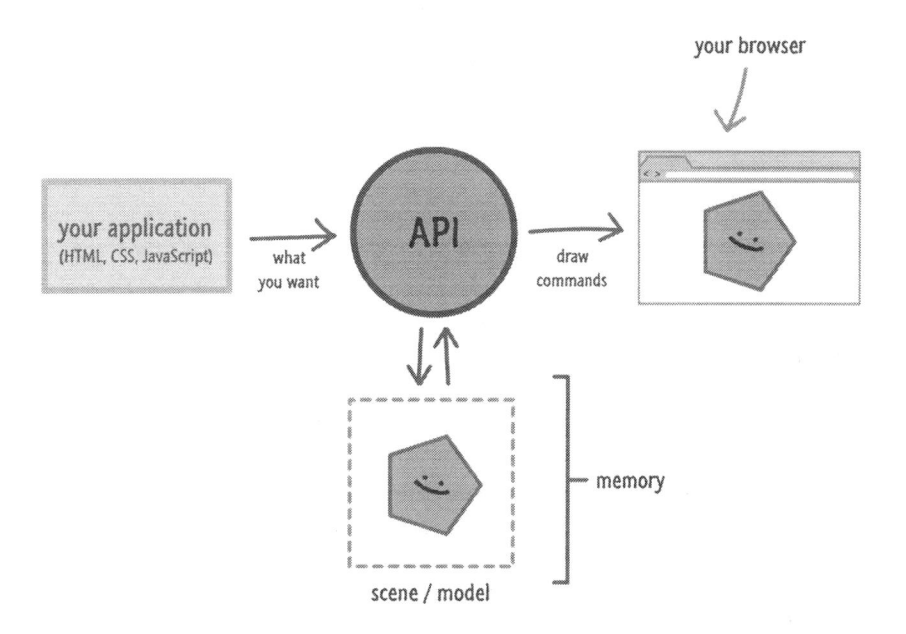

The yellow box represents the HTML, CSS, and JavaScript that makes up your application. While you may not have thought about your markup and code in quite this way, almost everything you specify is nothing more than a drawing instruction that tells your browser what to display on the screen.

This translation between your raw markup and code to something visual is handled by your browser's Graphics API. This API takes what you specify and creates an in-memory model (often referred to as a scene, object list or display list) of what the final output should look like. Once it creates this model, the final step is to translate the model into the arcane draw commands that your browser understands.

All of this happens very seamlessly behind the scenes. You simply define your application. The details of getting what you defined into something you can see is automatically handled for you.

Immediate Mode (Canvas)

Contrasting the gentle comforts of a retained mode system is the immediate mode one where...well, let's just look at the diagram first:

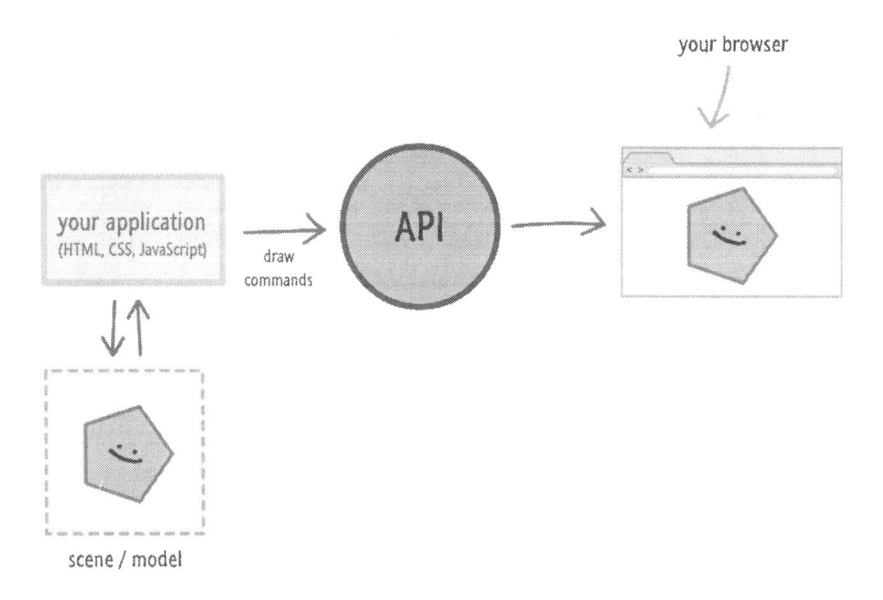

In an immediate mode system, you do all of the heavy lifting. You not only specify what needs to be drawn, you also create and maintain the model as well. As if all of this wasn't enough, you also specify the draw commands to get your browser to actually update! Your browser's Graphics API, the API that did so much for you in the retained mode world, doesn't do much here. It simply takes your draw commands and sends them off to the browser for execution.

In HTML, immediate mode comes into play when you are using the `canvas` element. Anything you wish to draw inside it requires you to issue primitive draw commands and handle all aspects of managing the scene and redrawing when changes happen.

When to Use Which?

Now that you have an idea of the two modes that compete for your attention, when do you use canvas and when do you use the DOM? Well, as with all questions of this sort, the answer is filled with exceptions. This time is no different. Choosing between the immediate mode-ness of the canvas and the retained mode-ness of your DOM is not an exclusive decision. It can actually be quite scandalous! You can choose just one, the other, or even both.

In this section, let's build on the overview you saw in the previous section and look at the advantages and disadvantages of each of the approaches. Much of this will seem very theoretical if you've never used a canvas before, but we'll fix that in the next chapter where you'll see the material presented here put to practice.

The DOM

Since we are talking about the DOM here, you will spend a majority of the time, possibly even all of your time, in this retained mode world. Despite the comforts it provides, it isn't perfect. Let's look at its perfections and imperfections in more detail.

The Good
The stuff we like about the DOM are:

- **Easy to use**. The DOM abstracts away a lot of the details that would otherwise get you bogged down. Examples of details that can bog down even the best of us include layout, event handling, clean up, selection/highlighting, accessibility, being DPI friendly, and so on.

- **Redrawing is handled for you**. You only specify what you want to display on the screen. The details of how to do that and how often to refresh are all left to the Graphics API to handle.

- **CSS! CSS! CSS!** You can easily modify the visuals of your DOM elements using CSS.

- **Animations are easy to define and modify**. Because of the CSS support, you can easily define animations or transitions, specify an easing function, make a few other tweaks, and you are good to go. This applies to JavaScript-based animations as well. If you are using JavaScript to animate an element's properties, you just have to get your `requestAnimationFrame` loop setup to update the property values. Everything else is taken care off...such as when to redraw or how to maintain a smooth frame rate.

The Bad
This is the stuff about the DOM makes us not want to invite it to your next birthday party:

- **Memory intensive**. You know all of the details that get taken care of for you when using a DOM element? Well, that care doesn't come cheap. Your DOM elements are very complex little things, and all of this complexity takes up space in your browser's memory. The more elements you are dealing with, the more resource hungry it all gets.

- **Less control over how things get drawn.** For certain graphics-related tasks, the default rendering may be a bit limiting. Browsers optimize for their particular needs, and those optimizations may go counter to what you want to do.

The Canvas

If this were a popularity contest, I would feel pretty bad for immediate mode and the canvas element that uses it. Fortunately, it isn't! Immediate mode systems certainly carry their own weight - even in the more limited cases they are used in. Let's look at some of their cool (and less cool) features in more detail.

The Good

If there was an award for awesomeness, we would give it to the canvas for the following reasons:

- **Fast. Really fast.** Because an immediate mode system doesn't maintain its own model, your code is all that stands between you and the browser redrawing. The many layers of abstraction that slow operations down simply do not exist in the immediate mode world.

- **You have a lot of flexibility.** Since your code controls all aspects of when and how something is drawn to the screen, you can tweak and customize the output any way you would like.

- **Great for dealing with many elements.** Compared to a retained mode system where every little addition to your scene takes up extra memory, immediate mode systems don't have that problem. Generally, an immediate mode system will always use less memory than a retained mode system - something that becomes more noticeable as you add more and more elements into the mix.

The Bad

This is the sort of stuff that makes you want to lock yourself inside an underground cave and never emerge:

- **It can be slow when drawing to large areas.** How quickly a redraw completes is proportional to the number of pixels you are re-drawing. If your addressing a really large area, things could get slower if you are not careful and do not optimize appropriately.

- **It is complex.** Because you are handling more of what it takes to get something to display on the screen, there are a lot more details for you to keep track of. Getting up to speed with the various draw commands and how they are used is no picnic either.

Summary

Understanding the retained mode and immediate mode differences makes it much easier to sympathize with the DOM on certain things and with the canvas on others. By now, hopefully you have a good idea of when to use one over the other. This book is focused entirely on the canvas and how awesome it is for helping bring your pixels to life. We won't be covering the DOM much at all outside of the `canvas` element that you need. More on that later.

Anyway, in the next many chapters, we'll cover everything canvas-related from drawing to animating to dealing with interactivity. It's going to be a fun ride, so let's get started!

Chapter 2: Getting Started with the Canvas

In the previous chapter, we got a high-level overview of the mysterious canvas by comparing it to the more-familiar DOM. That article was missing something crucial, though. It was missing the part where you get your hands wet writing markup and code. We are going to fix that up in this chapter.

We are going to put some of that conceptual knowledge you gained to good use by creating a simple example using the `canvas` element. I know that sounds a little scary, but you'll have a lot of help along the way. As you will find out soon enough, getting bizarre lines of JavaScript to draw something on the screen is a whole lot of fun.

Onwards!

Meet the Canvas Element

The first thing we are going to do is add a `canvas` element to our page and make some adjustments to make it easier to work with. Before we get to any of that, you need a blank HTML page that we will be working on. If you don't have a blank HTML page and need some help creating one, go ahead and create a new document and add the following lines of markup into it:

```html
<!DOCTYPE html>

<html>

<head>

    <title>Simple Example</title>

</head>


<body>
```

```
</body>

</html>
```

Once you have a blank HTML document setup, it's time for the main event you have been eagerly waiting the past 30-ish seconds for!

Adding the Canvas Element

The `canvas` element is represented by the appropriately named `canvas` HTML tag, and it behaves just like any other HTML element you might have used in the past. To add a `canvas` element to your page, simply add the following opening and closing tag inside your `body`:

```
<canvas></canvas>
```

With this line, you have successfully added a `canvas` element to your document!

All that said, let's not celebrate too soon. If you preview your page right now, you'll be greeted with a deafening blank screen. The reason is that your canvas element by itself has nothing interesting going for it. It is merely a screen that JavaScript will *eventually* project pixels onto.

Visualizing our Canvas

Working with something invisible isn't fun. To help us visualize our `canvas` element, let's specify some CSS to give it a border. Add the highlighted `style` block to your document inside your `head` tags:

```
<!DOCTYPE html>
<html>

<head>
  <title>Simple Example</title>
  <style>
    canvas {
      border: #333 10px solid;
    }
  </style>
</head>
    .
    .
    .
</html>
```

Once you've added that CSS, preview your page now. If everything worked out properly, our page will look as follows:

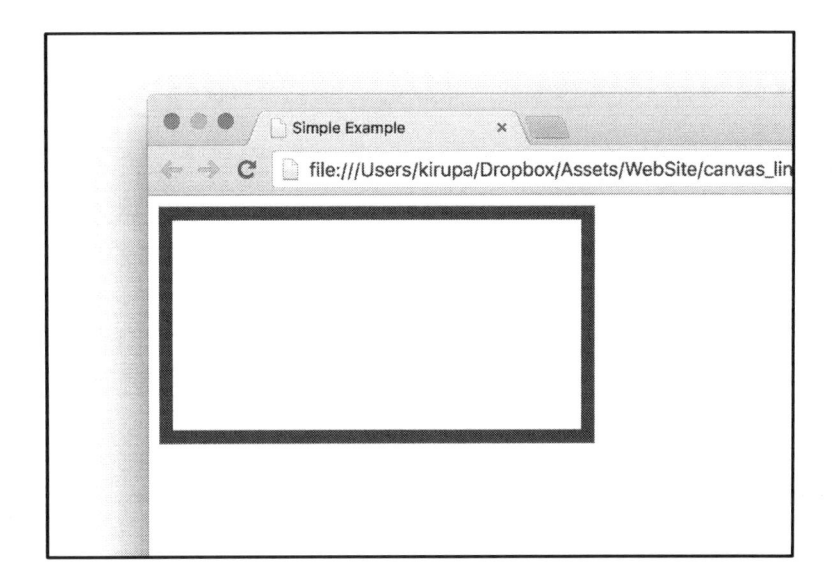

[Screenshot of browser window showing a canvas with a dark gray border]

As expected, our CSS gave our canvas a 10 pixel wide dark gray border! While this is *normally* nothing to write home about, in our case, we can at least see some evidence that the canvas element is indeed alive...and possibly well. Now that we can see our `canvas` element, doesn't it look a little too small? Let's fix that next!

Resizing our Canvas Element

By default, your `canvas` elements are 300 pixels wide and 150 pixels tall. That might be a good size, but we want something bigger...like 550 pixels by 350 pixels. Our initial reaction might be to add some `width` and `height` properties to our existing style rule that targets our `canvas`. As it turns out, you can't really do that and get the intended result.

To properly change your canvas element's dimensions, add the **width** and **height** attributes to your `canvas` element's HTML directly:

```
<canvas width="550px" height="350px"></canvas>
```

Yes, I know that looks a bit odd given that we have been told to use CSS for setting the size of elements in HTML. I am not saying that you can't use CSS for setting the size. You can use CSS for setting the size on one condition: **you preserve your canvas element's aspect ratio**. If you aren't (like we are), then setting the size via HTML is the only way to get the proper size without having all the pixels inside our canvas look all stretched and weird.

As you will keep finding out, there are some quirks about working with the `canvas` element that we all have to tolerate above and beyond the usual silliness commonly found with HTML elements :P

Giving Our Canvas Element an ID

The last and probably most important step is to give our `canvas` element an ID value so that you can reference it via JavaScript. On the `canvas` element, add the **id** attribute and give it a value of **myCanvas**:

```
<canvas id="myCanvas" width="550px" height="350px"></canvas>
```

The full markup for everything you should have in your document so far should look something similar to the following:

```
<!DOCTYPE html>
<html>
<head>
  <title>Simple Example</title>
  <style>
    canvas {
      border: #333 10px solid;
    }
  </style>
</head>
```

```
<body>

    <canvas id="myCanvas" width="500" height="500"></canvas>

</body>


</html>
```

At this point, I would say don't preview what you have in your browser. The reason is that you still won't see anything different or drastic from what you had earlier. That is about to change, though!

Drawing Things

In the previous section, we basically defined our `canvas` element in markup. While important, what we've just done is a very VERY minor part of working with the `canvas` overall. The real work is about to happen in this section when we write the JavaScript that interacts with the `canvas` element to get pixels to show up on the screen.

Adding the Script Tags

Before we can write JavaScript, we need a `script` tag that will house the JavaScript we write. You can use an external JavaScript file or keep all of the code in the same document. For simplicity, I'll be keeping all of our code in the same document, and that will look something like the following:

```
<!DOCTYPE html>

<html>


<head>

  <title>Simple Example</title>
```

```
  <style>

    canvas {

      border: #333 10px solid;

    }

  </style>

</head>


<body>

  <canvas id="myCanvas" width="550px" height="350px"></canvas>


  <script>

  </script>


</body>


</html>
```

With this minor addition, you are now set to write some JavaScript that will interact with our `canvas` element!

Accessing our Canvas Element

When it comes to working with the `canvas`, the first line of JavaScript you will almost always write will involve getting a reference to the `canvas` element in your HTML. This will allow you to start doing all sorts of canvas-ey things using JavaScript.

Now to get the reference, inside your script tag, go ahead and add the following line:

```
var canvas = document.querySelector("#myCanvas");
```

All we are doing here is initializing our **canvas** variable to our **myCanvas** element we defined in HTML earlier. We get a reference to the **myCanvas** element by relying on the **querySelector** function. This function is the cooler (and more flexible) way of finding elements in HTML compared to the older **getElementById** and **getElementsByClass** functions you might have seen in the past.

Getting the Rendering Context

Here is some useful trivia. Our **canvas** element has two modes of operation. One mode is designed for drawing things in 2D, and this is the mode we care about for now. The other mode is all about supporting drawing in 3D. These modes are more formally known as **rendering contexts**. To be able to draw to our **canvas** element, we need to first specify the rendering context we want to use. That is done by calling the **getContext** method on our canvas object and passing in the argument for the 2D rendering context we want:

```
var canvas = document.querySelector("#myCanvas");
var context = canvas.getContext("2d");
```

The context variable now stores a reference to our **canvas** element's 2d rendering context and all the sweet drawing-related properties and functions that go along with it. To put all of this more simply, with a hook into the rendering context, you now have a pipeline through which you can issue commands to get pixels to show up inside your **canvas**!

Issuing Draw Commands

All that remains at this point is to use the various tools JavaScript provides to get things drawn on the screen. We've covered a lot of ground here already, so I won't overwhelm you with what all the various draw commands are and how to use them. Instead, I am going to first provide some code for you to copy/paste/write to see our **canvas** element in action.

Go ahead and add the following lines below where you have defined your `context` variable:

```
// draw a diagonal line
context.moveTo(50, 50);
context.lineTo(450, 300);

// close the path
context.closePath();

// specify what our line looks like
context.lineWidth = 45;
context.strokeStyle = "steelblue";

// get the line drawn to the canvas
context.stroke();
```

Once you have done this, preview your HTML page in your browser. If everything went well, this time you will actually see something drawn with a thick blue diagonal line showing up:

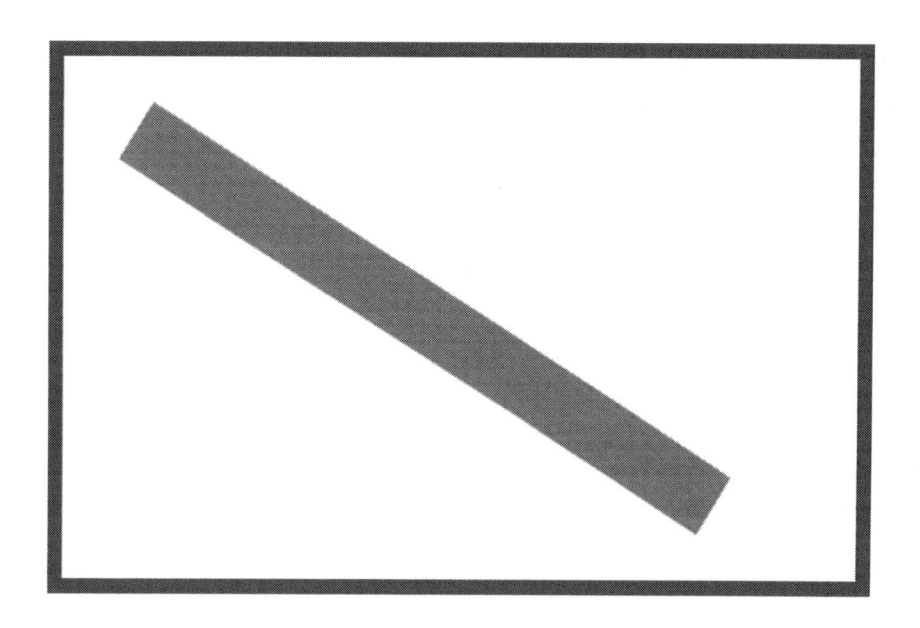

All of the code you just pasted is responsible for getting this line to show up. Take a few moments to look at what each line of code does. Don't worry if it doesn't fully make sense! For this introduction, just notice that we are doing what looks like moving a virtual pen around and specifying the starting and ending co-ordinates:

```
// draw a diagonal line
context.moveTo(50, 50);
context.lineTo(450, 300);
```

There is even some code that seems to specify the thickness and color of the line that gets drawn:

```
// specify what our line looks like
context.lineWidth = 45;
context.strokeStyle = "steelblue";
```

In future chapters, we will dive much deeper into what each of these commands do and learn precisely how they work. We will also look at the supporting code that is very important...despite me ignoring them in this lightning-fast overview. For now, just be proud of the massive amount of progress you made!

Conclusion

In this chapter, we created a basic template that all future `canvas`-related content will follow. You have your `canvas` element in the HTML with some optional CSS and inline HTML attributes to help style it. You then have your JavaScript where you reference the `canvas` element, gain access to its rendering context, and then issue the draw commands needed to get pixels to appear. All of this sets the groundwork for the topic you are about to see next: DRAWING!

Part I
Drawing

Chapter 3: Drawing Lines (aka The Basics)

Well, we got really REALLY close to actually drawing something in the previous chapter. Yes, you manually entered some code to get a line to appear, but that doesn't really count since we didn't look at why the code works the way it does. Let's fix that in this article where we will both take a look at what exactly drawing on the canvas entails and meet a lot of the cohorts responsible for getting pixels to the screen.

Onwards!

How Drawing in the Real World Works

Putting pixels on the canvas is really no different than how you would sketch or doodle using a pencil:

This is a pencil!
(some people write using it)

Using a pencil, let's say you want to draw a funny four-sided shape that looks as follows:

Four-sided and funny!

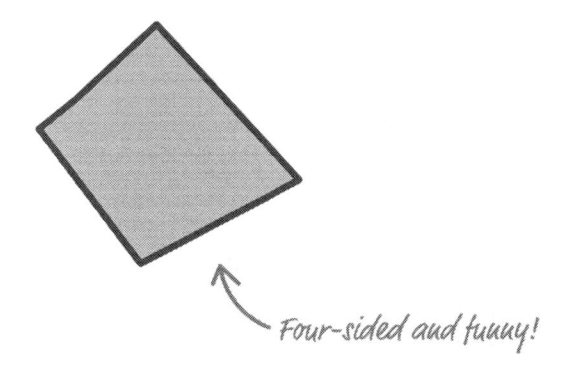

The way you would do this is as follows:

1. Find a spot on a piece of paper or a sketchpad
2. Pick up the pencil
3. Move pencil to the point you want to start your drawing
4. Press pencil down and draw a line to create one side of this shape
5. Press pencil down from where your last line ended to draw another line to create another side of this shape
6. Keep drawing lines until your shape is complete. Your last line will end at the point you started from to create a closed shape
7. Adjust the thickness and color of the outline by going over it a few times with a different and thicker pencil
8. Color the insides of your shape yellow

These steps seem really simple, right? Some of them you perform without even thinking about it! There is a reason why I am pointing out the obvious here. Drawing on the canvas is very similar to drawing manually using a pencil. The only difference is that your pencil in the canvas world is powered by lines of JavaScript as opposed to your actual hands. It's time to get familiar with what these lines of JavaScript entail.

Drawing in the Canvas World

Our `canvas` provides you with a bunch of handy methods that make drawing things to it pretty easy. We will cover almost all of them in time, but right now we are going to focus on just the methods needed to help us draw the funny four-sided shape you saw earlier. The methods we are going to look at are the following: `beginPath`, `moveTo`, `lineTo`, `closePath`, `lineWidth`, `strokeStyle`, `fillStyle`, `stroke`, `fill`. I know this list of methods seems really long, but once you see them in use, it will all make sense.

Starting Point

Let's pick up from where we left off in the previous chapter by starting with a mostly-empty HTML document that already has a `canvas` element defined inside it:

```html
<!DOCTYPE html>
<html>

<head>
  <title>Simple Example</title>
  <style>
    canvas {
      border: #333 10px solid;
    }
  </style>
</head>

<body>
  <canvas id="myCanvas" width="550px" height="350px"></canvas>
```

```
<script>

  var canvas = document.querySelector("#myCanvas");

  var context = canvas.getContext("2d");

</script>


</body>


</html>
```

The only difference is that the content inside our `script` tag doesn't contain the code for drawing the blue line to the `canvas`. We just have the two lines that we need for getting the rendering context, and that detail is important. All of the drawing methods that we talked about earlier work off of the `context` object, so without this code, nothing in your `canvas` will actually work.

Picking our Starting Point

With the rendering context in our sights via the context object, we have the digital equivalent of a piece of paper where we can draw on. Right now, our `canvas` (aka the paper) is 550 pixels wide and 350 pixels tall:

550 pixels by 350 pixels

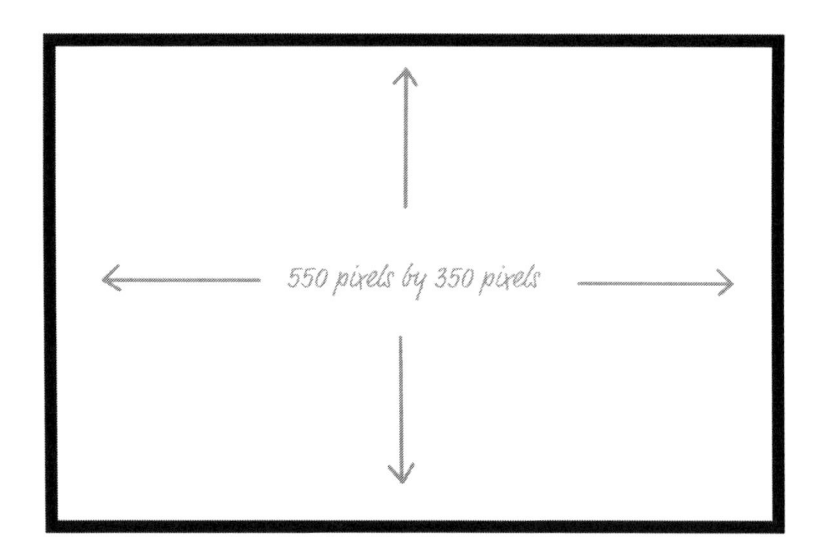

We want to have our shape appear somewhere inside that box, and for that we need a starting point. Before we can do that, there are *two things* you need to know and understand sorta kinda really well.

Thing #1

The first thing to know is that the method responsible for specifying the starting point is moveTo, and it looks like this:

```
context.moveTo(x, y);
```

It takes two arguments that correspond to our starting point's x and y co-ordinates. That brings us to the next point...

Thing #2

The second thing to know is that our canvas uses an **Inverted Cartesian Coordinate System**. This means that the origin (0, 0) is at the top-left of the canvas and the **x** and **y** values increase as you go right and down:

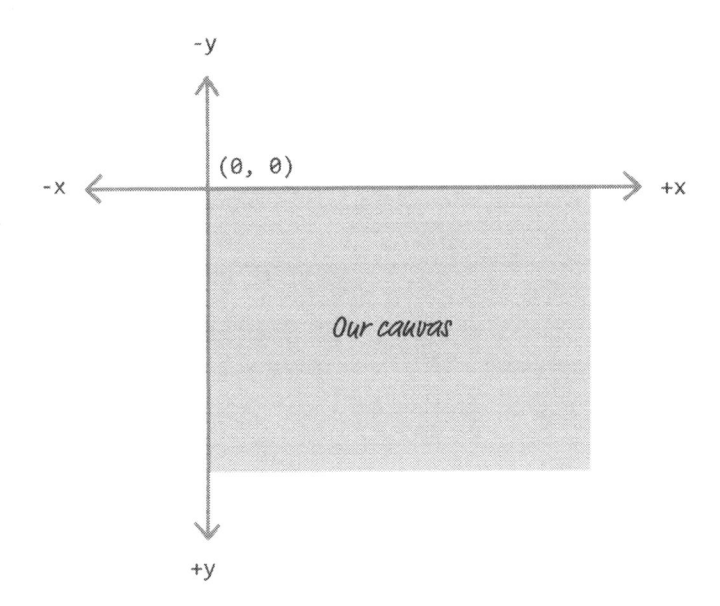

```
                    -y
                    ↑
                    |
              (0, 0)|
    -x  ←───────────┼──────────────→ +x
                    |░░░░░░░░░░░░░
                    |░░░░░░░░░░░░░
                    |░░░ Our canvas
                    |░░░░░░░░░░░░░
                    ↓
                    +y
```

This kind of co-ordinate system is very common in computer graphics, so if this is your first time running into something like this, embrace the weirdness until it feels natural!

Ok, getting back on track here, what we want to do is specify our starting position using the moveTo method. Let's go with a starting point of **160** for x and **130** for y, so add the following highlighted line just after your existing code:

```
var canvas = document.querySelector("#myCanvas");

var context = canvas.getContext("2d");


context.moveTo(160, 130);
```

When this code runs, our `moveTo` line ensures our virtual pencil will start at the (160, 130) mark. All of this happens silently with no visual cues, so if you preview in your browser, you will not see anything. That is because we haven't actually pressed down and drawn anything yet.

Drawing a Line

Now that we have our starting point figured out, it is time to actually draw something. We are going to draw a line that is going to make up one side of our four-sided shape. The way you draw a line is by using the `lineTo` method:

```
context.lineTo(x, y);
```

This method draws a line from your current position (aka where your virtual pencil was seen last) to the x and y coordinates you specify as arguments. Let's specify an x and y value of **75** and **200** respectively to draw a line from our starting point (160, 130) to (75, 200).

Go ahead add the following highlighted line to your code:

```
var canvas = document.querySelector("#myCanvas");
var context = canvas.getContext("2d");


context.moveTo(160, 130);

context.lineTo(75, 200);
```

Once you have done this, go ahead and preview this page in your browser. Do you see something that looks like this:

Why is this still blank?

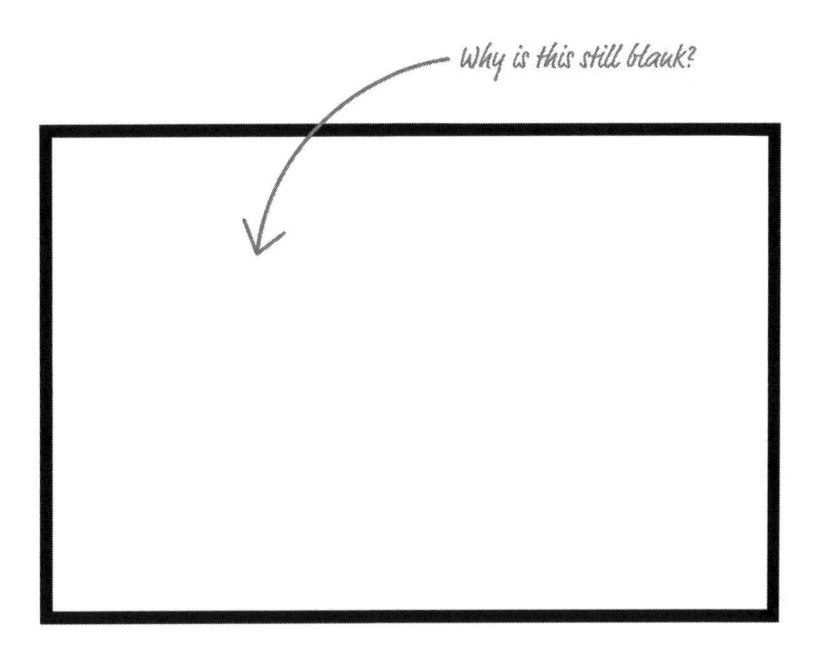

The reason for this emptiness that you need to specify an explicit "draw stuff to the canvas" command to actually...um...draw stuff to the `canvas`. For displaying a line, that command takes the form of the `stroke` method. Add the following highlighted line to our code:

```
var canvas = document.querySelector("#myCanvas");

var context = canvas.getContext("2d");


context.moveTo(160, 130);

context.lineTo(75, 200);

context.stroke();
```

After you have done this, preview your page now. You should now see a diagaonal line appear:

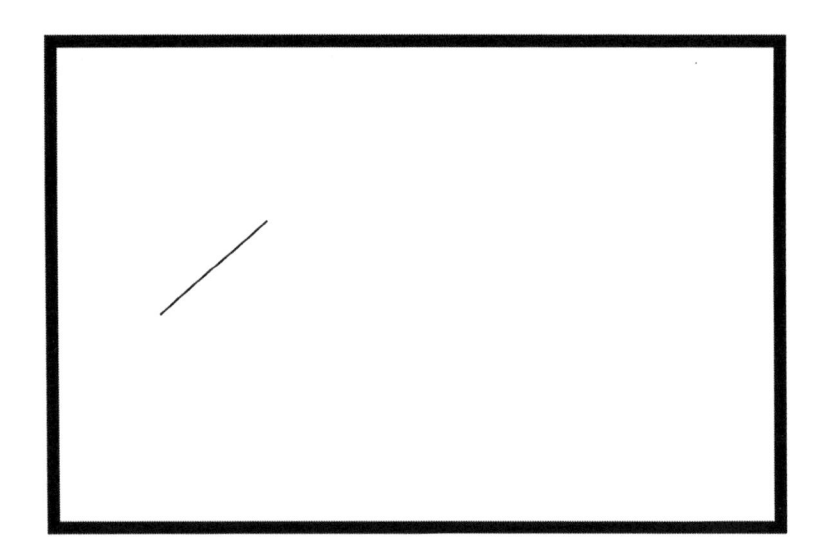

One side of our shape is done. Let's go ahead and add another line. Our virtual pen is currently at (75, 200), for that was the point specified by our last `lineTo` method. As to our next stop, let's go to (150, 275). Go ahead and add the following highlighted line:

```
var canvas = document.querySelector("#myCanvas");
var context = canvas.getContext("2d");


context.moveTo(160, 130);
context.lineTo(75, 200);
context.lineTo(150, 275);
context.stroke();
```

Note that we add this line just *before* our `context.stroke()` call. That detail is important, for any line-related drawing commands you specify after your `stroke` call will be ignored unless you call `stroke` again separately.

At this point, when you preview your page in your browser, this new line will now make its grand appearance:

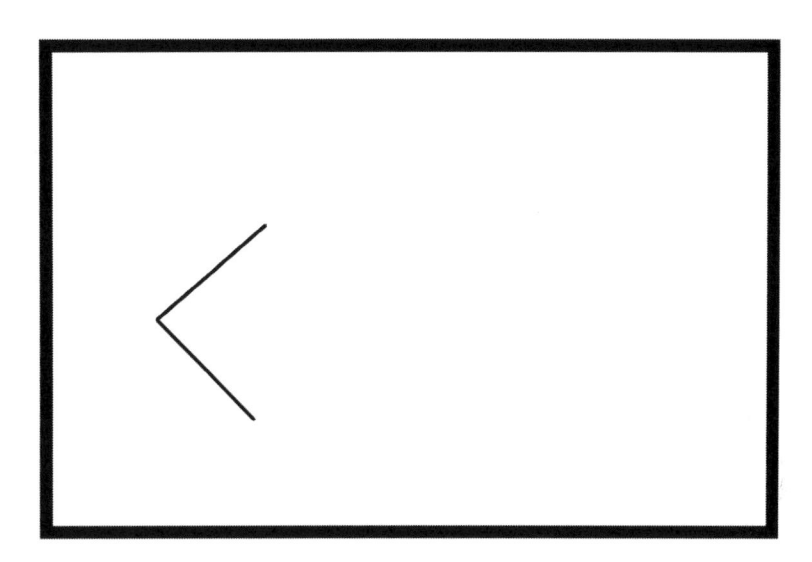

We are making great progress, so let's not slow down now. In fact, let's speed things up a bit. We are on to our third line, and this time let's go all the way to (250, 230) by adding the highlighted line you see next:

```
var canvas = document.querySelector("#myCanvas");
var context = canvas.getContext("2d");


context.moveTo(160, 130);

context.lineTo(75, 200);

context.lineTo(150, 275);

context.lineTo(250, 230);

context.stroke();
```

Once you've added this line, preview this change in your browser to see this third line appear:

Page | 39

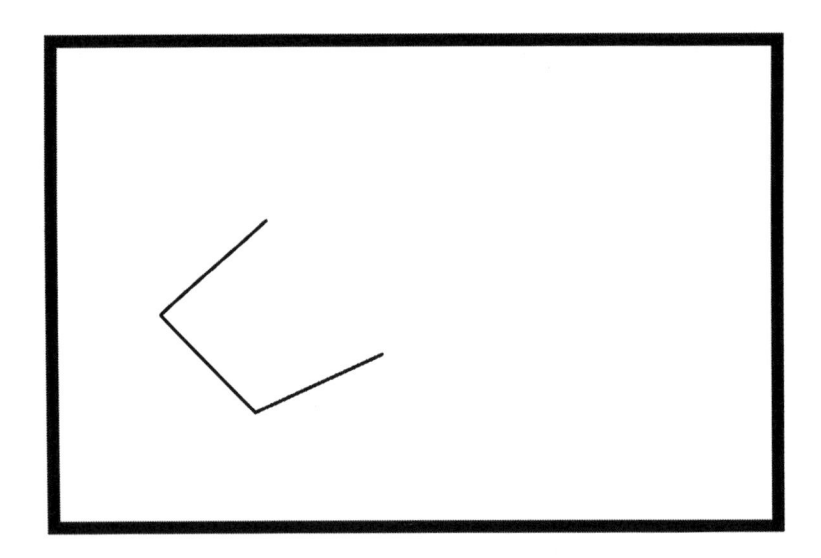

Ok - we just have one more line to draw to close our shape. Now, there are two ways to go about this. One way is to add another `lineTo` call and specify our starting point of (160, 130). The other more ninja way is to use the `closePath` method that accomplishes pretty much the same thing.

Go ahead and add the following highlighted line to your code:

```
var canvas = document.querySelector("#myCanvas");

var context = canvas.getContext("2d");


context.moveTo(160, 130);

context.lineTo(75, 200);

context.lineTo(150, 275);

context.lineTo(250, 230);

context.closePath();

context.stroke();
```

When you preview this in your browser, you will now see our funny four-sided shape in all its black and white glory:

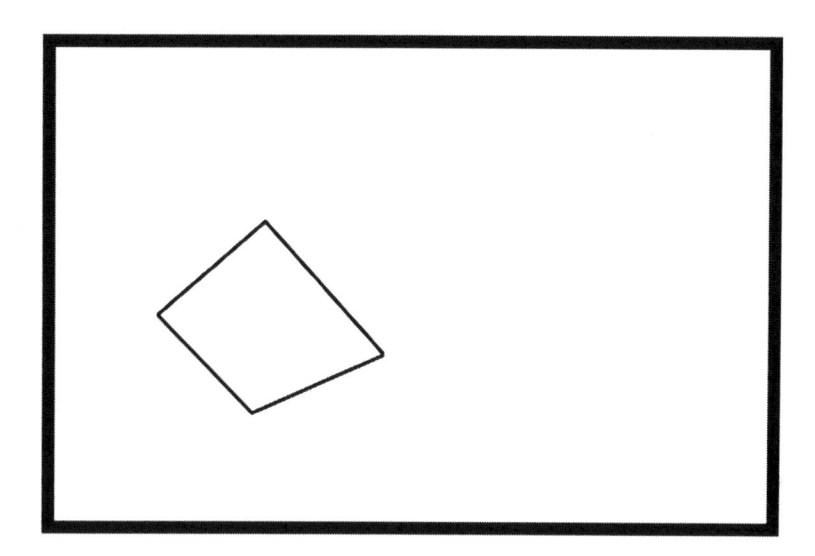

We are getting there! We have our shape, but it doesn't look complete yet. The outline is too thin, and where is the awesome yellow fill color? We will address that next.

Modifying the Appearance

Full disclosure - fully covering how to style and modify the appearance of our `canvas` content is something we will tackle in the future. There are far too many cool things that we need to look at in detail, but (for today) let's take a sneak peak at what to expect by looking at a few appearance-related properties and methods to get our funny four-sided shape looking nice.

Some of the players responsible for helping style our content are:

- `lineWidth`
  Allows you to specify the thickness of the lines.

- `strokestyle`
  Allows you to specify the line color.

- **fillStyle**

  Allows you to specify the background color for your shape.

- **fill**

  Similar to the `stroke` method, takes any fill-related pixels and pushes them live.

As you can see by the descriptions, these properties and methods are pretty straightforward to use...at least for what we are going to be using them for. To increase the thickness of our shape, adjust the shape color, and to give it a yellow background, add the following highlighted lines:

```
var canvas = document.querySelector("#myCanvas");
var context = canvas.getContext("2d");


context.moveTo(160, 130);

context.lineTo(75, 200);

context.lineTo(150, 275);

context.lineTo(250, 230);

context.closePath();


context.lineWidth = 5;

context.strokeStyle = "#333333";

context.fillStyle = "#FFCC00";


context.fill();

context.stroke();
```

Once you have done this, take a look at what our canvas looks like in the browser:

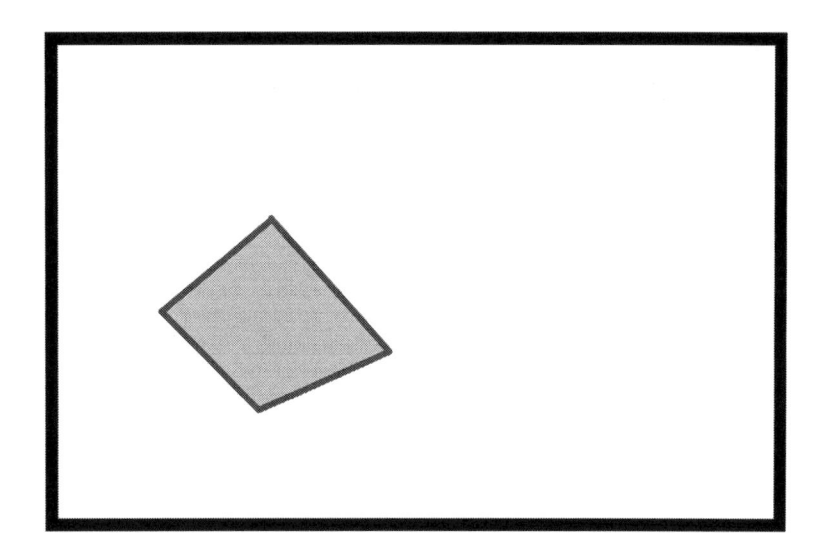

Doesn't that look pretty awesome? Well, I certainly think so!

Getting back to our code for a second, the `stroke` method ensures all of the stroke-related commands such as drawing our line, adjusting our line thickness, and setting the line color are all pushed live. You already knew that, but it is worth re-iterating for we'll do some clever things with that fact in the future. The `fill` method ensures that anything related to the fill of the shape are pushed live as well. In this example, the only thing the fill method really had to deal with is the `fillStyle` property that set the background color, but we'll look at more fill-related commands as we dive deeper into exploring everything you can do with the `canvas` in later chapters.

Conclusion

Tying up something we started with, drawing on the canvas is really not that much different than drawing on a piece of paper. The real-life gestures and movements you perform is replaced by the near-exact equivalent in the digital world defined by a few lines of JavaScript. This similarity will carry over to not only simple examples such as this, but you'll see parallels in even the more advanced `canvas`-related scenarios as well.

Chapter 4: Drawing Beziér Curves

Straight lines are cool and all, but sometimes you need to create lines that are not straight. Sometimes you need to create curved lines:

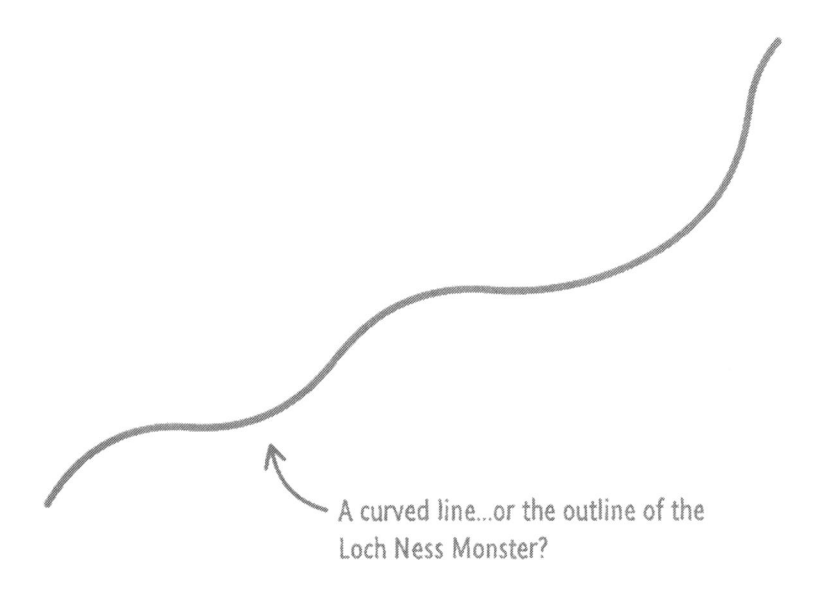

A curved line...or the outline of the Loch Ness Monster?

In this chapter, you will learn how to create not just any old curved line. You will learn how to draw something known as a **Beziér Curve**. Ignoring all of the boring academic stuff behind it, the elevator pitch for what they are is as follows: **Beziér curves allow you to easily create curves that are smooth.** That's the only important detail for you to keep in mind...for now.

Onwards!

Did you know?

Even if you don't know what Beziér curves are or have only heard about them in passing, there is a very good chance you've actually used them. If you've ever drawn a path in a vector illustration tool like Flash or Illustrator, you were indirectly manipulating a Beziér curve under the covers. Isn't that cool?

Drawing a Quadratic Beziér Curve

The first kind of Beziér curve we will learn to draw is the quadratic version. A quadratic Beziér curve is made up of a starting point, ending point, and a single control point that determines the nature of the curve:

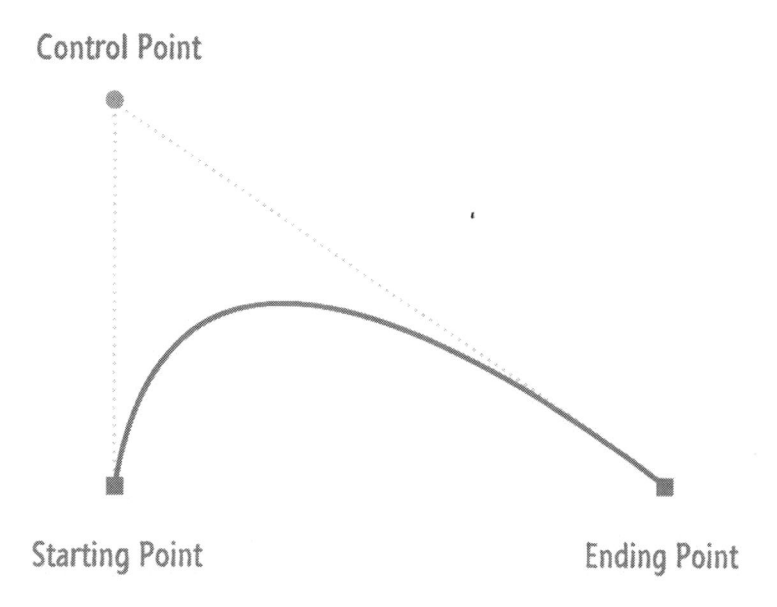

By adjusting any of these three values, you can customize how your curve looks. In the `canvas` world, you represent these three values as arguments you pass in to the `quadraticCurveTo` method:

```
context.quadraticCurveTo(c1_x, c1_y, e_x, e_y);
```

The first two arguments determine the x and y positions of the control point. The last two arguments specify the x and y positions of the ending point. You may have noticed that we don't specify the starting point anywhere. The reason for that is simple: The starting point is automatically calculated based on where your virtual pen is - either based on what you had drawn earlier or explicitly positioned using the `moveTo` method.

Here is an example of of the `quadraticCurveTo` method in action:

```
var canvas = document.querySelector("#myCanvas");
var context = canvas.getContext("2d");


context.moveTo(50, 130);
context.quadraticCurveTo(200, 400, 490, 100);
context.closePath();


context.lineWidth = 15;
context.strokeStyle = "#FFCC00";


context.stroke();
```

To run this code, simply add all of it between the `script` tags to the starting point HTML you saw earlier:

```
<!DOCTYPE html>
<html>


<head>
    <title>Simple Example</title>
```

Page | 46

```html
    <style>
      canvas {
        border: #333 10px solid;
      }
    </style>
  </head>


<body>
  <canvas id="myCanvas" width="550px" height="350px"></canvas>


  <script>


  </script>


</body>


</html>
```

When you run your code, you will see something that looks as follows:

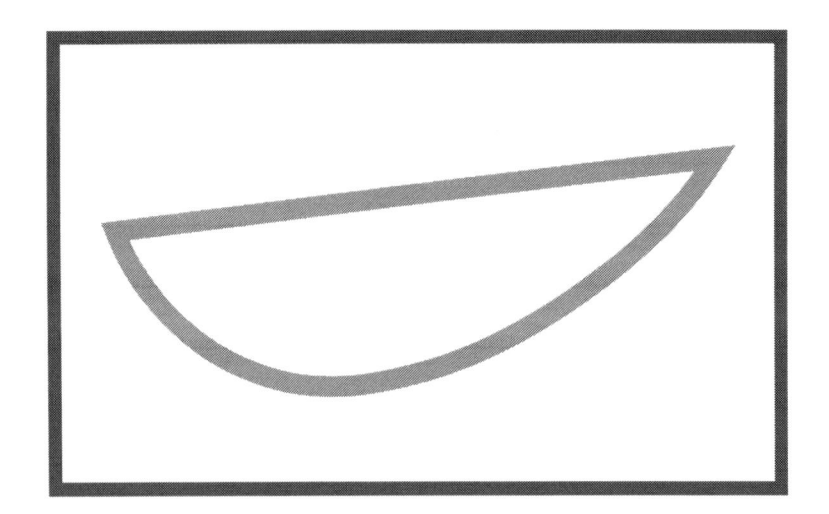

The main thing to keep in mind is that drawing curves is really no different than drawing lines or any other shape. The same rules about drawing, closing shapes, applying a fill, and other `canvas`-specific things apply here as well. If you look at the code, except for the `quadraticCurveTo` method, all of the various drawing methods we used should be very familiar for you.

Drawing a Cubic Beziér Curve

The cubic Beziér curve is almost identical to the quadratic one we just looked at. The only (and very important) difference is that it contains an additional control point:

Control Point #2

Ending Point

Starting Point

Control Point #1

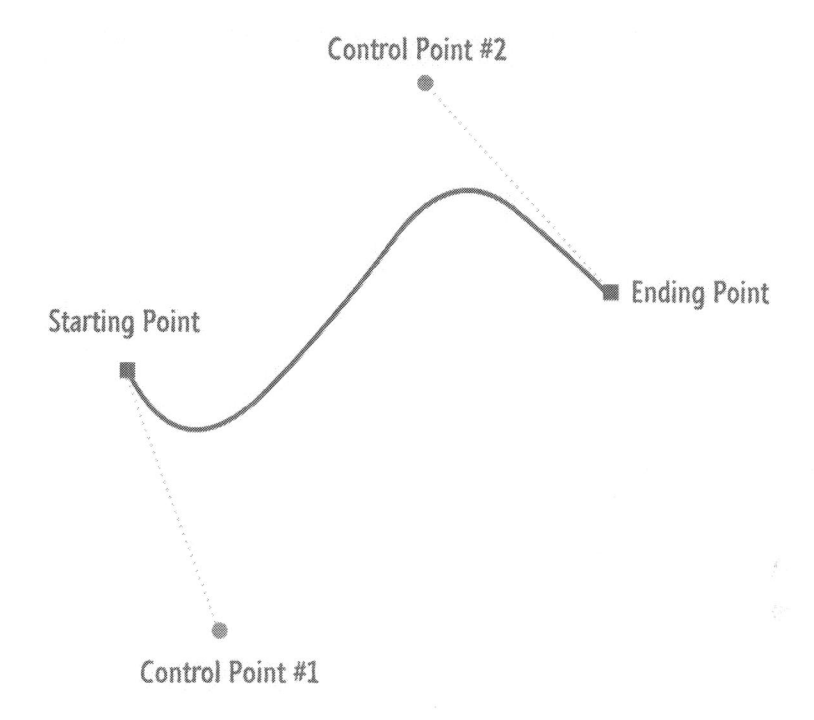

This additional control point gives your cubic Beziér curve the ability to be smoother and more awesome (such as what you see above) than the quadratic Beziér curve with just a single control point. The way you draw a cubic Beziér curve is by using the `bezierCurveTo` method and specifying the six arguments it needs:

```
context.bezierCurveTo(c1_x, c1_y, c2_x, c2_y, e_x, e_y);
```

The first four arguments specify the coordinates of our two control points. The last two arguments specify the coordinates of our ending point. Just like with our quadratic Beziér curve, the starting point is inferred based on where your virtual pen is prior to calling the `bezierCurveTo` method.

Below is an example that highlights the `bezierCurveTo` method at work:

```
var canvas = document.querySelector("#myCanvas");
```

```
var context = canvas.getContext("2d");


context.moveTo(50, 130);

context.bezierCurveTo(300, 50, 200, 400, 490, 100);

context.lineTo(490, 300);

context.lineTo(50, 300);

context.closePath();


context.lineWidth = 15;

context.strokeStyle = "#FFCC00";

context.fillStyle = "#FFDE58";


context.stroke();

context.fill();
```

If you test this code out on your own, you will see something that looks like this:

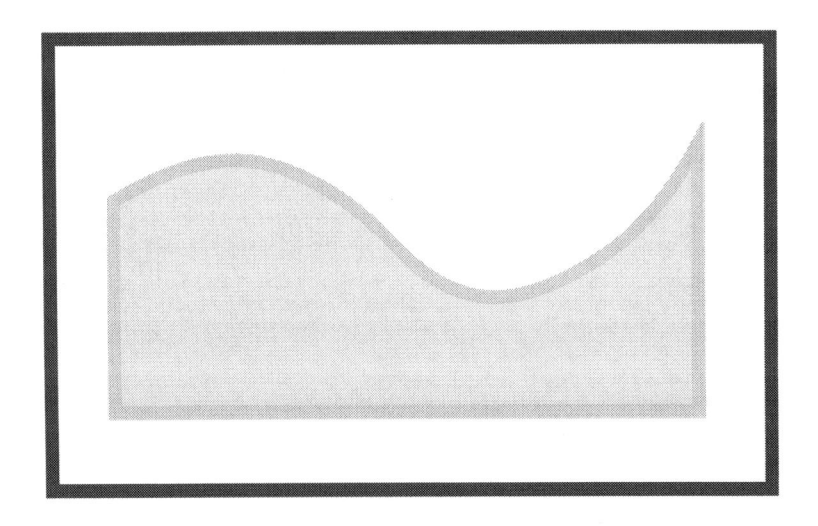

This example is a little bit more complex than having a single call to the `cubicBezierTo` method, but it does a good job highlighting how well all of the various drawing methods we've looked at so far play together.

Conclusion

Drawing Beziér curves on the canvas is not very fun. The reason is that you are often drawing blind. In various image editing tools, when you edit Beziér curves (via the more common Path features), you get immediate visual feedback on how your curve looks and what adjustments you can quickly make. When using the `quadraticCurveTo` and `bezierCurveTo` methods, changing various x and y values to get your curve looking right is pretty tedious because you will need to refresh your page to see how your curves ultimately look. That is no fun. To make all of this more digestible, one solution I employ is to the awesome *Mathlets: Beziér Curves* tool (http://bit.ly/MathletBC) that makes editing and visualizing these curves much easier.

Our Starting Point – Save for Later!

Throughout this book, we will be writing code to help our canvas do interesting things. To save you some time, we will be using the same HTML document as our starting point. It is the one you've seen several times already:

```html
<!DOCTYPE html>
<html>

<head>
  <title>Simple Example</title>
  <style>
    canvas {
      border: #333 10px solid;
    }
  </style>
</head>

<body>
  <canvas id="myCanvas" width="550px" height="350px"></canvas>

  <script>
    var canvas = document.querySelector("#myCanvas");
    var context = canvas.getContext("2d");
```

```
    </script>

  </body>

</html>
```

Keep this section close to you, for whenever you see a code snippet being thrown with no supporting markup provided, it means you need to use this starting HTML document and put your code in question inside it.

Chapter 5: Drawing Multiple Things

Up until now, we were engrossed in the details of drawing just a single thing. That had its own set of fun little details for us to learn, but in most practical situations, you'll never draw just a single thing. You will draw many MANY things all inside the same `canvas` element, and in this chapter we will look at the `beginPath` method and learn a few other tricks along the way to make all that possible.

Onwards!

This Seems Simple, No?

Earlier, we looked at an example where we drew a simple four-sided shape. The `canvas` code for that looked as follows:

```
context.moveTo(160, 130);

context.lineTo(75, 200);

context.lineTo(150, 275);

context.lineTo(250, 230);

context.closePath();


context.lineWidth = 5;

context.strokeStyle = "#333333";

context.fillStyle = "#FFCC00";


context.fill();

context.stroke();
```

In your browser, this code translates to the following pixels that you see on the screen:

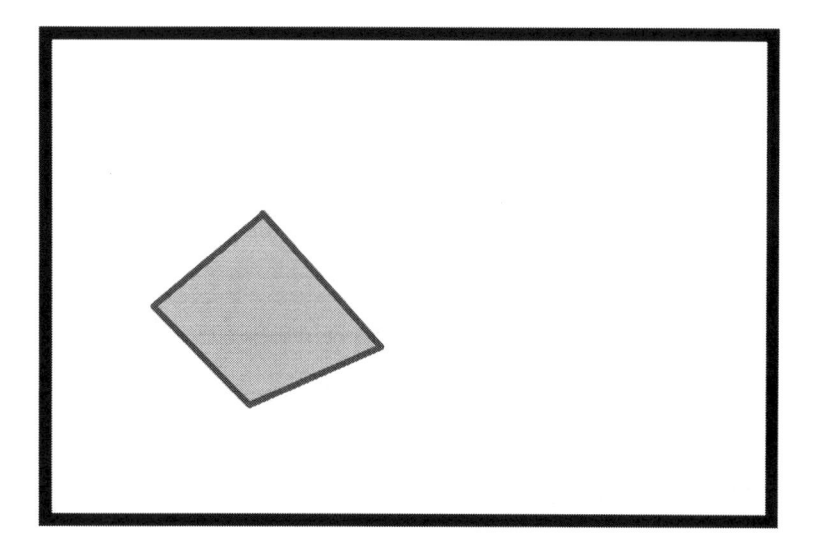

Now, let's say that we want to add another shape to what we have here. The shape we want looks something like this:

In code, it is represented as follows:

```
context.moveTo(50, 50);

context.lineTo(450, 300);

context.closePath();


context.lineWidth = 45;

context.strokeStyle = "steelblue";


context.stroke();
```

What do you think we should do to combine these shapes? One thing we learned from earlier is that the `stroke` and `fill` methods act as the big red button you push to get things displayed on our screen. One reasonable attempt might be to keep the common `stroke` and `fill` methods from earlier and merge in the lines of code that represent our diagonal line:

```
context.moveTo(160, 130);

context.lineTo(75, 200);

context.lineTo(150, 275);

context.lineTo(250, 230);

context.closePath();


context.lineWidth = 5;

context.strokeStyle = "#333";

context.fillStyle = "#FFCC00";


context.moveTo(50, 50);
```

```
context.lineTo(450, 300);

context.closePath();


context.lineWidth = 45;

context.strokeStyle = "steelblue";


context.fill();

context.stroke();
```

On the surface, this seems like a reasonable thing to do. The first part of the code deals with the four-sided shape and what it looks like. The second (and highlighted) part deals with our diagonal line and what it looks like. In my mind, this seems like a solid solution!

When we preview this in our browser, this is what you will see:

Not quite what we had in mind, right? Ok, so it turns out merging the relevant lines of code under one single `stroke` and `fill` call didn't work out properly. What if we decide to keep the code for these shapes separate and have duplicate `stroke` and `fill` calls for each shape?

The code for that would look like this:

```
// first shape
context.moveTo(160, 130);
context.lineTo(75, 200);
context.lineTo(150, 275);
context.lineTo(250, 230);
context.closePath();

context.lineWidth = 5;
context.strokeStyle = "#333";
context.fillStyle = "#FFCC00";

context.fill();
context.stroke();

// second shape
context.moveTo(50, 50);
context.lineTo(450, 300);
context.closePath();

context.lineWidth = 45;
context.strokeStyle = "steelblue";

context.stroke();
```

If you try this arrangement and preview in your browser, what do you see? **It's exactly the same thing as the weird jumble of shapes you saw earlier.** What do you think is going on? Let's figure this out in the next section.

Creating an Individual Shape

What we need to do is create individual shapes - shapes whose properties don't bleed into each other and cause a weird mashup like you saw previously. The solution to our problem is pretty simple. Everybody, say hello to the `beginPath` method:

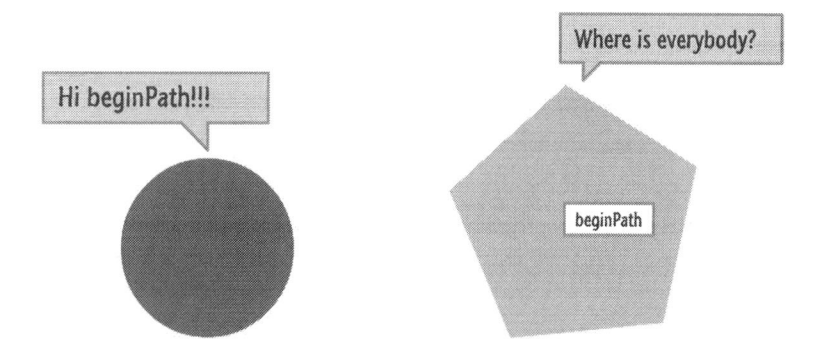

The `beginPath` method is called on your drawing context object (just like almost all of the methods we've seen so far!), and this method is responsible for telling your canvas that a new shape is about to be started. If we want to display multiple shapes, simply put a call to `beginPath` just before you are starting up your new shape.

This means, the solution to our multiple shapes situation from earlier would look as follows:

```
// first shape
context.beginPath();
context.moveTo(160, 130);
context.lineTo(75, 200);
context.lineTo(150, 275);
```

```
context.lineTo(250, 230);

context.closePath();


context.lineWidth = 5;

context.strokeStyle = "#333";

context.fillStyle = "#FFCC00";


context.fill();

context.stroke();


// second shape

context.beginPath();

context.moveTo(50, 50);

context.lineTo(450, 300);

context.closePath();


context.lineWidth = 45;

context.strokeStyle = "steelblue";


context.stroke();

context.stroke();
```

Notice that all we did as add a `beginPath` method before each individual shape we wished to draw. If you preview in your browser, you will now see both shapes displayed as intended:

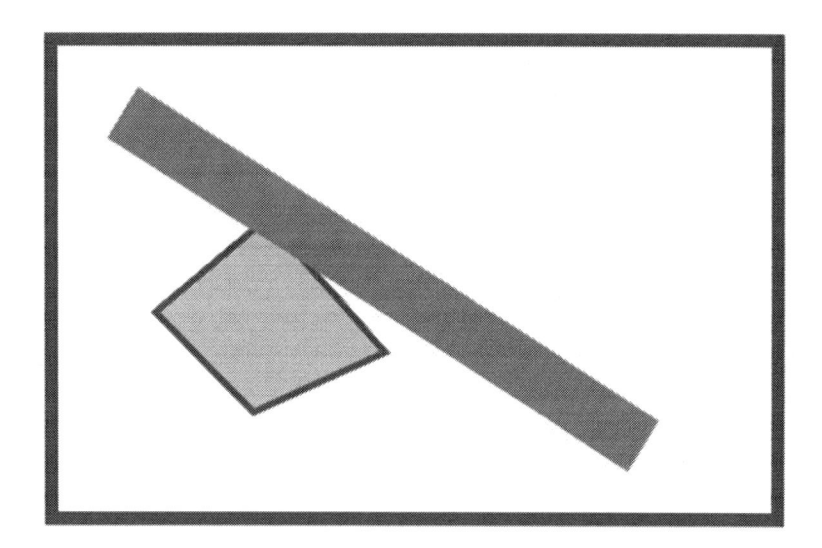

Pretty simple, right? Who knew that the solution to our problem was nothing more than a call to `beginPath`?

Draw Order Matters

We are almost done here. One last thing to call out is the order with which things get rendered on the `canvas`. The `canvas` follows what is known as the *painters model* of rendering. All of your draw operations are added to the canvas in the order they were specified in. This means the first shape you define in your code will be added to the canvas first. The second shape you define will be added next and drawn over the top of the first shape (if they overlap). The third shape will...you see the pattern:

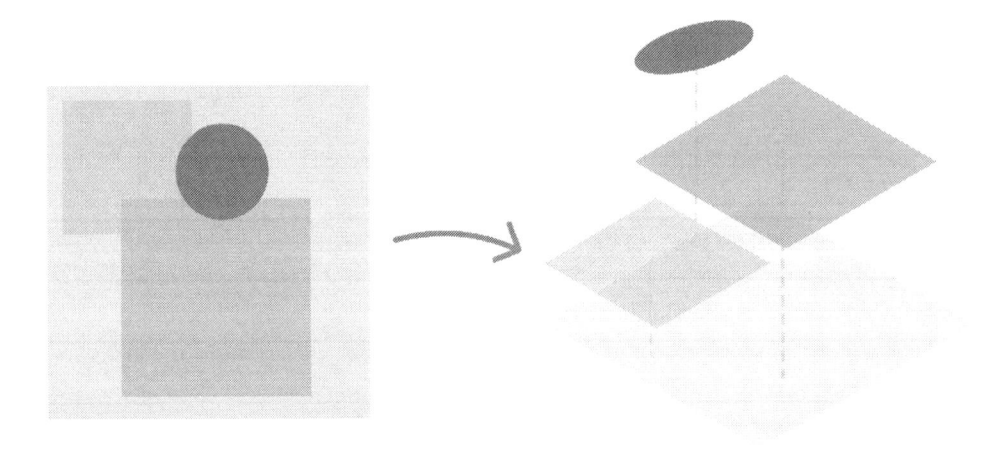

From a visual point of view, the implications of this model are huge. Each shape will be drawn on top of whatever shape preceded it. This means the order in which you specify your shapes matters just like it would in the real world where you are using a paintbrush and layering on colors. Once a shape has been layered on, you can't easily rearrange it unless you alter your code. You can thank the immediate graphics mode nature of the canvas element for that little gift!

Conclusion

The thing that confused me when working with the canvas is that beginPath is the only thing you need to signal your intent to draw a new shape. For every new shape you want to draw, just call beginPath. Any stroke, fill, or draw-related properties you set earlier stay with the earlier shape. Nothing gets carried over to your new shape. This confusion was compounded every time I saw the closePath method. As we saw in the previous chapter, all closePath does is draw a line from where you are now to your shape's starting point. You don't have to specify it if you are going to manually close the shape using lineTo, and you certainly don't need to pair it with beginPath to signal the closing of your shape.

Chapter 6: Drawing Rectangles (and Squares)

When drawing shapes on the `canvas`, you can actually go really REALLY far without ever having to draw a rectangle. The reason for that is simple. Rectangles are terrible things that nobody should ever have to deal with:

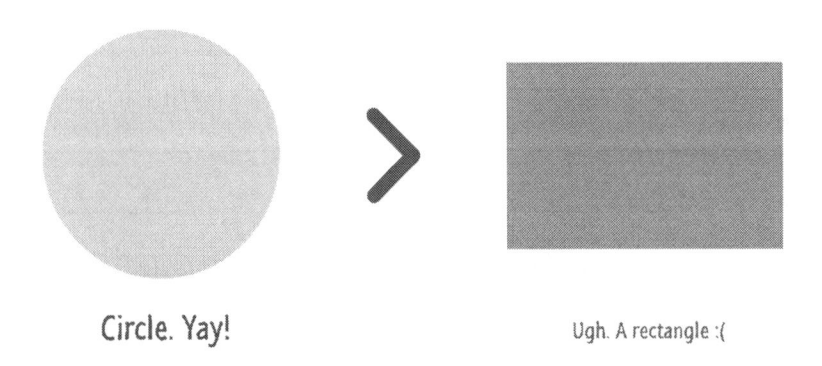

Circle. Yay!   Ugh. A rectangle :(

Putting my irrational hatred for our rectangular brethren aside, a rectangle is a shape that you must learn to properly represent on a `canvas`. Even if you can never envision yourself using rectangles, remember - **squares** are rectangles as well. They are rectangles whose sides are all the same size. In this short chapter, we'll walk through the basics of how to draw rectangles on our friendly little `canvas` element.

Onwards!

Meet the rect Method

The primary way you draw a rectangle is by using the `rect` method to define a rectangular path. This method takes four arguments that map to the following things:

- Starting x position the rectangle will start from
- Starting y position the rectangle will start from
- Width of the rectangle

- Height of the rectangle

Let's take a look at what this method looks like when used in a simple example. Feel free to use the same HTML page (with our **myCanvas** `canvas` element) we've been using since the beginning. Inside your `script` tag, add the following lines of code:

```
var canvasElement = document.querySelector("#myCanvas");
var context = canvasElement.getContext("2d");


// the rectangle
context.beginPath();
context.rect(75, 100, 250, 150);
context.closePath();


// the outline
context.lineWidth = 10;
context.strokeStyle = '#666666';
context.stroke();


// the fill color
context.fillStyle = "#51DCFF";
context.fill();
```

Once you've done this, preview your page in your browser. If everything worked out properly, you should see a blue rectangle appear:

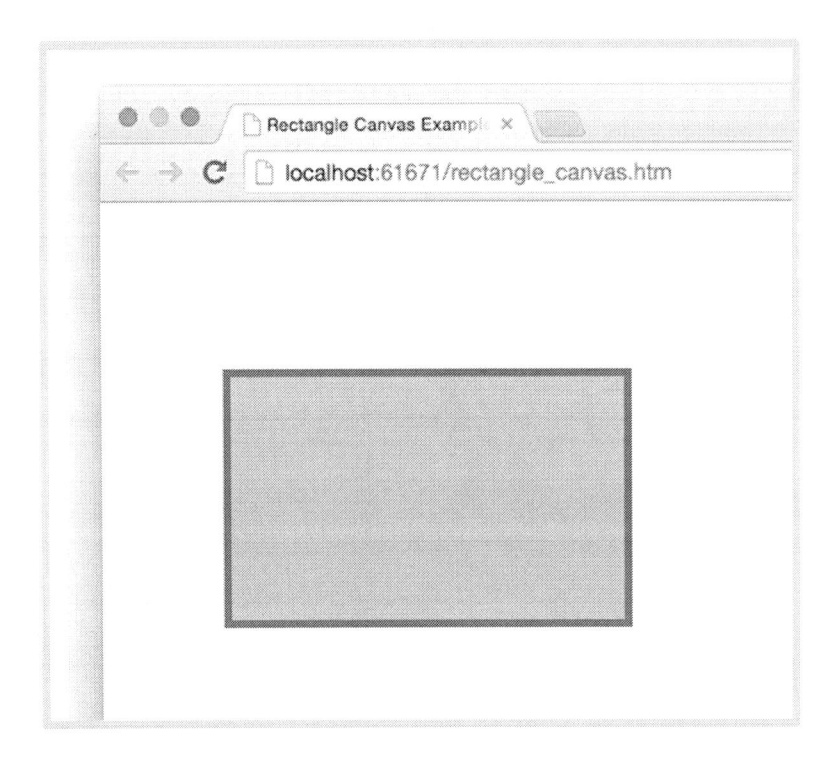

See, wasn't that easy? Now, let's look at how the lines of code you've written map to the rectangle that you see on the screen. The interesting stuff starts here:

```
// the rectangle
context.beginPath();
context.rect(75, 100, 250, 150);
context.closePath();
```

Because these lines are crucial to drawing our rectangle, I'm going to slow down and dive into greater detail on what each line does.

The first line sets it all up:

```
context.beginPath();
```

The beginPath method signals to the canvas that you intend to draw a path. We saw what it does in the previous chapter, so we aren't going to dwell on this one much further :P

The next line is our `rect` method that defines the starting point and size of the rectangle we wish to draw:

```
context.rect(75, 100, 250, 150);
```

We are specifying a rectangular path that starts at an x position of 75, y position of 100, is 250 pixels wide, and 150 pixels tall:

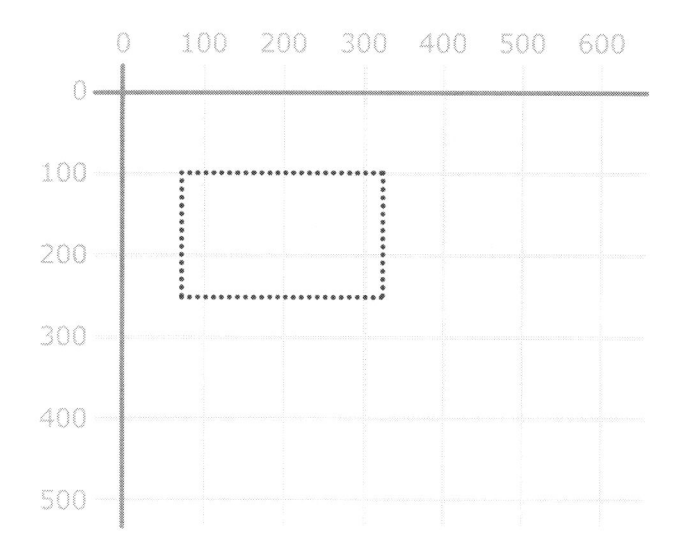

There is one other thing to note about where we are right now. What we've done so far isn't visible to the eye. That is because we've only defined the path. We haven't actually defined what exactly gets drawn, the next two chunks of code fix that up. The first chunk is where we define the rectangle's outline:

```
// the outline

context.lineWidth = 10;

context.strokeStyle = '#666666';

context.stroke();
```

The `lineWidth` and `strokeStyle` properties specify the thickness and color of the line we want to draw. You already know this, so that should hopefully be a review for you. **In fact, this and the next chunks of code should be things you know as well as the back of your hand.** The actual drawing of the line is handled by calling the `stroke` method. At this point, you will see a rectangle whose outlines are actually visible:

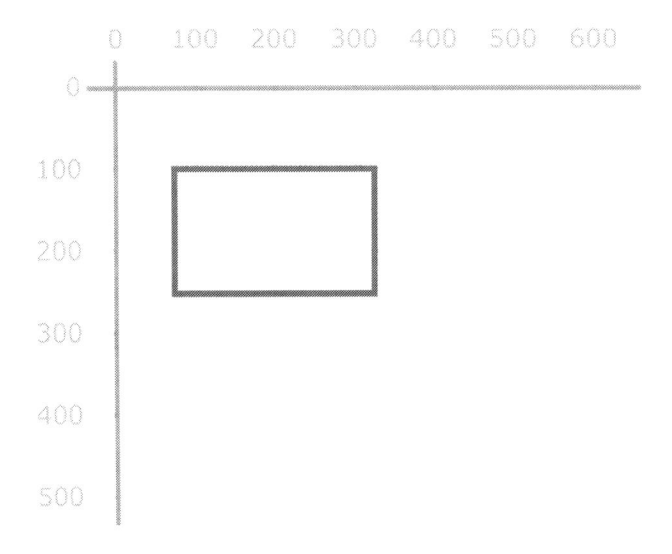

The second chunk of code gives our rectangle some color:

```
// the fill color

context.fillStyle = "#51DCFF";

context.fill();
```

The `fillStyle` property allows you to define the color. The `fill` method tells your `canvas` to go ahead and fill up the insides of our closed path with that color. After this line of code has executed, you will end up with the rectangle in its final form:

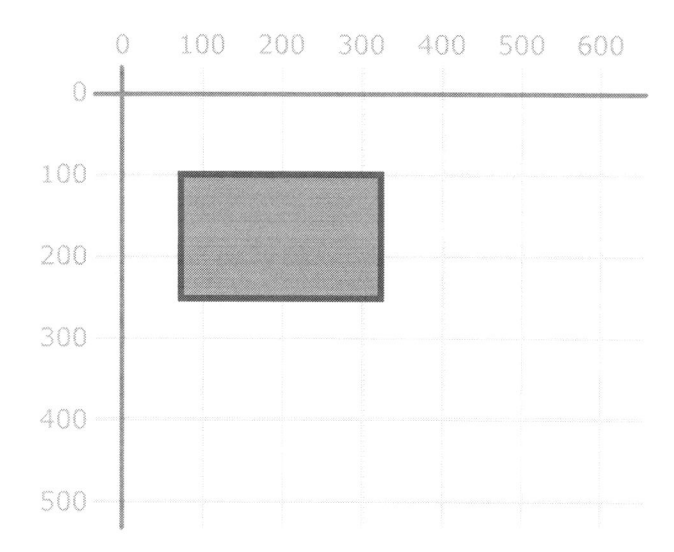

You now have a rectangle that has an outline and a fill. This would be a great moment of celebration if it weren't for a rectangular shape that we completed.

The fillRect and strokeRect Methods

If all the excitement from the `rect` method wasn't enough, you also have the `fillRect` and `strokeRect` methods that allow you to draw rectangles as well. To make things even more exciting, these two methods take arguments that are the same as what the `rect` method expects - the first two arguments specify the position, and the next two arguments specify the size.

To best explain what is going on, let's look at some code that uses both of these methods:

```
var canvasElement = document.querySelector("#myCanvas");
var context = canvasElement.getContext("2d");
```

```
// Outline
context.strokeStyle = "#FF3399";
context.strokeRect(300, 50, 200, 200);


// Filled
context.fillStyle = "#00CCFF";
context.fillRect(50, 50, 200, 200);
```

If you had to visualize this using our numbered grid, you would see two squares that look as follows:

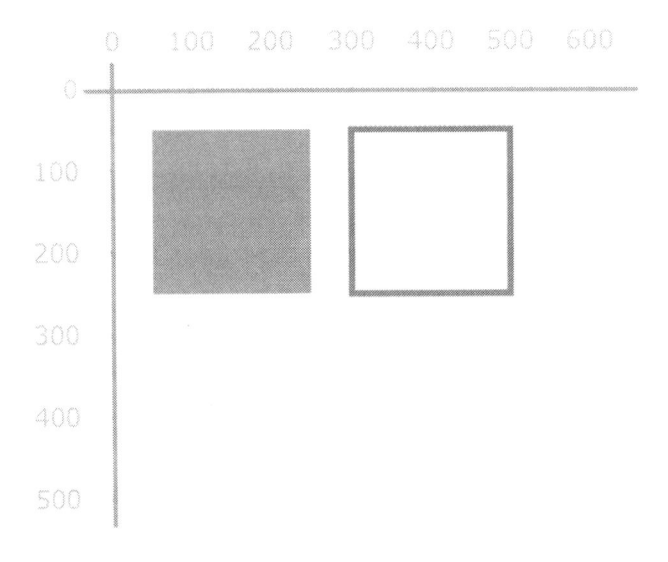

The `strokeRect` method draws an outline of a rectangle. The `fillRect` method draws a solid colored rectangle. These two methods are basically macro draw commands. You specify them and, just like magic, the rectangle of your choosing gets drawn.

That is very different than what the `rect` method provides. The `rect` method is part of your path commands. You specify a bunch of path commands that start with `beginPath`. Some of these commands may be related to your rectangle. Some may not. In the end, you have a giant grouping of path commands that tell your canvas all the various things it needs to draw.

Conclusion

So...there you have it! You just saw a quick overview of how to draw rectangles on the `canvas` using `rect`, `fillRect`, and `strokeRect`. You may be wondering which of the three methods you'll want to use. If you need to just draw a rectangle quickly, either the `fillRect` (solid shape) or `strokeRect` (outline of a shape) methods are fine. For drawing a rectangle as part of a series of other draw commands, the `rect` method is your best friend. In case it matters, I almost always use the `rect` method for the unfortunate times I need to draw a rectangle or square :P

Chapter 7: Drawing Triangles

When you are working with the canvas, you have some built-in functions that help you easily draw common shapes like circles (you'll see in a little bit), rectangles/squares, and lines. Guess what shape you don't have a built-in function to help you easily draw?

If you guessed any shape other than a triangle, I weep for you. Because there is no built-in triangle function, drawing triangles on the canvas is a bit more involved and error prone than the other shapes:

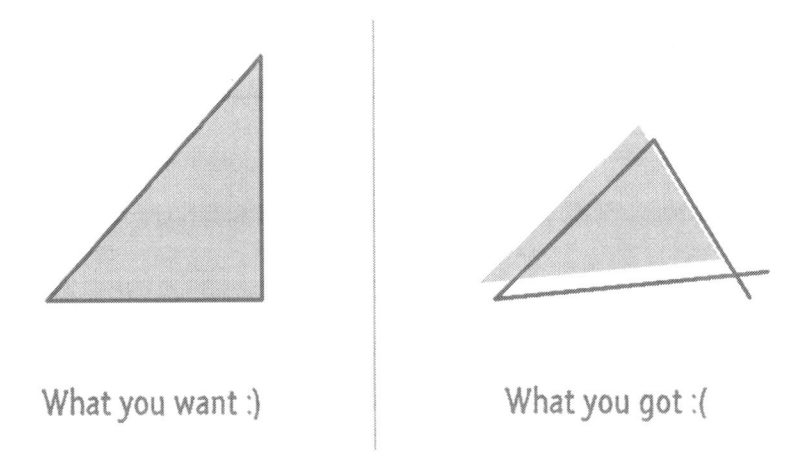

What you want :)   What you got :(

Not to worry, though! In this chapter, we will take a look at all the boring steps and how you can make drawing triangles really easy...and maybe even fun!

Onwards!

Drawing Triangles

First, make sure you have a canvas element defined in your HTML page, and give it an **id** of **myCanvas**. This is the starting point for all of the examples we've seen so far, and this is what that HTML looks like for it:

```
<!DOCTYPE html>
<html>
<head>
  <title>Simple Example</title>
  <style>
    canvas {
      border: #333 10px solid;
    }
  </style>
</head>

<body>
    <canvas id="myCanvas" width="500" height="500"></canvas>
</body>

</html>
```

It is inside this `canvas` element we will draw our triangle. Now that we got this boring stuff out of the way...

The way you draw a triangle is by putting into code the following steps:

i.   Declare your intent to draw lines so that the canvas knows what to expect

ii. Move your virtual pen to to the x and y co-ordinate where you wish to start drawing the triangle

iii. With your virtual pen at the starting point, use the `lineTo` method to draw lines between two points.

iv. Specify the fill color, line color / thickness, etc. to adjust how your triangle looks

These steps are deliberately pretty hand-wavy to not overwhelm you at this point. The overwhelming will take place next, so let's look at the code for drawing a simple rectangle first. We will weave these four steps in as part of explaining how the code works.

Inside the `script` tag, add the following lines of code:

```
var canvasElement = document.querySelector("#myCanvas");

var context = canvasElement.getContext("2d");


// the triangle

context.beginPath();

context.moveTo(100, 100);

context.lineTo(100, 300);

context.lineTo(300, 300);

context.closePath();


// the outline

context.lineWidth = 10;

context.strokeStyle = '#666666';

context.stroke();


// the fill color
```

```
context.fillStyle = "#FFCC00";

context.fill();
```

Once you've done this, preview your page in your browser. If everything worked out properly, you should see a yellow triangle appear:

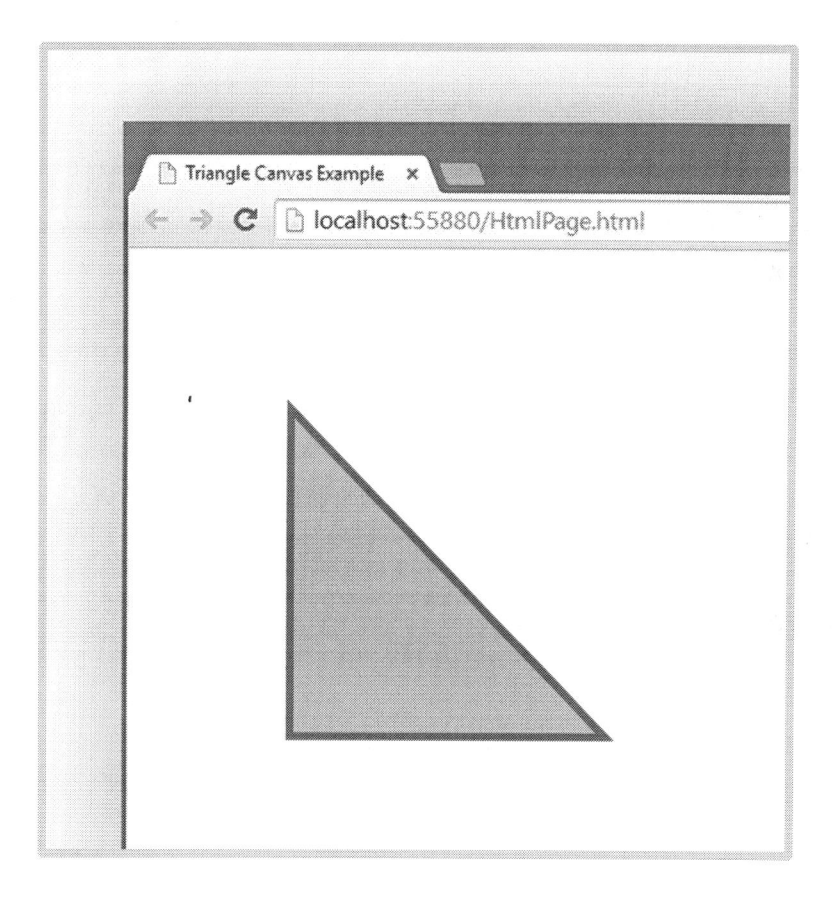

Let's look at how the lines of code you've written map to the triangle that you see on the screen. We are going to skip the `canvasElement` and `context` variables and start with the interesting lines that follow them:

```
// the triangle
```

```
context.beginPath();

context.moveTo(100, 100);

context.lineTo(100, 300);

context.lineTo(300, 300);

context.closePath();
```

Because these lines are crucial to drawing our triangle, I'm going to slow down and dive into greater detail on what each line does.

The first line sets it all up:

```
context.beginPath();
```

The `beginPath` method signals to the `canvas` that you intend to draw a path. The next line defines where to start our path from:

```
context.moveTo(100, 100);
```

That is handled by the `moveTo` method which takes an x and y co-ordinate value. In our case, we are going to be starting the path from a horizontal and vertical position of **100**:

With the starting point set, it's time to start drawing the lines that make up our triangle:

```
context.lineTo(100, 300);

context.lineTo(300, 300);
```

The first `lineTo` method draws a line from our starting point of (100, 100) to (100, 300):

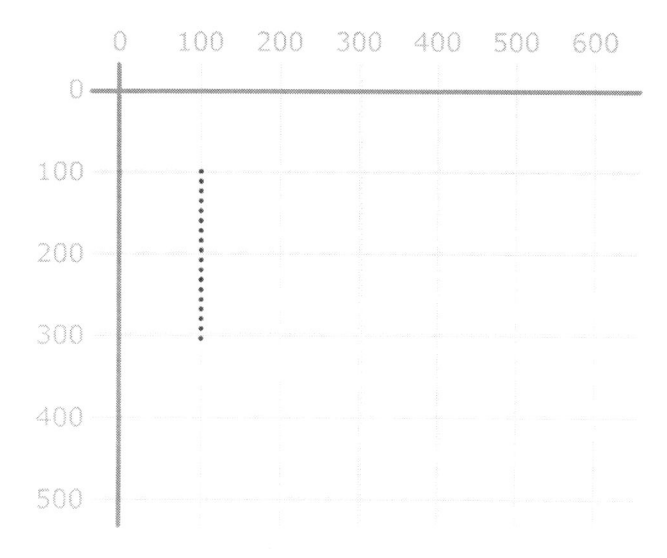

The second `lineTo` method picks up from where the pen currently is and draws a line from (100, 300) to (300, 300):

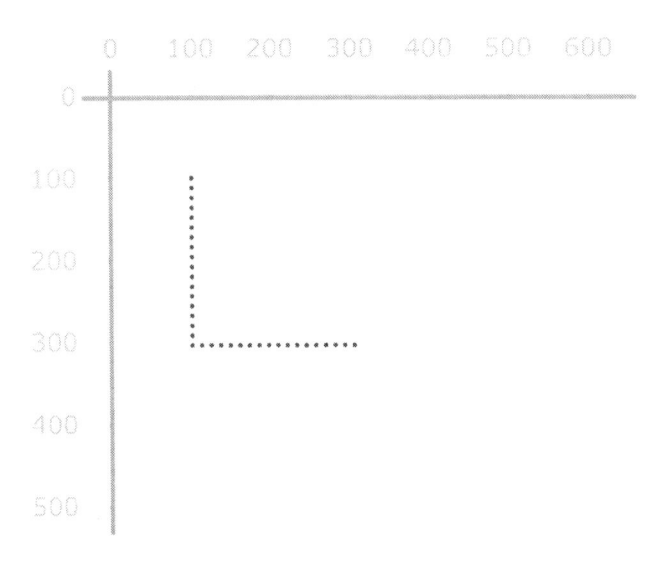

Right now, we have an L shape that isn't quite a triangle. To make this a triangle, we need to close this path by drawing a straight line from where we are back to the beginning. As you may recall, there are two ways to do this. One way is by by drawing a line using `lineTo` back to our starting point. The other way is by using `closePath`. The easiest way is to use closePath, and that is what our code shows as well:

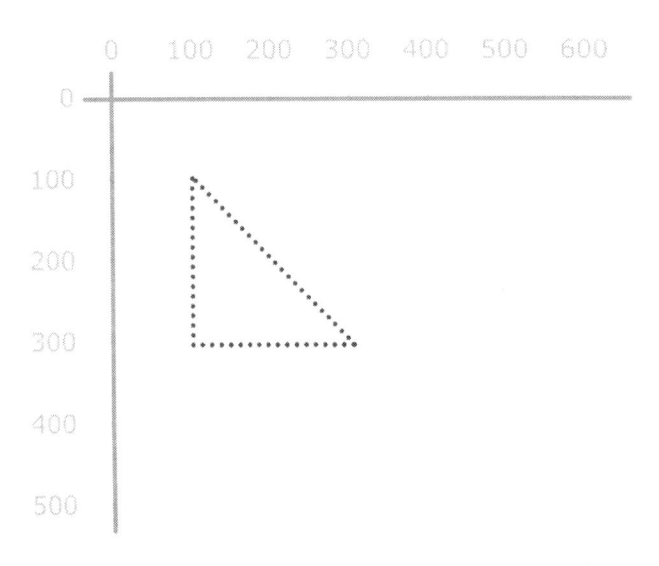

At this point, you may be wondering why our triangle looks dotted and ghostly. If you haven't been wondering that, take a few moments and wonder.

Now that you are done wondering, here is why I visualize the lines in the way that I have. The five lines of code you've seen so far don't actually help you to see the triangle. What you've basically done is draw something that is **entirely invisible**:

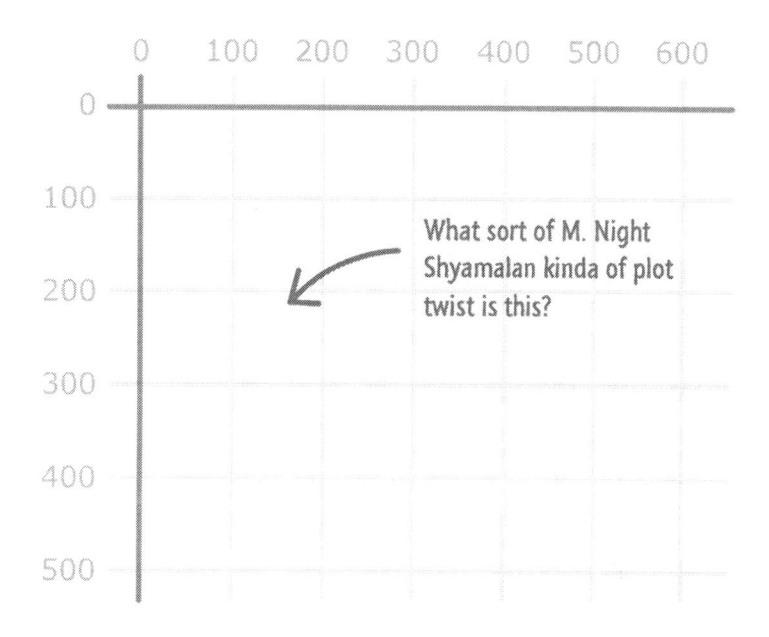

What sort of M. Night Shyamalan kinda of plot twist is this?

The next two chunks of code fix that up:

```
// the outline
context.lineWidth = 10;
context.strokeStyle = '#666666';
context.stroke();


// the fill color
context.fillStyle = "#FFCC00";
```

```
context.fill();
```

The `lineWidth` and `strokeStyle` properties specify the thickness and color of the line we want to draw. The `fillStyle` property allows you to define the color. The `fill` method tells your canvas to go ahead and fill up the insides of our closed path with that color. After this lines of code have run, our triangle will now take its final form:

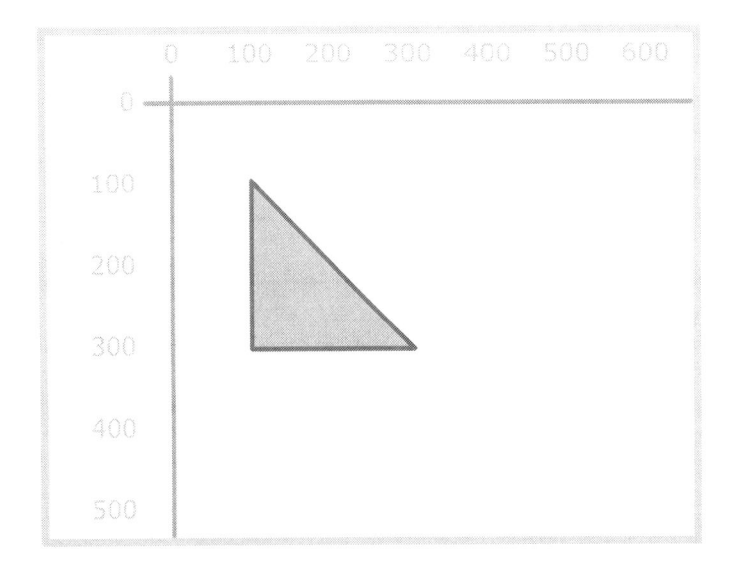

You now have a triangle that has an outline and a fill. It is, as some wise people say, complete.

Conclusion

Anyway, as you can see, drawing a triangle isn't particularly hard. At least, it should no longer be after seeing how easy it is to draw a few lines and set a few visual properties. It just requires you keeping track of where your virtual pen is at the end of a series of `moveTo`, `lineTo`, and `closePath` commands.

Chapter 8: Drawing Circles

When drawing in the canvas, a (very superior) shape you will often want to draw is a circle:

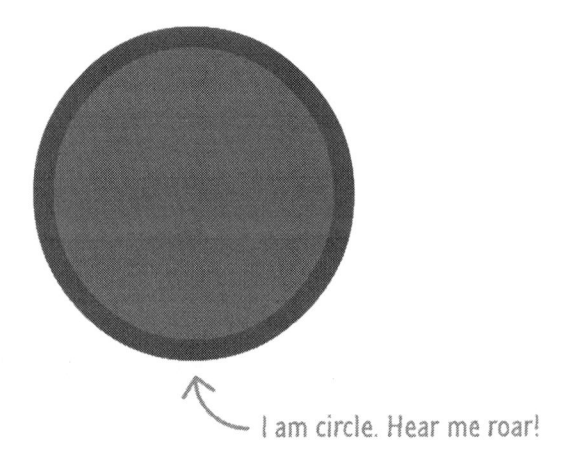

I am circle. Hear me roar!

While the circle seems like something that would be easy to draw, as you will see shortly, it has some bizarre behaviors that you need to know about. This chapter will help you out with that and more.

Let's get started!

Meet the Arc Function

The way you draw a circle in your canvas by using the handy `arc` function. This function and the arguments you need to specify in order to use it look as follows:

```
arc(centerX, centerY, radius, startAngle, endAngle, isAntiClockwise);
```

These arguments are important in helping you draw the circle that you want, so let's look in detail what all of these arguments do.

centerX and centerY

The `centerX` and `centerY` arguments are pretty straightforward to understand. They specify where the center of your circle will be positioned inside the `canvas`:

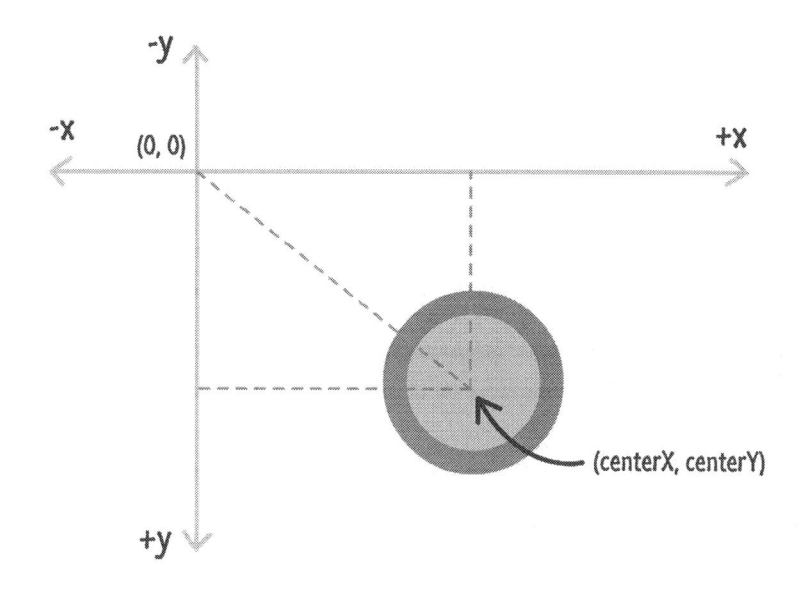

Remember, the canvas lives in an inverted Cartesian system. What this means is that the x value increases as you move right, and the y value increases as you go down. This might be a little different than what you may remember from graphing equations in school.

Radius

The radius specifies the straight line distance of your circle from its center to any edge:

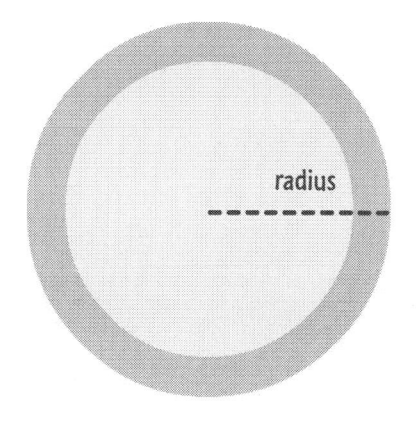

The larger your radius, the bigger your circle will be. The smaller your radius, the smaller your circle will be. If you provide a negative value, JavaScript will throw a nice `IndexSizeError` exception, so you don't want to do that.

startAngle, endAngle, and isAntiClockwise

Now, we finally get to the interesting stuff. These three arguments are interesting and closely related to drawing your circle. As you probably know, a circle is made up of 360 degrees:

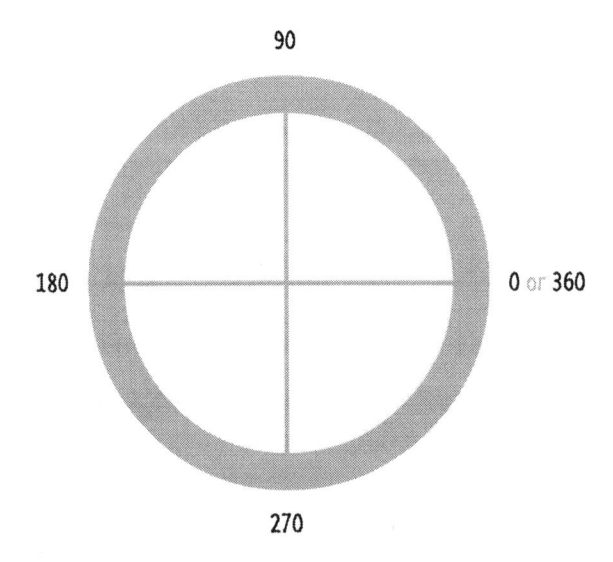

There are two important details to note - details that will probably shatter your belief in all that is good in this world. The first is that the angles increase clockwise for a circle when drawn in the canvas:

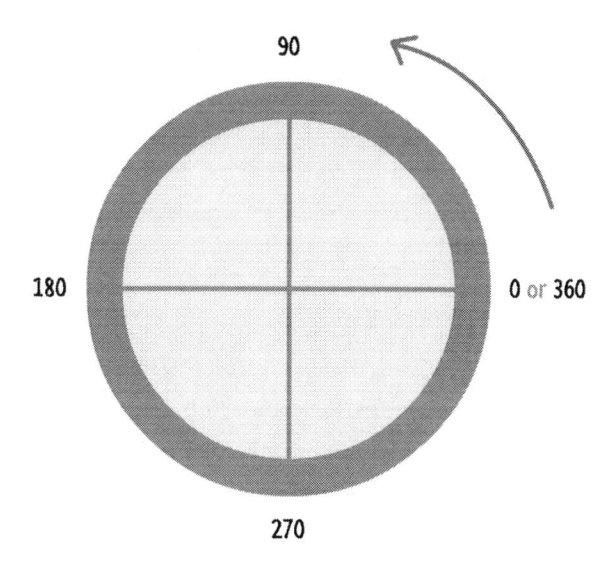

The second detail is that JavaScript doesn't work with degrees. In JavaScript land, you deal with everything in terms of radians:

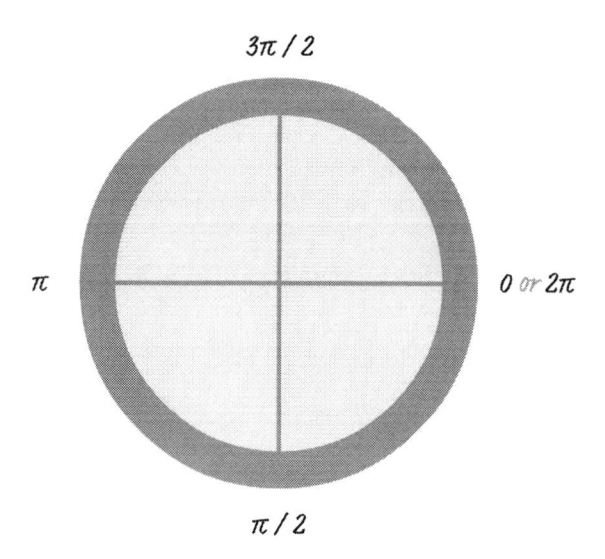

Once you understand these two details, you crossed a big hurdle in mentally being able to visualize what your `arc` function will create.

Note: Converting from Degrees to Radians

To convert from degrees to radians, just use the following expression:

`var radians = (Math.PI / 180) * degrees.`

Ok, let's now take a step forward and work through how the **startAngle**, **stopAngle**, and **isAntiClockwise** arguments play a role. There are three steps you need to follow:

1. Mark your **startAngle**.

2. Mark your **stopAngle**.

3. Draw a line on the circumference either clockwise or anticlockwise depending on whether your value for **isAntiClockwise** is `true` or `false`.

4. If you are filling in your circle, fill in the region enclosed by the circumference and the straight line between the points referenced by **startAngle** and **stopAngle**.

Let's look through an example of this. Let's say your start angle is π / 2, and your end angle is π. You are also anticlockwise and centered at 200, 200 with a radius of 93.

Given those values, the `arc` function would look as follows:

```
arc(200, 200, 93, Math.PI / 2, Math.PI, true);
```

If you had to visualize this, here is what your circle with just the stroke defined would look like:

$3\pi / 2$

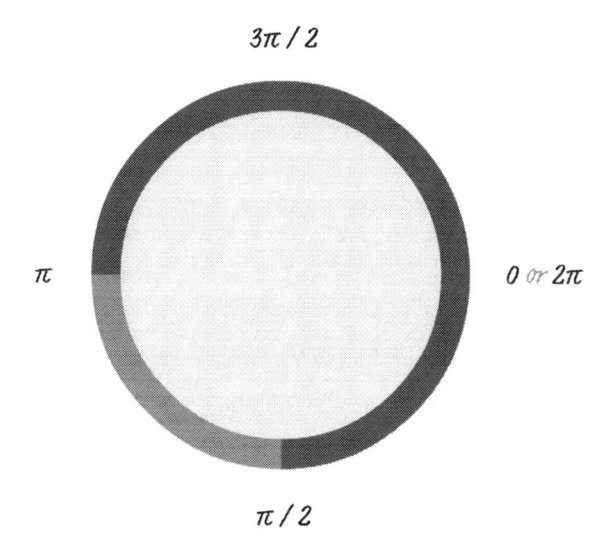

π *0 or 2π*

$\pi / 2$

If you filled in this circle, here is what you would see:

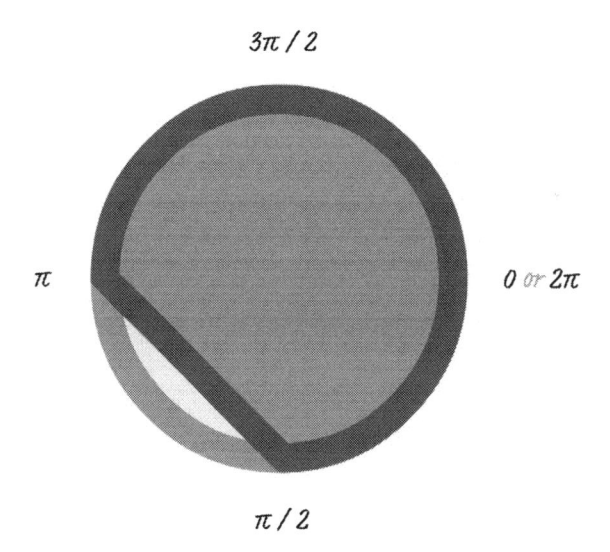

$3\pi / 2$

π *0 or 2π*

$\pi / 2$

Notice that your circle's start and end points are defined by your **startAngle** (π / 2) and your **endAngle** (π). Because you are going anti-clockwise, notice that the outline and the colored region goes all the way around the circle on the long side.

If you switch from being anticlockwise to being clockwise but keep all of your other values the same, your `arc` function now looks as follows:

```
arc(200, 200, 93, Math.PI / 2, Math.PI, false);
```

As a result of the direction being changed, your circle takes a different turn (ha!):

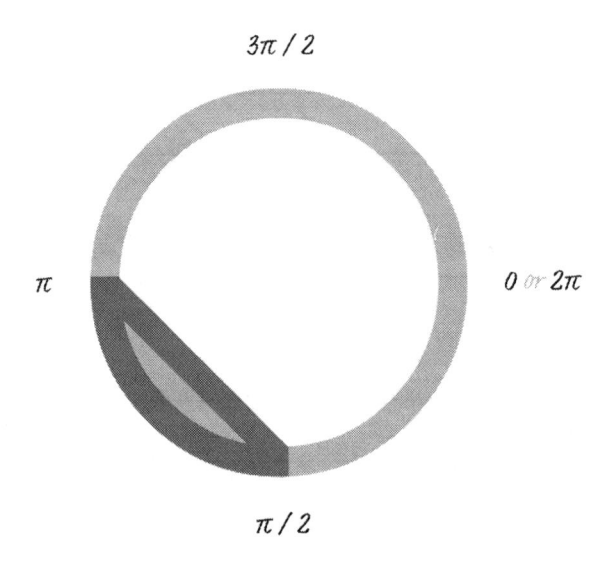

$3\pi / 2$

π 0 or 2π

$\pi / 2$

Whenever you run into the arc function and need to visualize what the final circle looks like, use the four steps I described earlier. Those steps hold for whatever combination of **startAngle, endAngle**, and **true/false** you provide for the anti-clockwiseness of your circle.

Displaying the Circle

Ok, now that you know all about the `arc` function and how you can mentally draw your circle, let's look at what drawing one looks like. Using the same starting example that you've been seeing for a billion chapters, here is what a 100% organic (and cage-free) semi-circle looks like:

```
// draw the colored region
context.beginPath();
context.arc(200, 200, 93, Math.PI / 2, Math.PI, true);
```

```
context.fillStyle = '#FF6A6A';

context.fill();


// draw the stroke

context.lineWidth = 20;

context.strokeStyle = '#FF0000';

context.stroke();
```

If you add this code to your page and preview in your browser, you will see something that looks as follows:

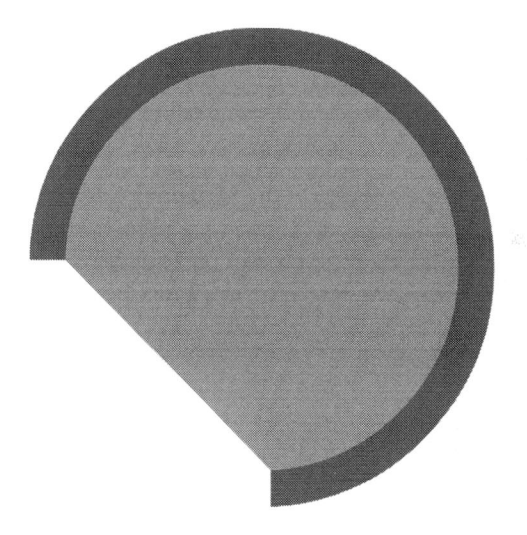

We've already seen this weird semi-circle in the previous section, it is nice to see it being drawn from actual code as opposed to just plain English words. Before we wrap things up, let's end (ironically) by looking at the code for how to draw a full circle:

```
// draw the colored region

context.beginPath();
```

```
context.arc(200, 200, 93, 0, 2 * Math.PI, true);

context.fillStyle = "#E2FFC6";

context.fill();


// draw the stroke

context.lineWidth = 20;

context.strokeStyle = "#66CC01";

context.stroke();
```

When you preview this in your browser, you'll see something that looks like this:

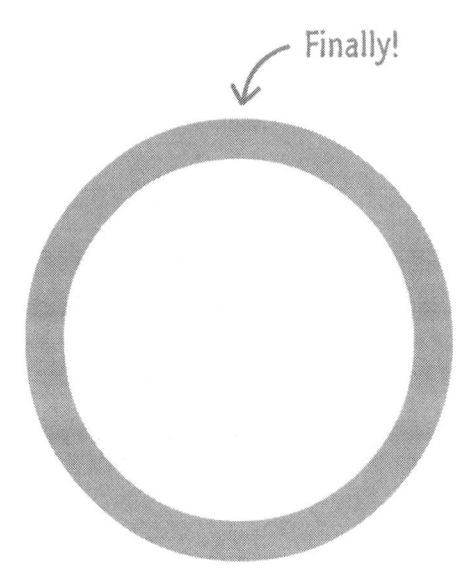

Finally!

You can tell by looking at the arguments we passed in to the arc method for why that is. The **startAngle** value is 0, and the **endAngle** value is 2π. We don't leave any room for any spoiled radians to go off and do something crazy.

Conclusion

Well, that's all there is to drawing circles on the `canvas`. As you've seen by now, there is no simple circle method that draws a circle for you. Instead, you have the more general `arc` method that provides you with a lot of little buttons to push and to customize what your circle looks like. With generality, you often get complexity. Where there is complexity, you'll probably find me writing about it. Now, isn't that the most cringe-worthy conclusion you've probably ever read? I certainly hope so :P

Chapter 9: Modifying How Corners Look

When drawing on the canvas, you create corners all the time:

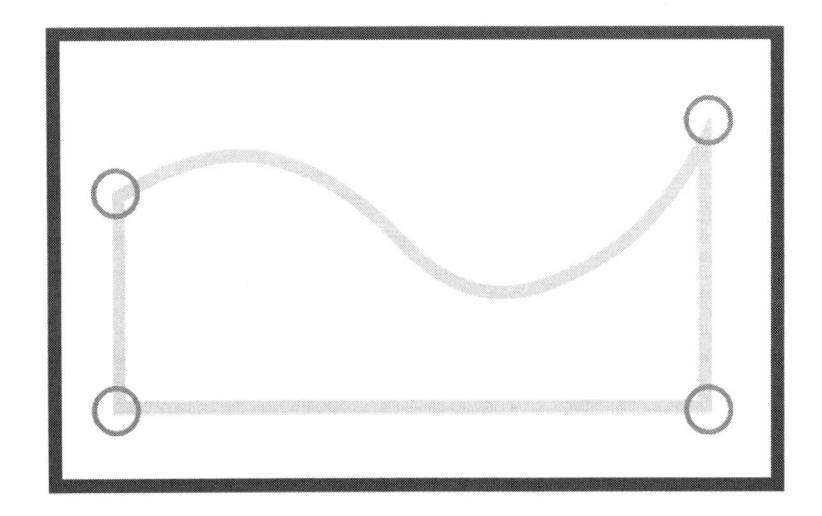

This is such a frequent occurrence, you normally don't even pay much attention to all the times it happens. We are going to change that with this chapter. In the next couple of sections, you will not only learn to notice what these corners look like, you will also learn all about the `lineJoin` property and how to adjust their appearance.

Onwards!

Meet the lineJoin Property

By default, your corners have a particular look to them. That default look is fine and all, but you can totally change what your corners look like. The way you do that is by setting the `lineJoin` property:

The lineJoin property specifies what this looks like.

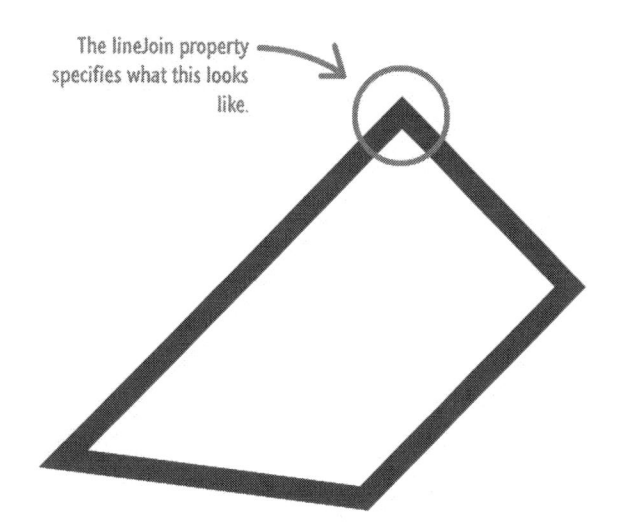

The `lineJoin` property takes three values: **miter, round, bevel**. A value of **miter** is the default behavior, and it creates sharp corners:

The **round** value, shockingly, creates rounded corners:

The **bevel** property creates triangular corners:

You set the `lineJoin` property on our drawing context object...just like almost all of the drawing-related properties that we've seen so far. To see the `lineJoin` property in action, take a look at the following code:

```
// the triangle
context.beginPath();
context.moveTo(100, 100);
context.lineTo(100, 300);
context.lineTo(300, 300);
context.closePath();
```

```
// the outline
context.lineWidth = 10;
context.strokeStyle = '#666666';
context.lineJoin = "round";
context.stroke();

// the fill color
context.fillStyle = "#FFCC00";
context.fill();
```

This code draws a triangle. What makes this relevant for this chapter is the highlighted line where we set the `lineJoin` property to a value of **round**. This would result in a triangle whose corners are all rounded. Simple bimple.

Did you know?

As if setting the lineJoin property to **miter** isn't exciting enough, you can set the `miterLimit` property:

```
context.miterLimit = 15;
```

This property stands for the ratio between half of the `lineWidth` value and the miter length. It acts as a threshold where if the value is too small, your `lineJoin` property value of **miter** will not kick in. I haven't found a use for it in real life, but I figured I would mention it here for the sake of completeness.

Conclusion

Putting my general snarkiness of this topic aside, it's admirable that we have so much control over something that seems trivial. The lineJoin property's default value of **miter** is appropriate for many situations, but when you are using the canvas to represent charts or other very line-heavy things, being able to customize how the corners look is essential...maybe!

Chapter 10: Working with Colors

Let's face it. The default black color everything on the `canvas` gets is cool at first, but it gets tiring after a while:

In this article, we'll do a deep dive into all the ways you have for giving your `canvas` content some much needed life via color.

Onwards!

Colors, strokeStyle, and fillStyle!

The primary way you colorize content is by setting the `strokeStyle` property for shape outlines and the `fillStyle` property for the shape insides:

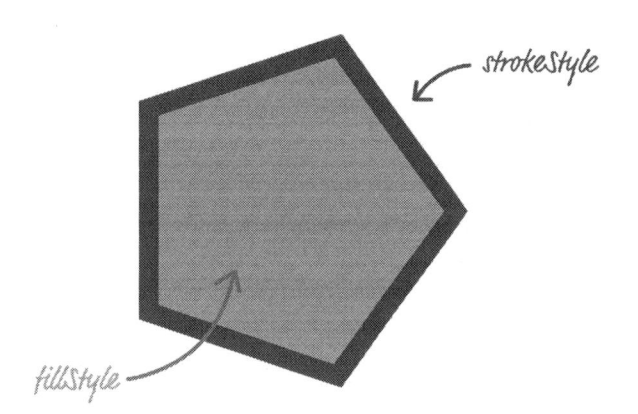

Between these two properties, you can color everything from lines to geometric shapes to text.

Let's say we have a rectangle that looks as follows:

The code responsible for this work of art looks like this:

```
var canvasElement = document.querySelector("#myCanvas");

var context = canvasElement.getContext("2d");

context.beginPath();

context.rect(75, 100, 250, 150);

context.fill();
```

To set the fill color of this element, add the following highlighted line that specifies the `fillStyle` property:

```
context.beginPath();

context.rect(75, 100, 250, 150);

context.fillStyle = "#FFCC00";

context.fill();
```

Let's not stop with just the fill. Since we are already here, we are going to next add a thick outline and give that a color via the `strokeStyle` property. Add the following three highlighted lines to your code:

```
context.beginPath();

context.rect(75, 100, 250, 150);

context.fillStyle = "#FFCC00";

context.fill();
```

```
context.lineWidth = 5;

context.strokeStyle = "#535353";

context.stroke();
```

Once you have made the change, preview what you have in your browser. You should see something that looks like this:

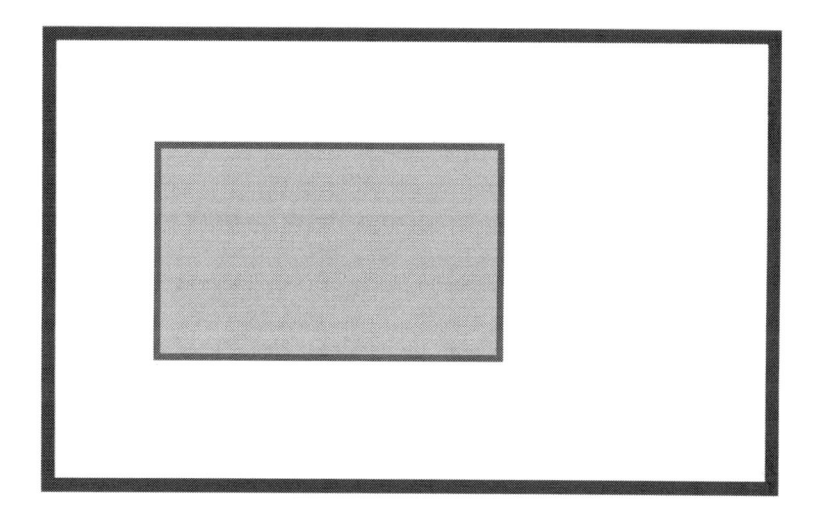

The two lines of code that took our pretty drab looking rectangle and helped make it a bit more lively are the `fillStyle` and `strokeStyle` properties. You can argue that the `fillStyle` probably had more to do with it since the outline is still a pretty dull shade of gray, but anyway...but what we are going to do from here on out is take a look at the various ways you have for specifying colors. While I will be focusing only on the `fillStyle` property, everything you see will apply equally to `strokeStyle` as well. Me ignoring `strokeStyle` is purely done for aesthetic reasons. After all, changing the fill color of a rectangle looks a lot more impressive than changing just the outline color!

Hex Color Values

Let us start our exploration by looking at what we have already specified for the `fillStyle` property in our code:

```
context.fillStyle = "#FFCC00";
```

Here, we've assigned a **hex color value** that corresponds to a nice shade of yellow. This hex value corresponds to the Red, Green, and Blue components of the color we are trying to represent. Chances are, if you are copying color values defined in an image editor, you are going to be seeing values in this format.

CSS Color Keywords

You can also specify CSS color keywords such as **yellow, navy, firebrick,** and a whole bunch of colors with really cool names:

```
context.fillStyle = "deepskyblue";
```

Have you ever wondered what **deepskyblue** looks like? Well, wonder no more:

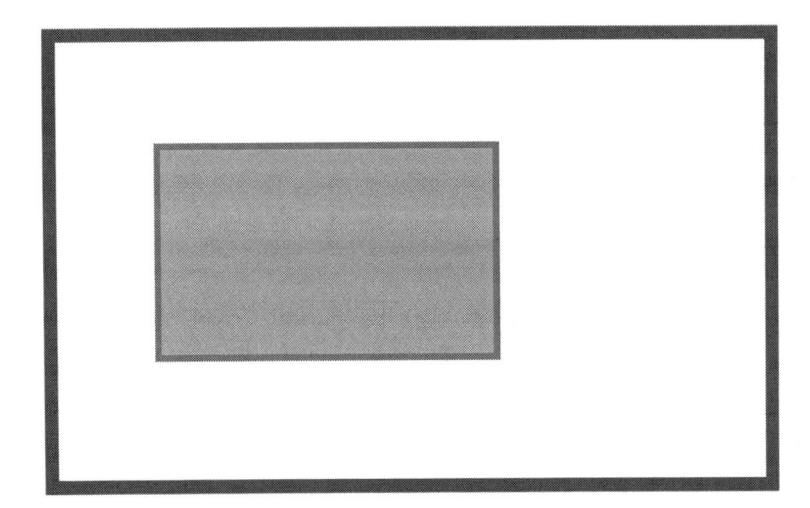

You can see the full range of color keywords in this MDN article (http://bit.ly/ColorKeywords). For the most part, you probably won't be using color keywords much. The reason is that these named colors are extremely web-specific, and most image editing tools have no idea to either accept or export color keywords. Instead, many image editing tools prefer good old RGB. Speaking of which...

RGB Values

As it turns, you can also specify colors to the `fillStyle` and `strokeStyle` properties as an RGB value by using the **rgb** function:

```
context.fillStyle = "rgb(204, 102, 153)";
```

Replacing our rectangle's `fillStyle` value with this RGB entry looks as follows:

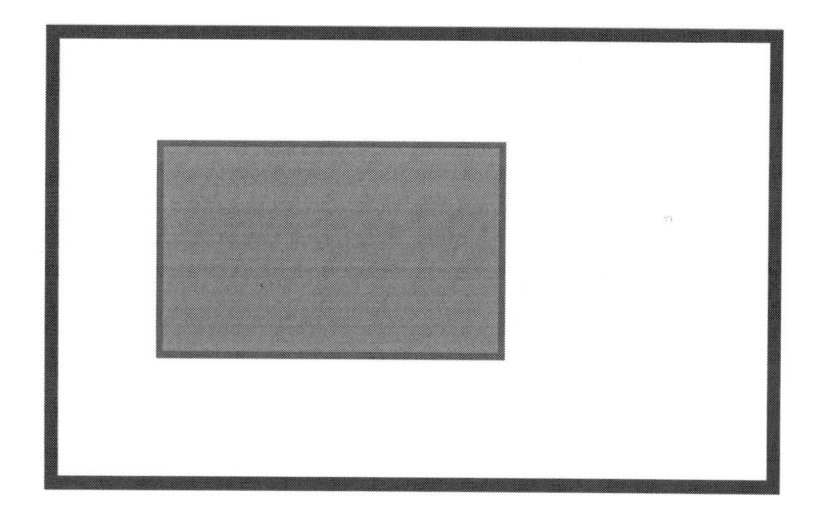

Your RGB function and the values are expected to be in the form of strings. That is why you see them wrapped inside quotation marks. With that said, we are inside JavaScript. Nothing prevents you from parameterizing the values by doing some good, old-fashioned string magic:

```
context.fillStyle = "rgb(" + r + ", " + g + ", " + b +")";
```

For many interactive scenarios, you will find yourself doing this quite often, so just be aware that you can totally do this.

Transparency and RGBA

So far, we've looked at specifying a color as a hex value, CSS color keyword, and a RGB value. There is just one more variant for specifying a single color, and that is RGBA. The "A" stands for alpha...or transparency, and you specify that value as a number between 0.0 (fully transparent) to 1.0 (fully opaque).

If we to extend the earlier example by giving our fill color a 50% transparency, here is what the **rgba** declaration would look like:

```
context.fillStyle = "rgba(204, 102, 153, .5)";
```

This will translate to a more muted version of the pink color we saw earlier:

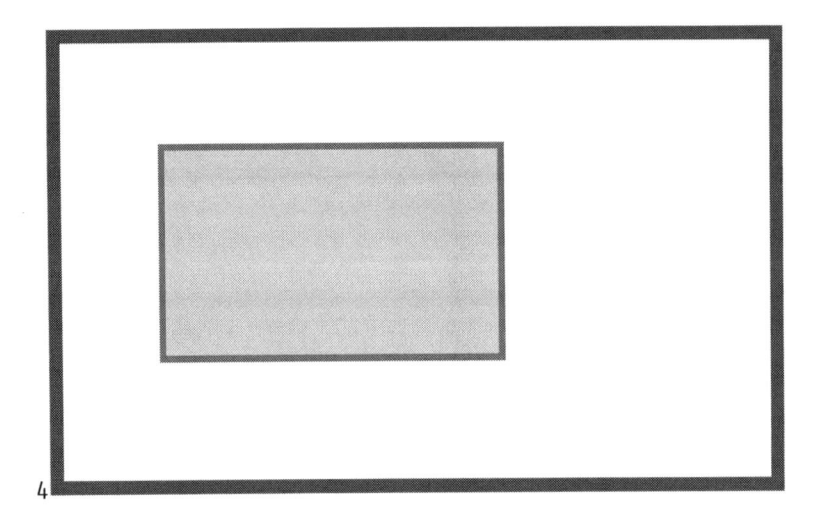

You do have one more way for setting the transparency, and that way is by setting it globally via the `globalAlpha` property:

```
context.globalAlpha = .3;
```

With this line, we are setting the opacity of *everything* in our `canvas` to be just 30 percent. Your strokes and fills will be impacted, and the `globalAlpha` property overrides any alpha value you may have specified inside your **rgba** function. Use this property at your own peril.

Using HSL Values

We've spent a lot of time taking about RGB values. While a lot of the colors you will use will be in that format, you aren't limited to just RGB, though. You can also specify colors in the HSL space. In HSL, you define a color by specifing values for **Hue**, **Saturation**, and **Lightness**.

You can think of HSL colors modeled as shown in the following three-dimensional cylinder (created by SharkD[1]):

---

[1] https://commons.wikimedia.org/wiki/File:HSL_color_solid_cylinder.png

Page | 105

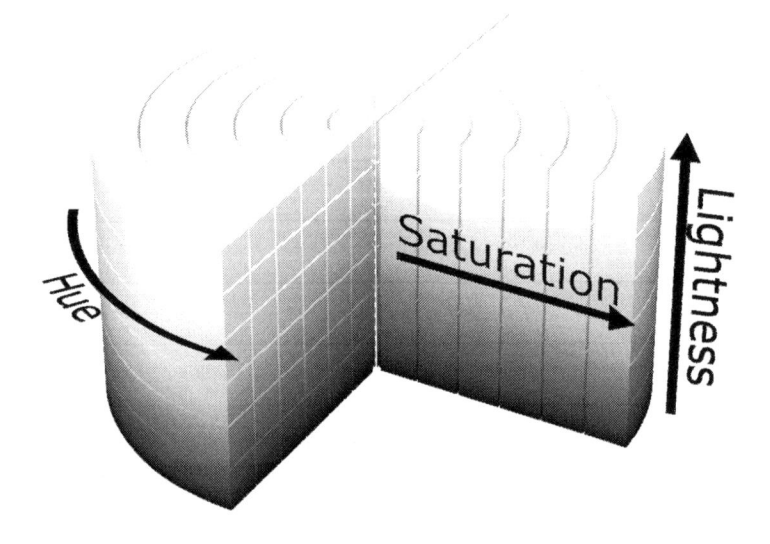

The value for Hue is specified in degrees going from 0 to 360. Both Saturation and Lightness are percentages that you specify as as percentage values. Below is what the `fillStyle` property set to a HSL value looks like:

```
// a salmon-ish color specified in HSL
context.fillStyle = "hsl(9, 83%, 70%)";
```

This translates into a rectangle that looks like the following:

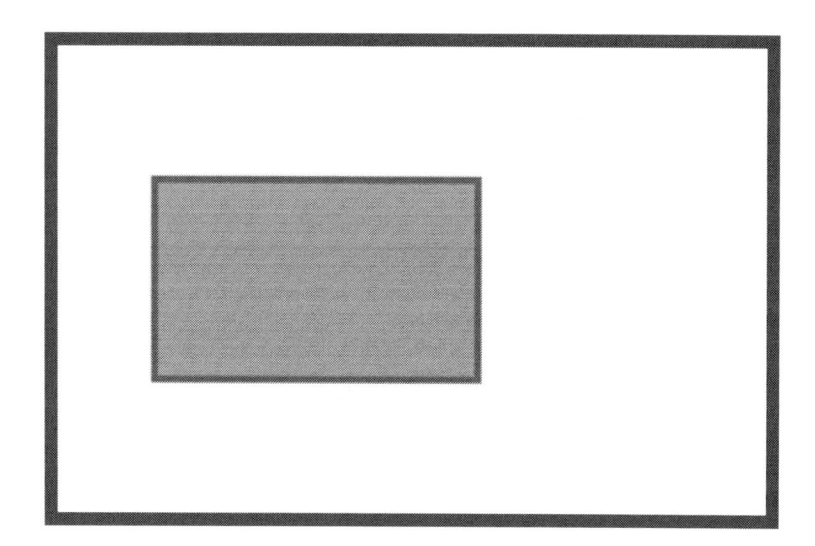

Just like what we saw with RGB values, you can tackle on a value for alpha to define a HSLA color. Below is an example of an HSLA color that is green-ish looking with an opacity of 50%:

```
context.fillStyle = "hsla(100, 83%, 70%, .5)";
```

HSL values are very common when working with colors from design tools, but they are great to use if you want to manipulate colors programmatically. Instead of dealing with three independent values like you have with RGB, in the HSL world, you can go through a range of colors by just modifying one of the H, S, or L values. That's a convenience you should totally not overlook if you ever find yourself manipulating color values in JavaScript.

Specifying Gradients

There is just one more thing we need to look at before our look into working with colors is wrapped up. That thing is **gradients**! So far, we've only specified a single color value for the various things we've been coloring. Gradients change all that. With gradients, you have the ability to specify multiple colors and how those colors blend in with each other. In the following sections, let's learn all about them.

The Linear Gradient

The first gradient variation we'll learn about is the linear one. A linear gradient is one where you have two or more colors on a virtual (invisible) straight line. These colors blend evenly as you move from one color to another on this line. That definition is probably more complicated than it needs to be, but hopefully the following image makes more sense:

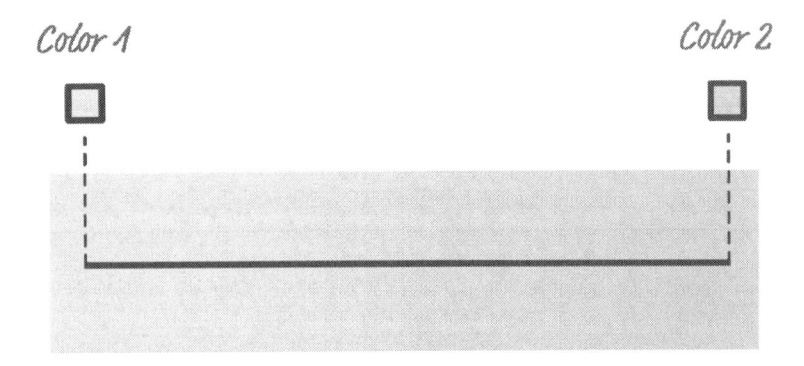

We have two colors one two ends of a rectangle. On one end is a light gray. On the other end is cyan. Between those two points, the colors gradually blend between the gray and cyan to give you this smooth look. That blending is one of the hallmark features of a gradient. Now, let's go a bit deeper.

These two points on either end of our gradient have a more formal name. They are known as **gradient color stops** or just **color stops**. You can have as many color stops as you want, and each color stop defines its own color and position on the virtual straight line:

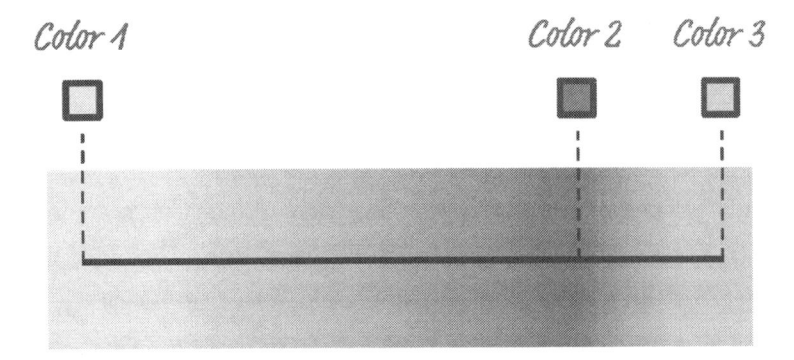

In this version, we modified our earlier example by adding a slightly darker blue gradient stop near the right. Notice that how our colors blend has changed to accommodate this new color that has been thrown in. By adding (or removing) gradient stops and positioning them in various places on our virtual straight line, you can create a variety of different gradient effects.

There is just one more thing to cover before we start looking at how to use this linear gradient to colorize what we draw on the `canvas`. This virtual line all of our gradient stops live on can be rotated in all sorts of ways:

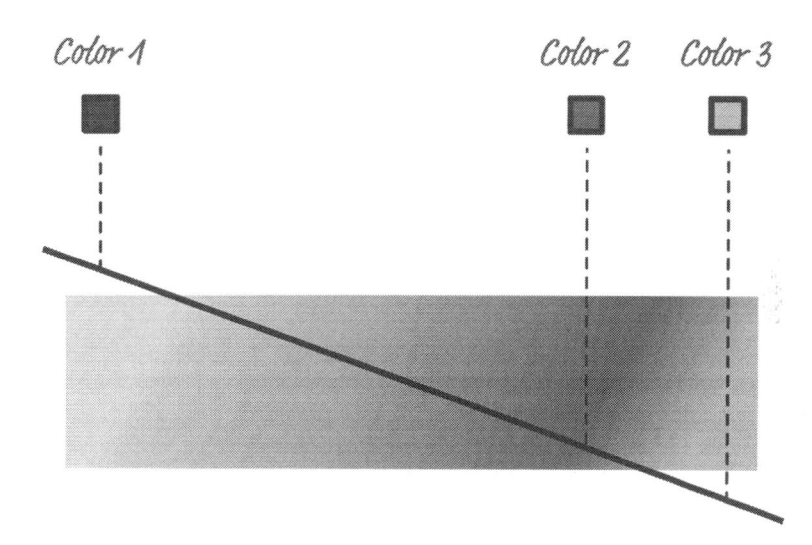

This rotation ends up changing the angle our colors transition from one value to another. By rotating the straight line, you can create gradients whose colors change horizontally (like we saw earlier) to ones where the colors are stacked like pancakes to ones that change in any other angle in-between.

Now that we have seen all of this, let's learn how to use linear gradiens in our `canvas`! The way you specify a linear gradient is by using the `createLinearGradient` method. This method takes four arguments that map to the starting and ending X and Y points of our virtual straight line:

```
context.createLinearGradient(x_0, y_0, x_1, y_1);
```

What this method returns is a `CanvasGradient` object that you can then add your color stops to using `addColorStop`. Let's re-create the gray/blue/cyan gradient that we've been seeing so far.

Take a look a the following code where anything gradient-related is highlighted:

```
context.beginPath();

context.rect(75, 100, 250, 150);


// virtual line length matches our rectangle's dimensions

var gradient = context.createLinearGradient(75, 0, 325, 0);


// our three color stops

gradient.addColorStop(0.1, "#DDDDDD");

gradient.addColorStop(0.75,"#2D7BEC");

gradient.addColorStop(0.9, "#31FFFF");


// assigning the gradient

context.fillStyle = gradient;

context.fill();


context.lineWidth = 5;

context.strokeStyle = "#535353";

context.stroke();
```

Notice how we go from defining our `CanvasGradient` object to specifying our `colorStops` to ultimately assigning our `CanvasGradient` object to the `fillStyle` property. The end result of this looks as follows:

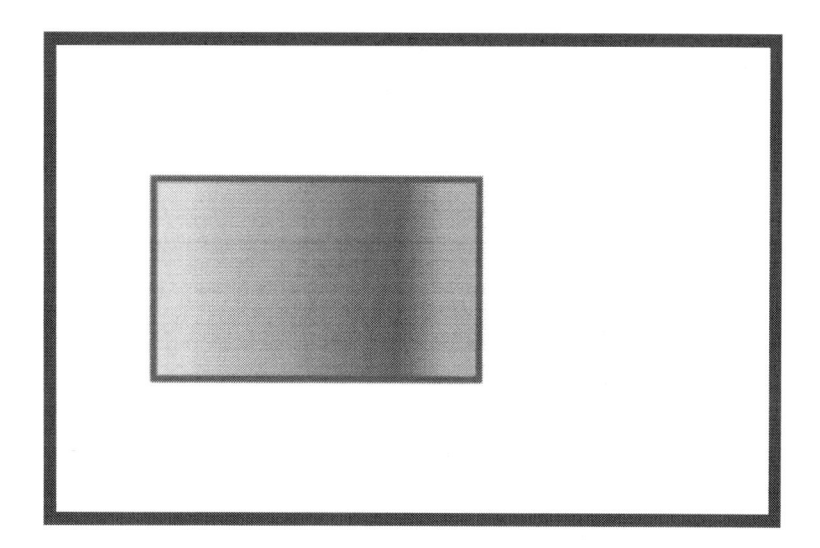

Our rectangle is filled with the linear gradient that we specified earlier. Before we move on to the next section, let's look at our gradient code in greater detail to truly understand what is going on.

The first line is where we define our `CanvasGradient` object very cleverly called `gradient`:

```
var gradient = context.createLinearGradient(75, 0, 325, 0);
```

The position of our virtual line matches the size of the rectangle we are trying to paint. Because our virtual line isn't going to be rotated, I left the Y value for both of the points to just be 0. The size of a gradient is infinite after all, so every Y position (in our unrotated virtual straight line) will have the same gradient value applied. Anyway, the X value maps to the starting and ending points of our rectangle, and it is important to get this value correct. If these values are off, our color stops will be placed at points you probably don't want. Speaking of color stops, gaze your eyes to the next chunk of code:

```
// our three color stops
gradient.addColorStop(0.1, "#DDDDDD");
gradient.addColorStop(0.75,"#2D7BEC");
```

```
gradient.addColorStop(0.9, "#31FFFF");
```

We call the `addColorStop` method on `gradient`. The `addColorStop` method takes two arguments. The first argument specifies where the color stop will be located. You specify the location in terms of a decimal value between 0 and 1 with 0 being the start of our virtual line and 1 being the end of our virtual line. The second argument takes a color value.

You put all of this together, we specify our three color stops at at the 0.1, 0.75, and 0.9 locations with a color value of #DDDDDD, #2D7BEC, and #31FFFF respectively.

All that remains is to now assign our `CanvasGradient` object to whatever any of the `canvas` properties that deal with color. The lucky winner in our example is `fillStyle`…again:

```
context.fillStyle = gradient;
```

This line and the subsequent call to the `fill` method ensure our linear gradient gets applied to our rectangle!

The Radial Gradient

The next (and last!) type of gradient we will look at is the radial gradient:

Look! A radial gradient!!!

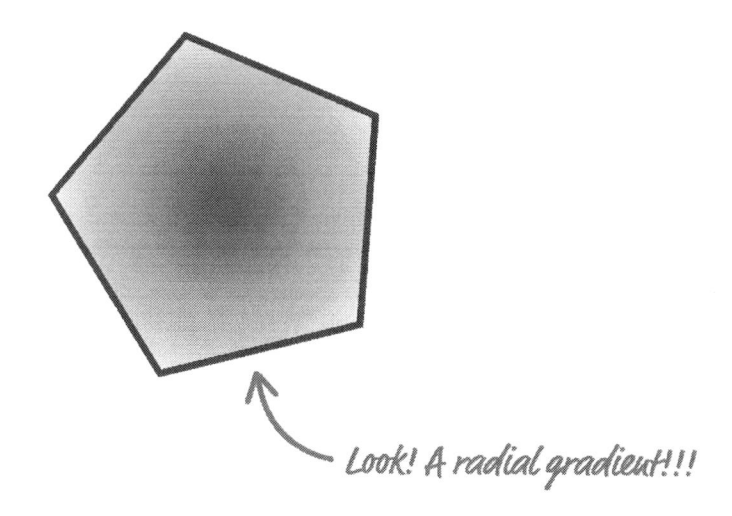

Radial gradients allow you to define a gradient that is all round and oval shaped. That sounds simple, but the way you visualize and actually use them is a whole another story. We will start at the very beginning and gradually ratchet up the complexity until we fully understand it.

With linear gradients, we had a virtual straight line that we specified our color stops on. That was easy to quickly understand. With radial gradients, we still have a virtual straight line. The difference is that this virtual straight line is bounded by two virtual circles. I know that last sentence makes no sense right now, so take a look at the following diagram:

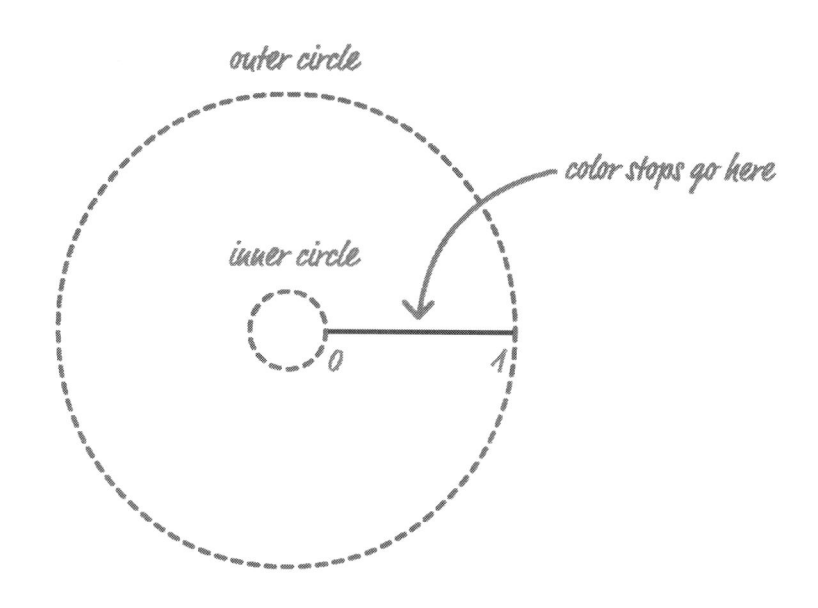

What we have here is a very literal representation of what a radial gradient looks like with no colors specified. We have an inner circle with a position and radius. We have an outer circle with a position and radius. Let's assume both of these circles are centered at the same location. If we drew a straight line from the center points of these two circles to the outer circle's edge, we have our virtual straight line that determines where our color stops will go. So far so good, right?

Let's throw some colors into the mix. At the 0 end of our virtual line, we are going to specify a yellow color. At the 1 end of our virtual line, we are going to specify a green color. Without doing any gradienting, given the two virtual circles we have, the two colors will look as follows:

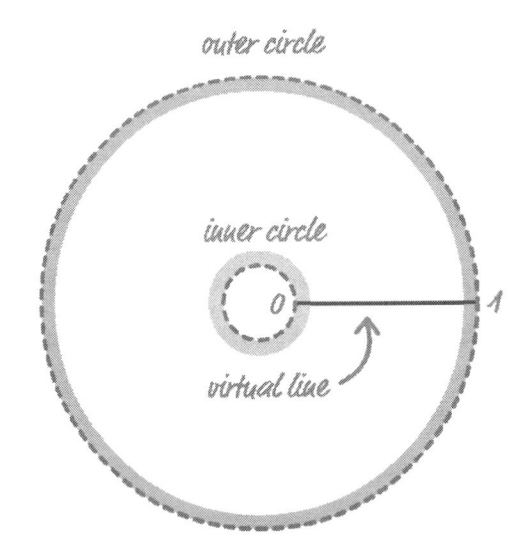

The way the colors move in a radial gradient is interesting and a little confusing at first. The easiest way to make sense of everything is to start by figuring out the coloring behavior for the inner circle and the outer circle.

The inner circle is affected by the first color stop. In our case, that is the yellow color stop at the 0 position. The outer circle is affected by the last color stop. That is the green color at the 1 position. Between the two color stops, the colors blend just like they had in the linear case. The yellow will slowly make way to the green:

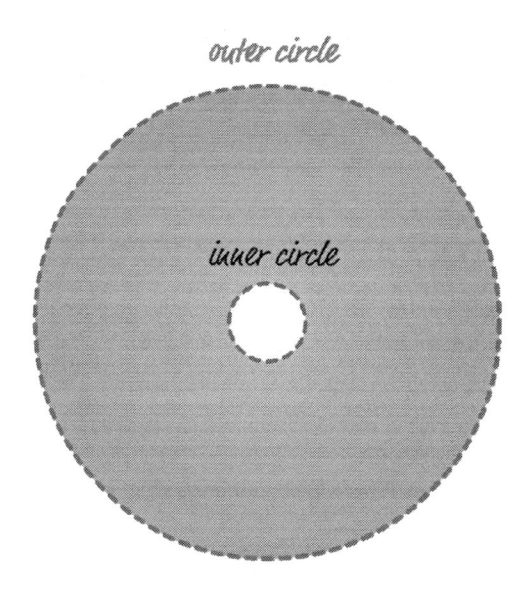

Inside the inner circle, the color will be the same as whatever the first color stop was. That means, the inside of our circle is going to be yellow:

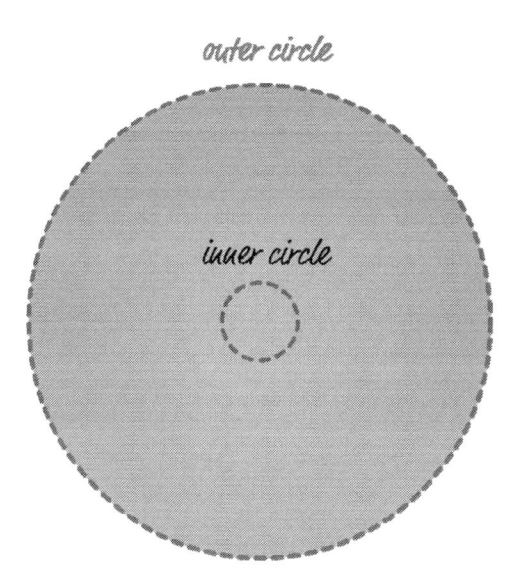

Outside of the outer circle, everything is going to be the same color as the last color stop. That means, everything is going to be green:

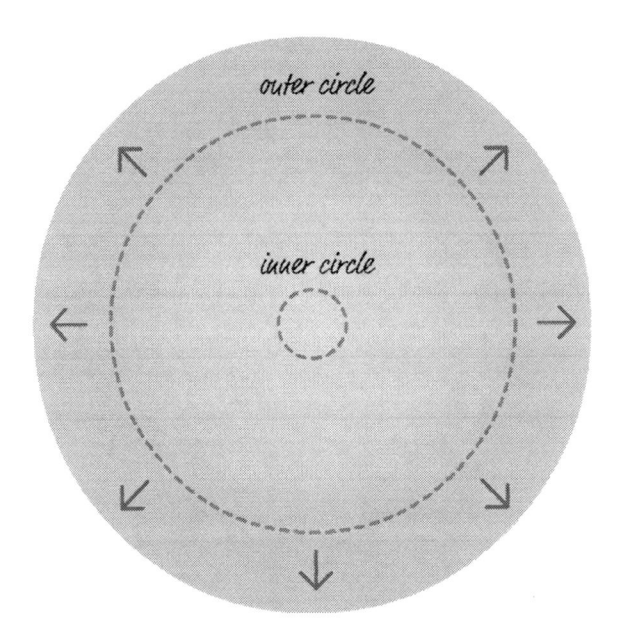

This green will go on forever in all directions. Any additional colors you specify only affect how the gradient behaves within the virtual straight line. The inside of the inner circle and the outside of the outer circle will always be a solid color that matches the color stop they are closest to.

> Ok. Pause for a moment. Did you know that we just fully explained how one variation of a radial gradient works?!!

You think we are done with this, right? Not yet! What we looked as is the ideal case where both the inner circle and the outer circle share the same center point. You can define a radial gradient where the inner and outer circles have different center points:

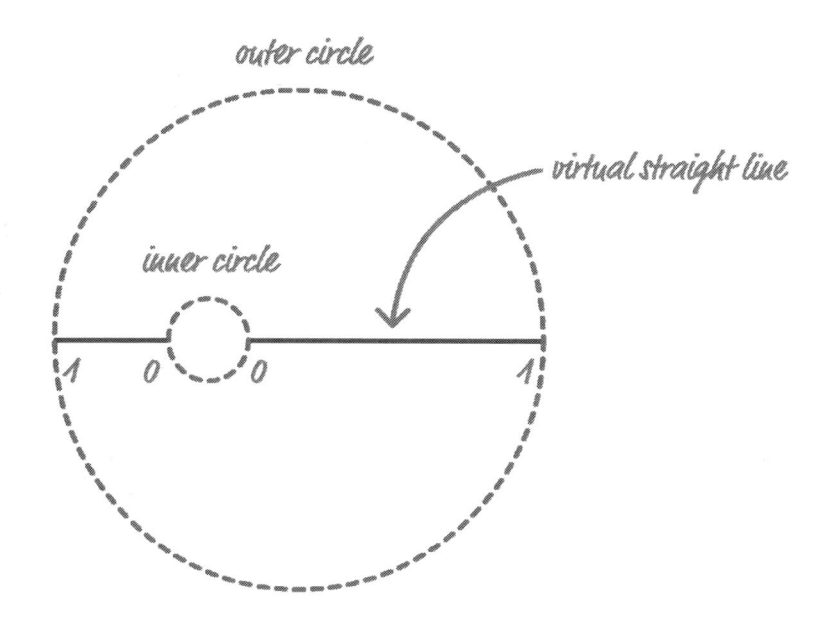

The behavior that we've seen so far is entirely identical even in this situation. The only difference is that your colors will look condensed on one side and more spread out on the other. Using the same yellow and green from before, the following is what you will see when the inner circle's center point is further left than our outer circle's center point:

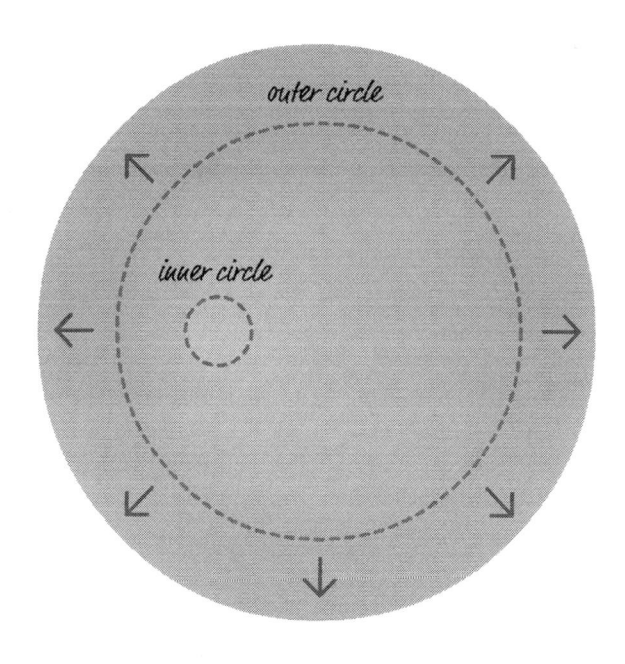

There are a few more quirks beyond the big ones we've seen so far, but enumerating all of those will take too much time. The hard part was learning the basics that you just saw, so let's next look at how to implement a radial gradient.

To create a radial gradient, you are going to use the `createRadialGradient` method. This method takes six arguments:

```
context.createRadialGradient(x_i, y_i, r_i, x_o, y_o, r_o);
```

The first three arguments stand for the inner circle's x position, y position, and radius. The last three arguments stand for the outer circle's x position, y position, and radius. The `createRadialGradient` method returns a `CanvasGradient` object that you can then add color stops to and assign to a property like `fillStyle` or `strokeStyle`.

Here is us applying our yellow and green colored radial gradient to our rectangle:

```
context.beginPath();
context.rect(75, 100, 250, 150);

// our radial gradient!
var gradient = context.createRadialGradient(150, 175, 0, 150, 175, 100);

// our two color stops
gradient.addColorStop(0, "#FFCC00");
gradient.addColorStop(1, "#B4CB02");

// assigning the gradient
context.fillStyle = gradient;
context.fill();
```

After all of this, our rectangle will look as follows:

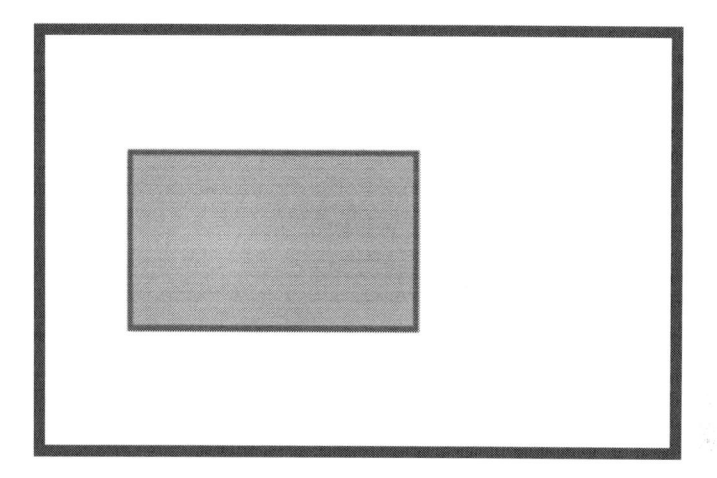

Once you understand the basics of how to work with radial gradients, the only tricky part is positioning the center points at the right location with regards to the thing you are painting. You can see where we positioned our inner and outer circles with respect to the rectangle - both in the code as well as visually.

Conclusion

When you are specifying values for `fillStyle` and `strokeStyle`, all of the approaches we looked at will help get you the colorful result that you want. You can even use multiple variations of these approaches in the same app. For the sake of consistency, I wouldn't recommend doing that, but that is a different issue of preference altogether. Also, isn't this probably the weakest conclusion for an epic chapter on color that you've probably ever seen? I certainly hope so! :P

Chapter 11: Drawing Text

This may come as a shock to you, so I encourage you to be seated for what I am about to say next. The things you can draw on the `canvas` aren't limited to just lines and shapes. You can also draw text. Not only that, you can extensively customize the text without breaking too much of a sweat. In this chapter, we will take a look at what all of this means.

Onwards!

From Text to Pixels

For getting text to appear in our `canvas`, we will primarily be using two methods: `strokeText` and `fillText`.

With the `strokeText` method, you end up drawing an outline of your text:

The `fillText` method allows you to display a solid / filled-in version of your text instead:

Now that you know this, let's wrap up this awkward introduction and get our hands dirty with some code! Make sure you have an HTML document ready or refer back to the **Prependix** where we have a simple starting point with a `canvas` element defined.

Using strokeText and fillText

Let's turn all of the English words in the previous section into some sweet code that showcases what `strokeText` and `fillText` have to offer. Now, the way you use both of these methods is nearly identical:

```
context.fillText("my text", xPosition, yPosition);
context.strokeText("my text", xPosition, yPosition);
```

You call them on your drawing context object, and you pass in three arguments:

1. The text you would like to display
2. The horizontal (x) position
3. The vertical (y) position

There is an optional fourth argument you can specify for setting the maximum width of your text, but that's not something you will use often. Just keep this knowledge under your hat for that rare rainy day when you'll need it.

Getting back to our original plan, let's add some code. Inside our `script` tag, go ahead and add the following lines:

```
var canvas = document.querySelector("#myCanvas");
var context = canvas.getContext("2d");


context.fillText("Canvas!", 40, 125);
context.strokeText("Canvas!", 40, 275);
```

The first two lines are the standard ones you have for getting at your canvas element's 2d drawing context! The interesting stuff happens with our `fillText` and `strokeText` lines:

```
context.fillText("Canvas!", 40, 125);
context.strokeText("Canvas!", 40, 275);
```

In these two lines, we are telling JavaScript to draw a solidly-filled version of the **Canvas!** text at (40, 125) and an outline version of the **Canvas!** text at (40, 275). If you preview what you have in your browser, you'll see something that looks as follows:

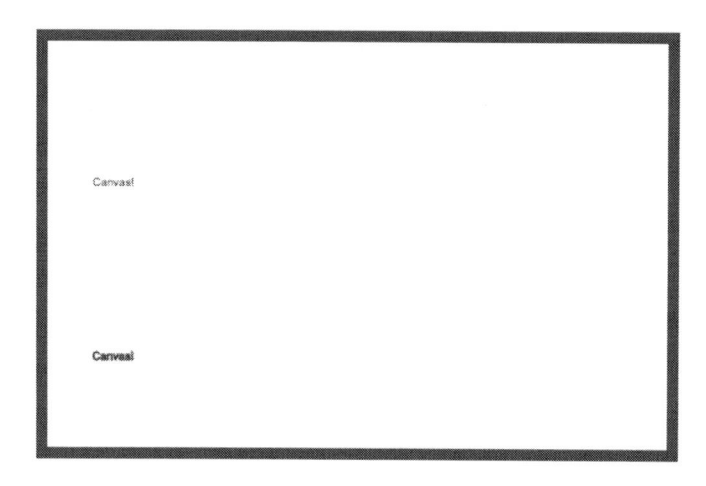

You did not make a mistake. That is what our text looks like by default when we don't specify any appearance details. We'll fix that right up in the next section.

Changing How Your Text Looks

Our `canvas`-bound text isn't destined to look like whatever hideous thing we have showing right now. **By default, your text shows up in a sans-serif font sized at 10 pixels.** Yikes! Fortunately, you have a handful of properties that help you to transform our almost unreadable text into something more appealing. The main awesome property for this is `font`, but you also have the lesser `textAlign`, `textBaseLine`, and `direction` properties that you can use as well. We'll look at all of these properties in the next handful of sections.

Changing the Font

Not to play favorites here, but the most frequently-used property you'll use for adjusting your text's appearance is the `font` property. This property mimics the quite complex CSS-equivalent property of the same name where you can specify all sorts of values to adjust how your text appears.

Instead of overwhelming you with everything the `font` property does, lets look at a few simple (and very common) cases where we just specify the font size and a font family with an optional **bold** or *italic* modifier.

Here is us setting the `font` property to display some 96 pixel-sized text in Helvetica, Arial, or sans-serif:

```
context.font = "96px Helvetica, Arial, sans-serif";
```

You can even add a **bold** or *italic* modifier to have the text appear bolded or italicized:

```
context.font = "bold 96px Helvetica, Arial, sans-serif";
```

Let's use this in our example to make our text more legible. Take the above line of code and add it just before the call to `fillText` and `strokeText` as highlighted below:

```
var canvas = document.querySelector("#myCanvas");
var context = canvas.getContext("2d");

context.font = "bold 96px Helvetica, Arial, sans-serif";
context.fillText("Canvas!", 40, 125);
context.strokeText("Canvas!", 40, 275);
```

Once you've added that line, go ahead and preview what you have in your browser. If everything worked well, you should now see that our text look as follows:

Doesn't this look much nicer? If you want greater customization of your font, you can specify any of the values that go to the font shorthand property:

```
context.font = "[style] [variant] [weight] [size]/[line height] [font family]";
```

For examples and more details on how to use the `font` property beyond the two common cases we looked at, head on over to MDN's amazing coverage of this at http://bit.ly/MDNFonts .

Changing Text Alignment

Something you might do every now and then is specify whether your text alignment is **left, center**, or **right** using the `textAlign` property. The behavior of the `textAlign` property is identical to what you might see when aligning text in a word editor:

Same as these three buttons here!

Page | 125

Getting back to JavaScript, here is an example of me setting the text alignment to be centered, for example:

```
context.textAlign = "center";
```

In addition, you can also specify a value of **start** or **end**. You may be wondering what makes **start** and **end** different from **left** and **right**? For those of us who are used to reading text in a left-to-right direction, there is no difference. For those of us who read text right-to-left, the "correct" thing happens when you use **start** and **end** as opposed to **left** and **right**. The default value if you don't specify anything for the `textAlign` property is **start**.

Changing Text Direction

Since we just talked about this, you can force your text direction to be **ltr** (left-to-right) or **rtl** (right-to-left). Below is an example of me forcing my text to appear in right-to-left mode:

```
context.direction = "rtl";
```

If you wish to respect your browser's (or your page's) default setting, you can specify a value of **inherit**. The **inherit** value also happens to the default value for `direction`, so unless you really care about setting **ltr** or **rtl** as the value, you don't have to ever set this property.

Setting the Baseline

The last text-related property we will look at is `textBaseline`, and it defines the baseline alignment your characters will appear in. This is a very simple way of describing something a bit complex. Your text can appear vertically aligned across several values defined by your font. These values are **top**, **hanging**, **middle**, **alphabetic**, **ideographic**, and **bottom**. To visualize these values, check out the WHATWG article at the following location that contains a really sweet picture: http://bit.ly/FontBaseline

To set any of these values, call the `textBaseline` property and pass in the alignment value you want:

```
context.textBaseline = "top";
```

The default value is **alphabetic**. I've never had to set this property, and (if you are lucky!) there is a good chance you never will have to either.

Changing the Text Color

The last thing we are going to look at is how to change our text's color. Right now, our text is colored black. To change the color of our text, we are going to use the familiar `strokeStyle` and `fillStyle` properties that we've seen a few times for setting the colors of our shapes. When you think of our text as nothing more than lines and shapes, it makes sense why these properties make an appearance!

To change the color of text created by `fillText`, use the `fillStyle` property. Similarly, to change the color of text created by `strokeText`, use the `strokeStyle` property:

```
var canvas = document.querySelector("#myCanvas");
var context = canvas.getContext("2d");


context.font = "bold 96px Helvetica, Arial, sans-serif";

context.fillStyle = "steelblue";
context.fillText("Canvas!", 40, 125);

context.strokeStyle = "#173b79";
```

```
context.strokeText("Canvas!", 40, 275);
```

If you add the code displayed in the highlighted lines and preview in our browser, our formerly black colored text will look a bit more blue-ish:

You can specify any valid CSS color keyword, rgb, or rgba value as what you assign to the `fillStyle` and `strokeStyle` properties. Now, why you would ever want to change these awesome blue colors is completely beyond me? :P

Measuring Your Text Size

One text-related property we didn't cover is the appropriately named `measureText` property. This property returns in pixels how wide or tall the text you are drawing is. For a great example of how this property works and why you would use it, check out the **Detect Whether a Font is Installed** article at the following location: http://bit.ly/FontInstalled

Conclusion

At the end of the day, even the text we generate for the `canvas` goes through the same torturous process as everything else `canvas`-related to end up as lifeless pixels on the screen. Your text can't be selected, cut/copied, read out-loud via a screen reader, or be part of a billion other things you take for granted when dealing with text on the DOM. Of course, with enough lines of JavaScript and time, you can re-implement a lot of that missing functionality if you really REALLY need to. I'm going to play some Fallout 4 instead.

Chapter 12: Drawing Images

As we saw in the previous chapter, the content on your `canvas` isn't just limited to lines and shapes. You can also have text. Sometimes, even all of that isn't going to be enough to allow you to create the kinds of things you want to display.

Your `canvas` can also work with predefined clusters of pixel data more commonly known as **images**. In this quick-ish article, we will take a look at what getting an image into our `canvas` entails and some of the totally fun things you can do.

Onwards!

Images and drawImage()

Getting an image to display into your canvas follows a very simple formula made up of these two steps:

1. Gain access to an image source (aka an image file, another canvas element, a frame from a video element, etc.)

2. Display the data from the image source to the `canvas`

That's really all there is to it, but like most things we've looked at so far, it's in the details where things get a little crazy. The first detail (that also happens to be crazy) is the `drawImage` method that is ultimately responsible for getting your image pixels to display on the `canvas`.

Just like all of the other drawing methods we've seen, it operates off of our rendering context object and looks as follows:

```
context.drawImage(image, x, y);
```

The `drawImage` method takes three arguments at its most basic level. The first argument refers to what we earlier called an **image source**. It is where we specify the image we would like to display. The second and third arguments point to **the x and y position** our image will be displayed in.

There is actually more to the `drawImage` method than what we've seen so far. It has two variations with different arguments, but we'll worry about those variations later when we stumble onto them. In the meantime, let's take what we've learned so far and actually write some code to load an image.

Displaying an Image

Here is the situation. You have an image on your server that you'd like to display inside your `canvas` element. From the previous section, you kinda know that there are two steps involved. You also know that the `drawImage` method is going to be used somewhere. If you are with me so far, that's good! The next few sections will be a breeze.

Finding an Image

The first thing you need is an image to display. You can display almost any image format your browser supports such as GIF, JPEG, PNG, SVG, etc. For walking through all of this with you, the image I will be using looks as follows:

https://www.kirupa.com/canvas/images/orange.svg

The images you can use don't have to be actual files. I know that sounds crazy, but your canvas can work with "images" that are base-64 encoded. Your image can be a frame from a `video` element. Your image can even by another `canvas` element where what is drawn there is the visual you have to work with.

For now, let's keep things simple and stick with a physical file. It will be the most common image type you'll be working with anyway, so it can't hurt to start with that!

Creating the Image Object

To get our image to display on the `canvas`, we need a JavaScript representation of it. The way you do that is by creating an `Image` object and setting the `src` property to the path where the image lives.

In code, this will look as follows:

```
var canvas = document.querySelector("#myCanvas");
var context = canvas.getContext("2d");


var myImage = new Image();
myImage.src = "images/orange.svg";
```

The first two lines are your standard `canvas` initialization stuff. The next two lines is where things start getting interesting:

```
var myImage = new Image();
myImage.src = "images/orange.svg";
```

In the first line we create a new `Image` object called `myImage`. In the second line, we set this object's `src` property to the path our image lives. This can be a relative path as I've shown. You can also specify an absolute path if you prefer, but ensure the domain you are specifying is the same as the domain your `canvas` element is in. There are some security issues you sorta kinda might run into otherwise.

Ensuring the Image Has Loaded

In the previous section, you may have thought that setting the `src` property is pretty much all you would need to do in order to get your image loaded and start working against that loaded image. As it turns out, it doesn't quite work that way. Because of bandwidth, network latency, and a bunch of other excuses, we need to actually ensure the image is loaded before we do anything that relies on it such as writing some code to get that image drawn to our `canvas`.

The way we do that is by listening for the **load** event on our `Image` object and calling an event handler once that event is overheard. All of that translates into the following highlighted lines of code that you should add to your document: triangle:

```
var myImage = new Image();
myImage.src = "images/orange.svg";
myImage.addEventListener("load", loadImage, false);


function loadImage(e) {
```

```
}
```

What these lines of code do is ensure the `loadImage` event handler is called when the **load** event on our `Image` object is overheard. That solves our problem of ensuring we have a way of running code only after our image has loaded. With that done, all that remains is to...

Displaying the Image...for Realz!

We created our `Image` object. We specified the image source. We even wrote some code to ensure the image was loaded before we took another step forward. All that remains is to actually display our image inside our `canvas` element. This part is actually a bit anticlimatic.

Inside the `loadImage` function, make a call to `drawImage` with our `myImage` object as the image source and a value of 0 for the x and y position.

Your code should look similar to the following highlighted line:

```
var myImage = new Image();
myImage.src = "images/orange.svg";
myImage.addEventListener("load", loadImage, false);

function loadImage(e) {
  context.drawImage(myImage, 0, 0);
}
```

After you have added this line, save your document and preview what you have in your browser. If everything worked well, you'll see your image loaded at the top-left corner of your `canvas` element:

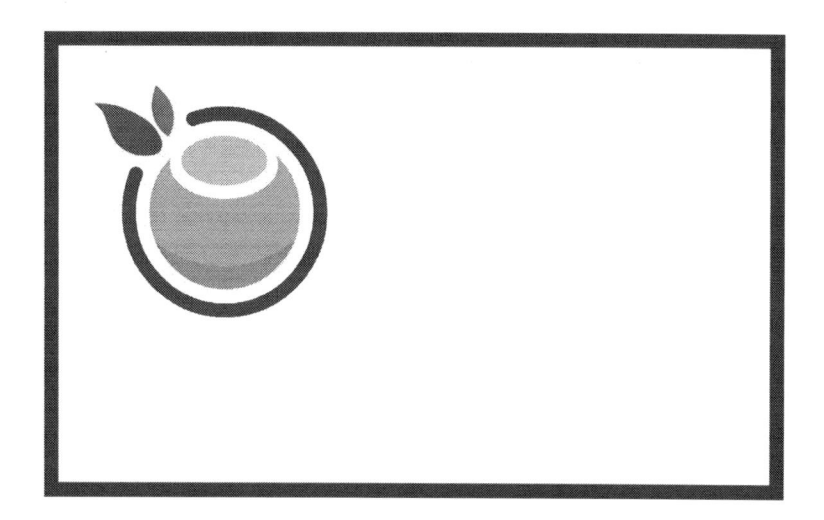

Pretty neat, right? What we've just looked at is the basic steps needed to go from having an image somewhere to having that image displayed inside a `canvas` element. At this point, you've learned the "80%" part of working with images on the canvas. You can safely step away and enjoy the outdoors (or play some video games in the great indoors!) as a celebration of what you've just learned.

With that said, the remaining "20%" is kinda cool as well. In the following sections, let's look at the other things you can do with images on the `canvas`.

Scaling the Image

By default, images you display in the canvas are displayed at whatever size they were created at. You can change that easily by specifying the final image size as part of your drawImage call. That might be news to you, for the drawImage method we looked at earlier takes only an image source and position values as its arguments:

```
context.drawImage(image, x, y);
```

As it turns out, our `drawImage` method has a few variants it can dress up as. An expanded variant of it allows you to also specify the width and height values you would like to display the image in:

```
context.drawImage(image, x, y, width, height);
```

If we took our earlier example and wanted our image to be displayed as a tiny 50x50 icon, our code would look like this:

```
var myImage = new Image();
myImage.src = "images/orange.svg";
myImage.addEventListener("load", loadImage, false);

function loadImage(e) {
    context.drawImage(myImage, 0, 0, 50, 50);
}
```

Notice that our `drawImage` call specifies a width and height value of 50. If we preview this code in the browser, we will see something that looks as follows:

Page | 136

Even though we are inside a `canvas` element, standard image scaling logic applies. Scaling down larger images is good. Scaling up smaller images is bad and might result in weird artifacts and blurry lines.

Speaking of blurry lines and weird artifacts, the `canvas` actually smoothens out your images when they are scaled. This smoothing is the default behavior, and you can disable this behavior by setting the `imageSmoothingEnabled` property on your drawing context to **false**: triangle:

```
context.mozImageSmoothingEnabled = false;
context.webkitImageSmoothingEnabled = false;
context.msImageSmoothingEnabled = false;
context.imageSmoothingEnabled = false;
```

This property is still pretty new, so you should specify the vendor-prefixed versions of this property (as shown) until the browser support catches up!

Slicing an Image

The last image-related manipulation we will look at involves taking an image, trimming the parts of it you don't care much about, and taking this smaller image to then display in our `canvas`. This manipulation is more commonly (and concisely!) known as **slicing**. The way it works is by using yet another variant of the `drawImage` method:

```
// this is another drawImage variant!
context.drawImage(image, x, y, w, h, x2, y2, w2, h2)
```

This variant takes nine (YES, NINE!) arguments, and they don't make any sense if you see them for the first time. Parsing the arguments, the x and y stand for position values. The w and h values stand for the width and height. Besides that, it's all still pretty nonsensical. We are going to make sense of all this by looking at all these arguments across two parts.

First Part: Cutting the Original Image

Let's say this is what our original image looks like:

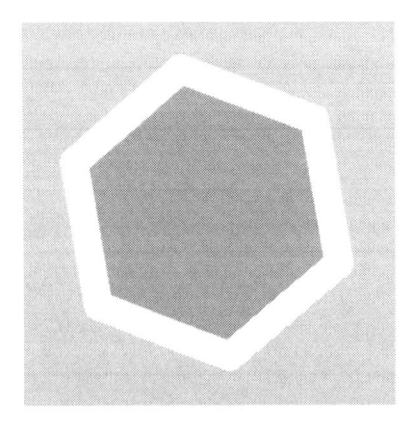

In this image, we would like to only keep the following highlighted region and discard everything else:

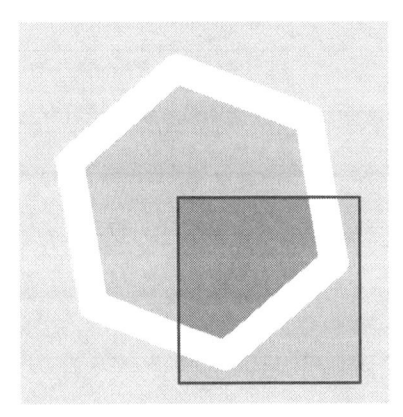

What I've just written is a roundabout way of stating that I basically want to cut out a chunk of our original image. The first five arguments to the `drawImage` method allow you to specify the location and size of the region you want to cut:

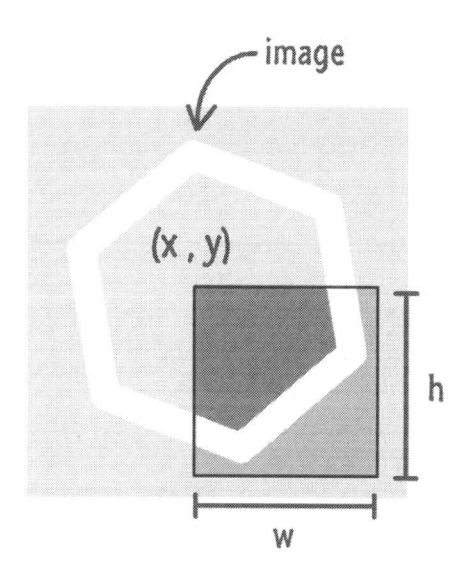

Let's pair this annotated image up with our `drawImage` definition from earlier:

```
context.drawImage(image, x, y, w, h, x2, y2, w2, h2)
```

The **image** argument points to our original image. The **x** and **y** arguments refer to the top-left position of the portion of the image we want to keep. The **w** and **h** arguments refer to the width and height of the portion of the image we want to keep. You put all of this together, we just figured out what more than half of the arguments to this variant of `drawImage` do!

Second Part: Pasting the Cut Image

What we are left with right now is just the part of the original image we decided to keep:

The remaining four arguments to our `drawImage` method help you to place and scale this image into the appropriate location on our `canvas`:

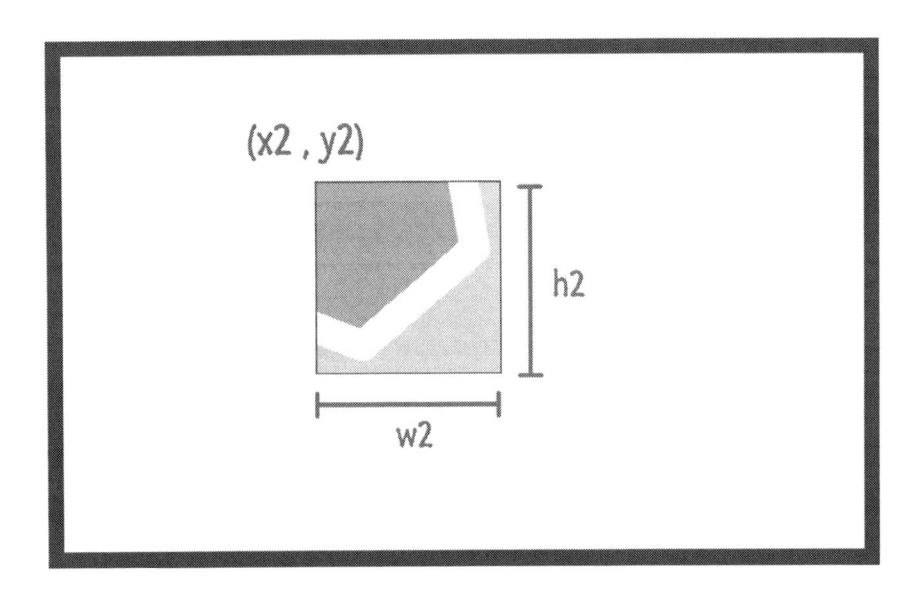

For reference, let's bring our `drawImage` method and its arguments back (this is the last time, I promise!):

```
context.drawImage(image, x, y, w, h, x2, y2, w2, h2)
```

What we've done is specified the last four arguments, and these arguments are identical to what you saw earlier when learning how to scale your image. The x2 and y2 arguments specify the location you want the image to appear on the canvas. The w2 and h2 arguments allow you to specify the width and height of your image. Keep these values the same as your w and h arguments if you do not wish to scale your image when "pasting" it into your canvas.

Conclusion

Once your images find their way onto the `canvas`, they become nothing more than pixels. All of this pomp and circumstance is to ensure your images get to their intended destination properly. That's it. Because your images become raw pixels, you now have the ability to manipulate the pixels in a bunch of different ways. We won't cover those ways here, but that might be something to tackle in the future…on your own!

Chapter 13: Transformations

So far everything we've drawn on the canvas was done without thinking much about exactly what our pixels are drawn into. Saying that our pixels are drawn on the canvas is only one part of the full picture. Under the canvas is an invisible virtual grid:

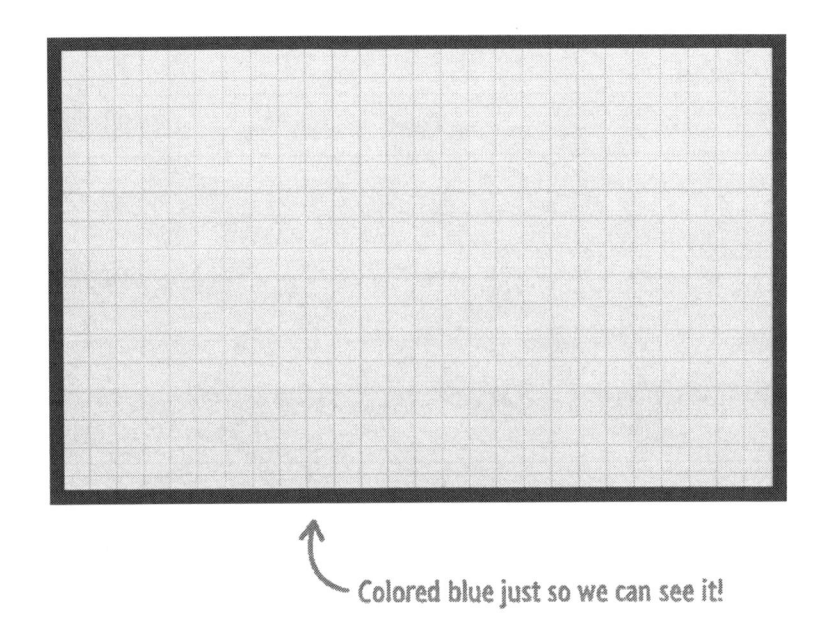

Colored blue just so we can see it!

It is this invisible virtual grid that all of the various draw commands we've seen map their pixels into. By default, this grid isn't very interesting. It becomes a whole lot more interesting when you transform it. You can rotate this grid:

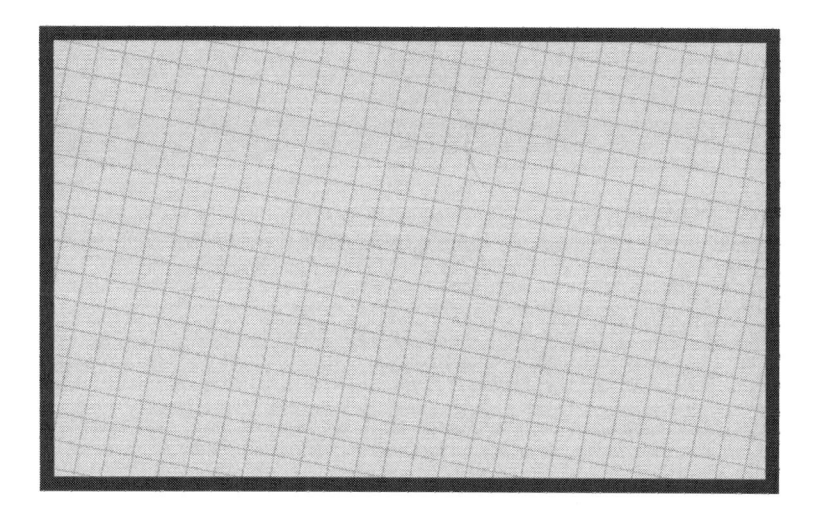

You can shift the starting point of this grid:

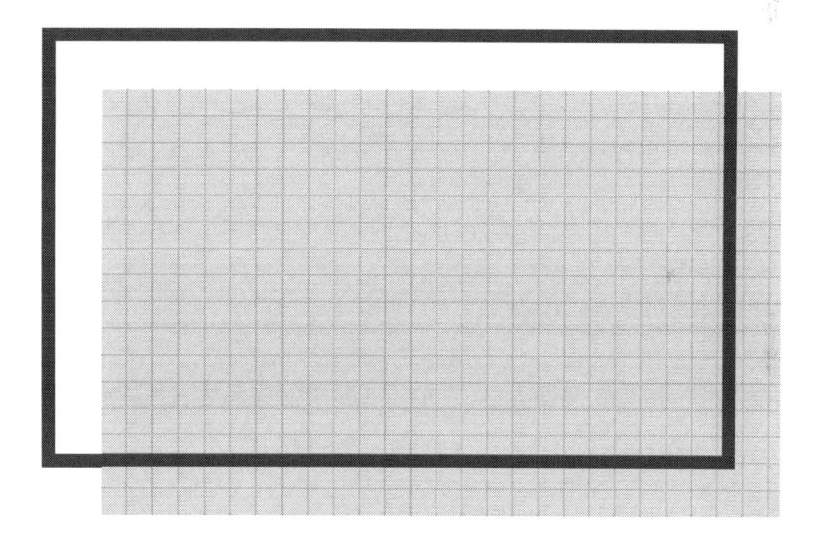

You can even scale each individual "cell" inside the grid to be larger or smaller:

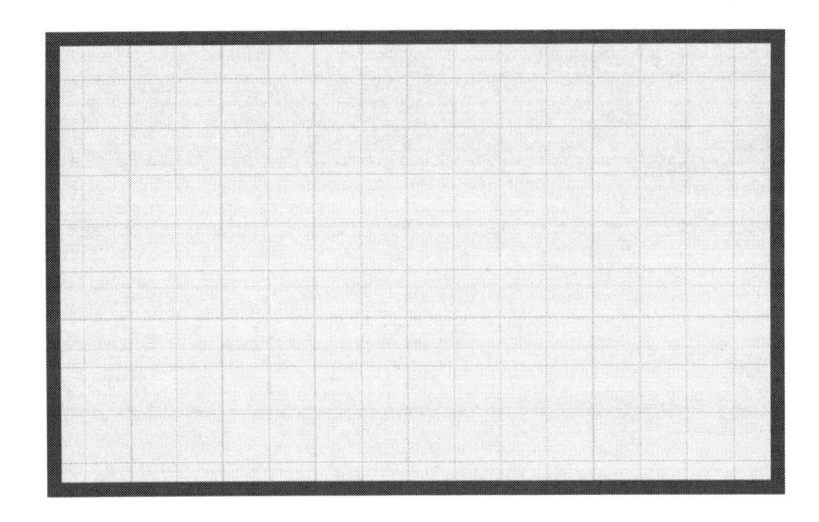

Why is this interesting? It is interesting because your `canvas` and anything you draw inside it will get scaled, rotated, or translated as well. This sort of makes up for the lack of interesting things you can do with the draw methods we've seen. At most, you can specify the size and position. That's not a lot, so transforms provide you with a few more ways of customizing what you draw. In this chapter, we are going to learn all about it.

Onwards!

Meet the Transformation Methods

The three methods you have for transforming your `canvas` are `translate`, `scale`, and `rotate`. In the following sections, let's look at how to use these methods.

Translating

If you want to shift your `canvas` and everything that gets drawn, you have the `translate` method:

```
context.translate(x, y);
```

The x and y arguments specify the number of pixels to shift your canvas horizontally and vertically by. Below is a simple example of what this looks like:

```
// Transform
context.translate(50, 50);


// Circle
context.beginPath();
context.arc(200, 200, 93, 0, 2 * Math.PI, true);
context.fillStyle = "#FF6A6A";
context.fill();


// Square
context.fillStyle = "#00CCFF";
context.fillRect(50, 50, 100, 100);
```

This code draws a circle and a square to our canvas. The call to the translate method at the top shifts both of the shapes over by 50 pixels. The following diagram shows the result of this translation:

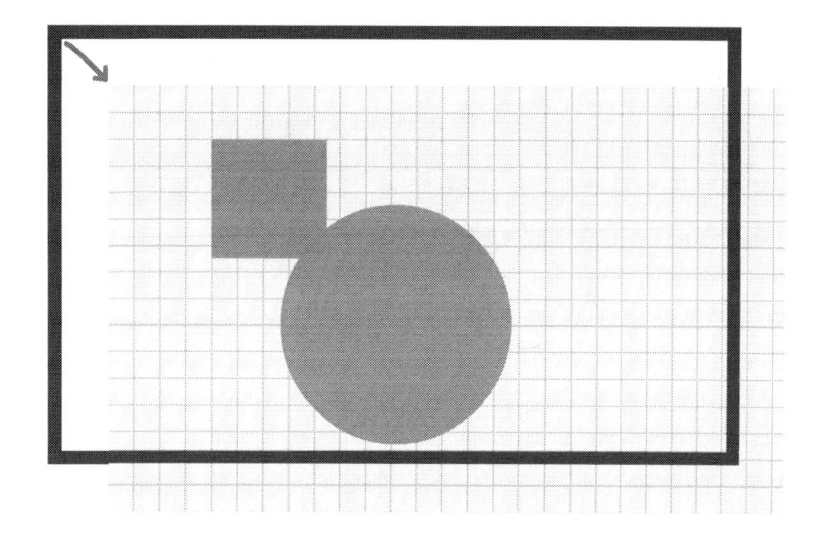

The entire canvas and the origin (0, 0) position is shifted, **so all future drawing operations will have their positions offset automatically**. Having a transform apply to all draw operations from here on out may be undesirable, and we'll look at how to address that in a little bit. Just ignore this minor annoyance for now.

Rotating

This is probably my favorite transform, for rotating the things you draw is really hard using the drawing commands we have available today. The way you rotate is by using the rotate method, and it looks as follows:

```
context.rotate(angle);
```

This method takes one argument that determines the angle (in the form of radians) you wish to rotate the canvas by. Here is an example of us rotating some text that we draw by 45 degrees:

```
// Transform
context.rotate(45 * Math.PI / 180);

// Text
context.font = "bold 48px Helvetica, Arial, sans-serif";
context.fillStyle = "steelblue";
context.fillText("Wheeeee!", 150, 0);
```

Here is what this looks like:

I chose a text example to highlight the **rotate** transform because text is one of the things you draw that is nearly impossible to re-create using rotated angled lines and curves. Without the `rotate` method, you'd be spending a lot of time trying to get a single character to look right - much less an entire word or a series of words! By comparison, rotating geometric shapes is much easier. With that said, you should still use the `rotate` method whenever you can instead of rotating manually...like an animal.

Scaling

The last individual transform we will look at is the scale method that is responsible for scaling what you draw:

```
context.scale(x, y);
```

This method takes two arguments that specify the horizontal and vertical scale accordingly. You can specify the arguments in the form of decimal values with 1 representing the original scale. A number between 0 and 1 means that what you draw will be scaled down, and a number greater than 1 means that what you draw will be scaled up.

The following code highlights an example where a poor square is stretched horizontally to twice its size:

```
// Transform
context.scale(2, 1);


// Square
context.fillStyle = "#FFCC00";
context.fillRect(50, 100, 100, 100);
```

If we had to visualize this, this would look as follows:

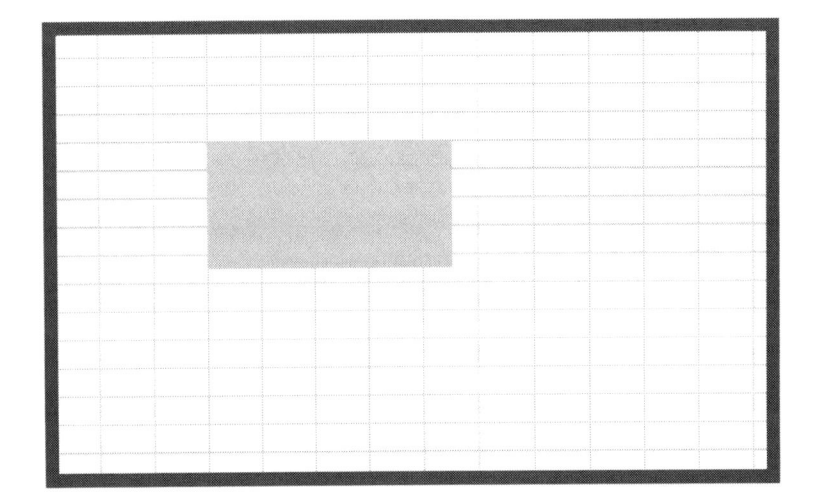

You can even specify negative values to flip our canvas horizontally or vertically. In the following code, we flip some text horizontally and scale it down by 50%:

```
// Transform
context.scale(-.5, 1);


// Text
```

```
context.font = "bold 96px Helvetica, Arial, sans-serif";

context.fillStyle = "#CC6699";

context.fillText("Confused", -700, 100);
```

This would look as follows:

The negative value for the `scale` method's x argument flips our `canvas` horizontally. The value of .5 squishes things by 50%.

Note: Combining Transforms

You aren't limited to using only a single transform to torture your `canvas` with. You can apply multiple transforms very easily:

```
context.scale(-.5, 1);
context.rotate(45 * Math.PI / 180);
```

```
context.translate(40, 10);
```

The reason this is possible has to do with how these transforms are implemented. There is a transform matrix that represents all of the transform values you can use:

transformation matrix

$$\begin{bmatrix} x\_scale & y\_skew & x\_translate \\ x\_skew & y\_scale & y\_translate \\ 0 & 0 & 1 \end{bmatrix}$$

These values aren't dependent on any other values, so you can independently set multiple transforms without stepping on any numerical toes. Don't worry if that doesn't make any sense. Just remember that all the `translate`, `rotate`, and `scale` methods end up affecting are the values stored by this matrix. You can set this matrix directly by using the `setTransform` method, but covering that goes beyond the scope of what you would use frequently in the real world.

Undoing Transforms

This may be the part you have been eagerly waiting for. As you probably realized by now, transforming the `canvas` isn't an operation that resets itself with each thing you draw. It's not like a `fillStyle` or `strokeStyle`. The transformation is always there for any draw operation you perform in the future. That isn't always desirable, right?

To handle this, you need to explicitly turn the transforms off. There are several ways you can do with this. We'll look at two approaches in this section and focus on a slightly different (and heavy-handed) approach in a future chapter where we look at how to save and restore state.

Resetting the Transform...the Easy Way

The easiest way to reset a transform is to call the `resetTransform` method:

```
// Transform
context.translate(50, 50);
context.scale(2, 2);

// Circle
context.beginPath();
context.arc(200, 200, 93, 0, 2 * Math.PI, true);
context.fillStyle = '#FF6A6A';
context.fill();

// Reset the Transform
context.resetTransform();

// Square
context.fillStyle = '#00CCFF';
context.fillRect(50, 50, 100, 100);
```

The `resetTransform` method performs the magic needed to the transformation matrix you saw earlier to get everything back to how it was before a transform was even applied. In our example, the circle will be drawn on the transformed canvas. The square will be drawn on the untransformed canvas. Because of how drawing on the canvas works, untransforming the canvas with our circle already on it won't affect how the circle displays. Only future draw operations after resetTransform will be impacted.

Manually Resetting the Transform

Before we go on, I should mention this upfront: **I don't recommend you reset the transform with using the approach I am about to show you**. The only reason I am showing you this is to give you a better understanding of how transforms affect the `canvas`. Plus, it inflates the length of this chapter and helps make all of us look really smart by learning about this.

The more tedious way to reset your `canvas` to its untransformed state involves setting new transforms to undo what your earlier transforms did. That seems straightforward, but as you will see in a few seconds, there are some complications here that you'll need to deal with.

Here is an example of what this madness looks like:

```
// Transform
context.translate(50, 50);
context.scale(2, 2);

// Circle
context.beginPath();
context.arc(200, 200, 93, 0, 2 * Math.PI, true);
context.fillStyle = '#FF6A6A';
context.fill();

// Reset the Transform
context.scale(.5, .5);
context.translate(-50, -50);

// Square
context.fillStyle = '#00CCFF';
context.fillRect(50, 50, 100, 100);
```

Pay attention to the highlighted lines where we set the transform first and then reset the transform next. Resetting a transform in this approach isn't as simple as specifying the default transform values for translate and scale:

```
context.scale(1, 1);
context.translate(0, 0);
```

That seems like the logical thing to do, but that only works in a world where the `canvas` can intelligently access its previous state. The moment our canvas gets transformed, it only sees the world through its transformed lenses. Setting a `scale` value of 1 or a `translate` value of 0 means that you just stay at the current transformed state. The fix is where the tediousness comes in:

You have to account for the earlier transform that has been applied and negate it.

If the original transform called for everything to be scaled by 200%, you need to reset the scale by scaling everything by 50% instead. If your `translate` transform shifted everything by 50 pixels horizontally and vertically, you undo this by translating back by 50 pixels in the horizontal and vertical directions.

That's what our code highlights:

```
context.scale(.5, .5);
context.translate(-50, -50);
```

There is one more wrinkle. The order you perform this reset is important. Notice that we first undo the scale before resetting the position. If you didn't do this, you will have changed the position of an element that will then be repositioned again as a result of the scale operation. Getting the position right at this point will require more calculations, and that isn't particularly fun. This whole section isn't fun!

Conclusion

The most difficult thing about learning how to transform the canvas is how bizarre it is. If you are familiar with transforms in CSS, you know that you only affect the element or elements you are targeting. In the wacky world of the canvas, there is no concept of an element. Everything is either the canvas itself or raw pixels. If you wish to draw something rotated (or scaled or translated), you transform the canvas first and then draw whatever you were planning on drawing. The strangeness of this all goes away with practice...and a lot of therapy.

Chapter 14: Structuring Your Drawing Code

Up until this point, we've been drawing each shape individually. That was fine for learning how the various draw commands work. In real life, you'll rarely issue draw commands directly. You'll instead delegate the drawing to a helper function or custom object or something else that makes drawing things more maintainable.

For example, take a look at the following, um…work of art:

What you see is a bunch of randomly overlaid semi-transparent circles. That's not the most interesting thing we are going to be focusing on. The interesting thing is looking at how this example was implemented. We bring these circles to life using two approaches that help make your canvas drawings easier to re-use and maintain, and we'll learn all about how to do that here.

Onwards!

Using Functions

As you probably know, functions help make your code reusable. They also ensure your code isn't duplicated unnecessarily throughout your app. You place the code you want to re-use inside a function, and that function is what you tell the rest of your app to call. That is pretty straighforward.

When it comes to drawing stuff on the canvas, the biggest advantage of functions is that you can pass arguments that your drawing code then uses to customize what gets drawn. Before I bore you any further, here is the full code for the circles example:

```
var myCanvas = document.querySelector("#myCanvas");
var context = myCanvas.getContext("2d");

for (var i = 0; i < 40; i++) {
  var r = Math.round(15 + Math.random() * 150);
  drawCircle(r);
}

function drawCircle(radius) {
  var xPos = Math.round(Math.random() * myCanvas.width);
  var yPos = Math.round(Math.random() * myCanvas.height);

  context.beginPath();
  context.arc(xPos, yPos, radius, 0, 2 * Math.PI, true);
  context.fillStyle = "rgba(41, 170, 255, .1)";
  context.fill();
}
```

Take a few moments to walk through this code and see how the various pieces of it work. The biggest chunk of code (and the star) is the drawCircle function:

```
function drawCircle(radius) {
  var xPos = Math.round(Math.random() * myCanvas.width);
  var yPos = Math.round(Math.random() * myCanvas.height);


  context.beginPath();
  context.arc(xPos, yPos, radius, 0, 2 * Math.PI, true);
  context.fillStyle = "rgba(41, 170, 255, .1)";
  context.fill();
}
```

This function neatly contains everything our canvas needs to get a circle drawn on the screen. It takes care of defining the circle, placing it in a random position on the screen, setting the size using the passed in argument for the radius, and ultimately drawing the whole thing with a semi-transparent blue color.

We call this function from inside the for loop just a few lines earlier:

```
for (var i = 0; i < 40; i++) {
  var r = Math.round(15 + Math.random() * 150);
  drawCircle(r);
}
```

This loop runs 40 times. Each time it runs, it calls the drawCircle function with a random value passed in for the radius. At the end of each of these calls, a blue circle gets placed somewhere on the screen. If we wanted to customize what gets drawn further, we can modify the drawCircle function and add more arguments really easily. If we ever added more entry points that would draw more circles, we can just call `drawCircle` directly without duplicating any code. Gotta love functions!

Using Objects

What we've done with functions so far is nice and all, but for the purposes of this example, it doesn't add a whole lot of value. We could have just stashed the contents of `drawCircle` into the `for` loop itself, and everything would have been just fine:

```
for (var i = 0; i < 40; i++) {

  var r = Math.round(15 + Math.random() * 150);

  var xPos = Math.round(Math.random() * myCanvas.width);

  var yPos = Math.round(Math.random() * myCanvas.height);

  context.beginPath();

  context.arc(xPos, yPos, r, 0, 2 * Math.PI, true);

  context.fillStyle = "rgba(41, 170, 255, .1)";

  context.fill();

}
```

While I totally get the advantage functions bring to the table when it comes to code clarity and reuse, let's go further.

For the ultimate level of control that leaves the functions-only approach in the dust, **we can use objects**. As you probably noticed by now, once things are drawn to the `canvas`, there really isn't much you can do. You can't access what you've just drawn as a single entity. It doesn't matter if you are calling draw commands directly or relying on a custom function like we saw in the previous section. Once the pixels get placed on the `canvas`, they lose any individuality and become just another brick in the wall. This is one of the things that makes drawing on the canvas more difficult compared to DOM elements.

We can't (at least not today :P) fundamentally alter how the canvas works. What we can do is come up with ways to track and manipulate the things we draw on the canvas using good old **JavaScript Objects**. If you aren't familiar with JavaScript objects and creating them using `Object.create`, I highly recommend you take a few moments to brush up on them. The **Introduction to Objects** and the **Deeper Look at Objects** tutorials on KIRUPA (https://www.kirupa.com) should help you out.

What sets our object-oriented approach apart is that each circle we draw will be associated with a corresponding object. This object looks as follows: triangle:

```
// the circle object!!!
var circle = {
  idValue: -1,
  radius: 0,
  xPos: 0,
  yPos: 0,
  color: "rgba(41, 170, 255, .1)",

  setup: function (x, y) {
    this.xPos = x;
    this.yPos = y;

    this.radius = Math.round(15 + Math.random() * 150);
  },
  setColor: function (newColor) {
    this.color = newColor;
  },
  draw: function () {
```

```
        context.beginPath();

        context.arc(this.xPos, this.yPos, this.radius, 0, 2 * Math.PI, true);

        context.fillStyle = this.color;

        context.fill();

    }

};
```

Notice that we have a few properties that help determine our shape's size, position, and color. We then have a few functions that are responsible for setting up each of our circles and drawing them to the screen.

To use this object as part of our example, all we need to do is create new objects based on `circle`, initialize it using the custom `setup` method, and then call `draw` to get the circle to appear on screen. Using our `for` loop approach that we saw earlier, this will look as follows:

```
function drawAllCircles() {
  for (var i = 0; i < 40; i++) {
    var r = Math.round(15 + Math.random() * 150);


    var xPos = Math.round(Math.random() * myCanvas.width);
    var yPos = Math.round(Math.random() * myCanvas.height);


    var newCircle = Object.create(circle);
    newCircle.setup(xPos, yPos);
    newCircle.idValue = i;
    newCircle.draw();

  }
}
```

```
drawAllCircles();
```

If you add this code along with the circle object that we saw a few moments ago, your canvas will display the semi-transparent blue circles that we had originally started off with. Now, I mentioned that this approach makes it easier to track each of the circles we've drawn. Right now, we aren't taking advantage of that capability.

The easiest way to track each circle we've drawn is to store its corresponding `circle` object inside an array:

```
var circles = [];

function drawAllCircles() {
    for (var i = 0; i < 40; i++) {
        var xPos = Math.round(Math.random() * myCanvas.width);
        var yPos = Math.round(Math.random() * myCanvas.height);

        var newCircle = Object.create(circle);
        newCircle.setup(xPos, yPos);
        newCircle.idValue = i;
        newCircle.draw();

        circles.push(newCircle);
    }
}
drawAllCircles();
```

Our `circles` array now contains data about every single circle that we've drawn. If you want to change the color of a particular circle, you can just retrieve it from the `circles` array and use the `setColor` and `draw` methods to update that circle.

For example, if we wanted to set the color of the first circle we drew to a yellow color with no transparency, we could do something like this:

```
var firstCircle = circles[0];
firstCircle.setColor("rgba(255, 204, 0, 1)");
firstCircle.draw();
```

If everything worked out properly, you'll see something that closely resembles our earlier example with the exception of one circle that will be yellow colored:

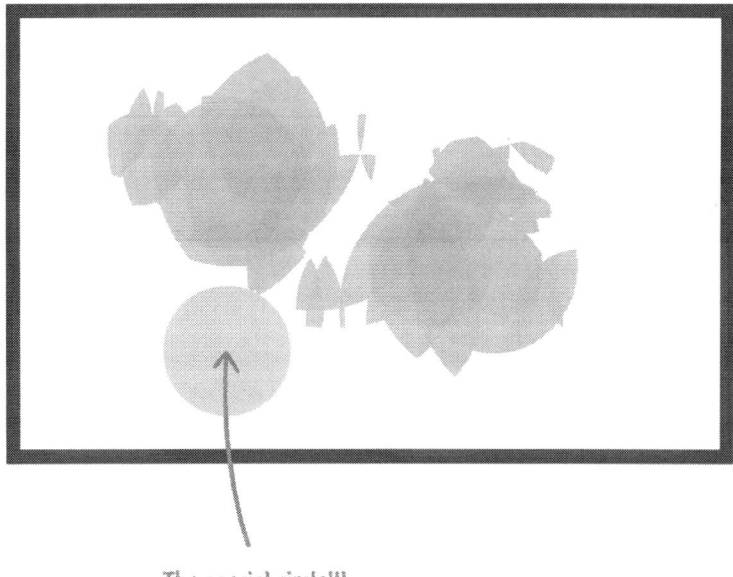

The special circle!!!

Here is how this works. When the `draw` method is called, we re-draw our first circle from the `circles` array with the same position and radius values it had initially. The only thing that has changed is the color...which we updated by calling the `setColor` method that updated our `circle` object's public `color` property.

Now, there is one other thing to note. When we re-draw our circle, it gets drawn over everything else. That's just how the `canvas` works, and maintaining the exact draw order is tricky. If we had to try to maintain that, we would need to redraw all of the overlapping circles in the exact order they originally were drawn in. That gets really complicated really quickly, and unless you really need that optimization, it would probably be easier to just redraw all of the circles at once at that point.

Conclusion

There are many ways to organize your `canvas`-related drawing code. What we looked at here are just two approaches that broadly describe how to think about this problem. For simple drawings, all of this is overkill. That's why we didn't do anything like this in many articles prior to this where we looked at each drawing method by itself. Now, as you start to create more complex designs or add animation (as we will see shortly), this fast-and-carefree way will end up hurting you in the long run. At that point, you'll be glad to use something like the functions-only or the functions/object approach we looked at in this article.

Part II
Animation

Chapter 15: Creating Animations

So far, the things we've drawn have kinda just sat there. That's about to change with this chapter. One of the coolest things you can do with the `canvas` is create animations where our once static pixels move or visually change over a period of time. Getting all of that right requires learning a few more tricks, so grab a cold one (or a hot one) and let's learn how to animate on the `canvas`!

Onwards!

Animation 101

Before we jump into the deep end, let's take a few steps back and talk about what an animation is. At its most basic level, **an animation is nothing more than a visualization of change** - a change that occurs over a period of time.

Let's look at that in more detail.

The Start and End States

If visualizing change is an important part of an animation, we need to create some reference points so that we can compare what has changed. Let's call these reference points the **start** state and the **end** state. To better explain what is going on, let's come up with an easy-to-understand example as well.

Let's say our start state looks as follows:

You start off with a blue circle that is small and located to the left of the screen. At the end state, your blue circle now looks sorta kinda like this:

Based just on the information you have on what our blue circle looks like in the start and end states, what can you tell is different?

One change is the position. Our blue circle starts off on the left side of the screen. It ends up on the right hand side. Another change is the size. Our circle goes from being small to being much larger.

How do we make an animation out of this? If we were to just play the start and end states repeatedly, what you would see is something that just bounces from left to right very awkwardly. That is, as Charles Barkley impersonated by Frank Caliendo would say, *pretty turrible. Just terrible!* What we need is a way to smooth things out between the start and end states. What we need is a healthy dose of what is known as **interpolation**.

Interpolation

Right now, what we have are two discrete states in time. At the beginning, you have your start state. And the end, you have the end state. If you were to play this back, this wouldn't be an animation...at least, not a very good one. In order to make an animation out of what we have, we need a smooth transition that creates all the intermediate states. This creation of the intermediate states is known as interpolation.

This interpolation, which occurs over a **period of time that you specify**, would look similar to the following diagram:

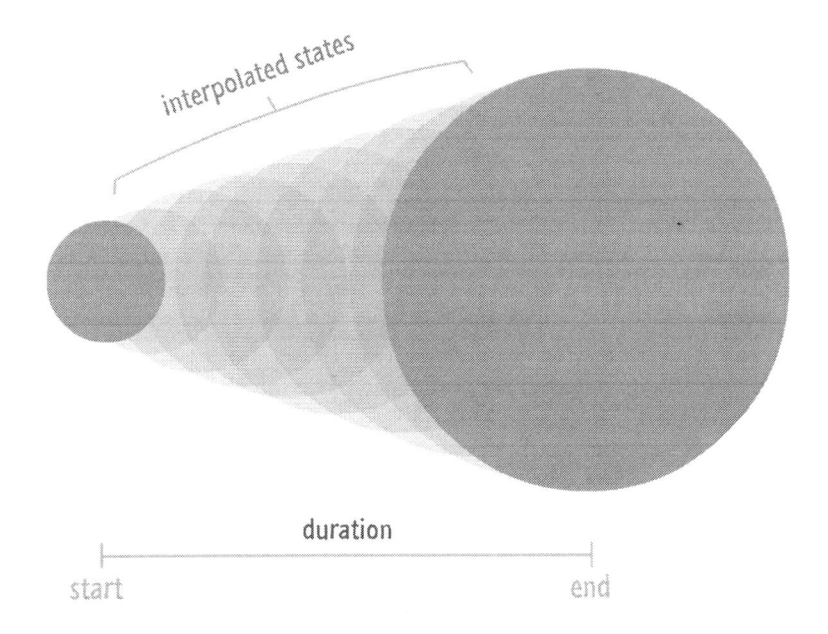

You may be wondering who specifies the interpolated states. The answer, which you should brace yourself for, is you! When creating animations on the canvas, you will need to specify the **starting state**, the **ending state**, the **duration**, and the **intermediate states**. Once you have all of these things, you have an animation! Now, I know this seems like a lot to deal with and process, but it isn't too bad as you will see shortly.

Animating on the Canvas

In the previous sections, we looked at some basic things about animations and how to think about them. It's time to move beyond that and focus a bit more on the details. The way you draw and animate on a canvas is very similar to how people created animations manually back in the day.

Initially, your canvas is completely blank. Let's call this initial state **frame 1**:

frame 1

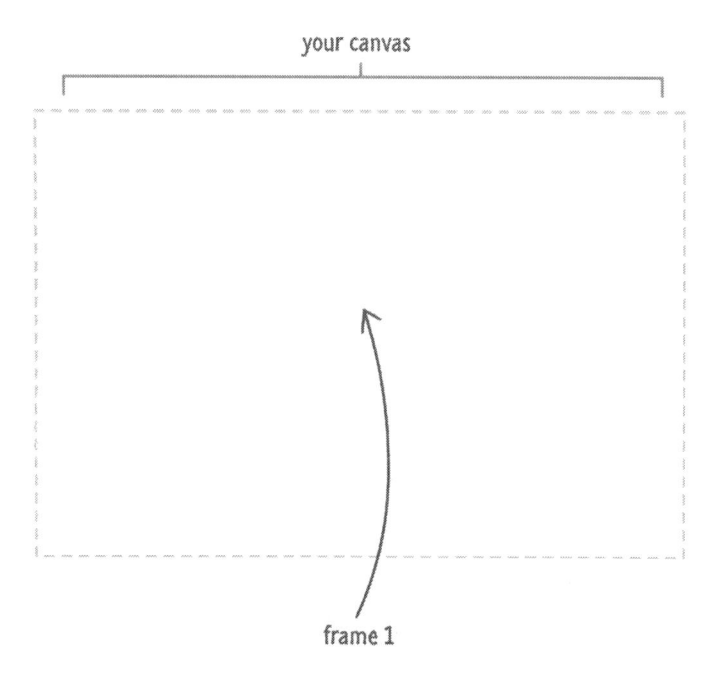

In this blank frame, you draw what you want to show as part of your starting state:

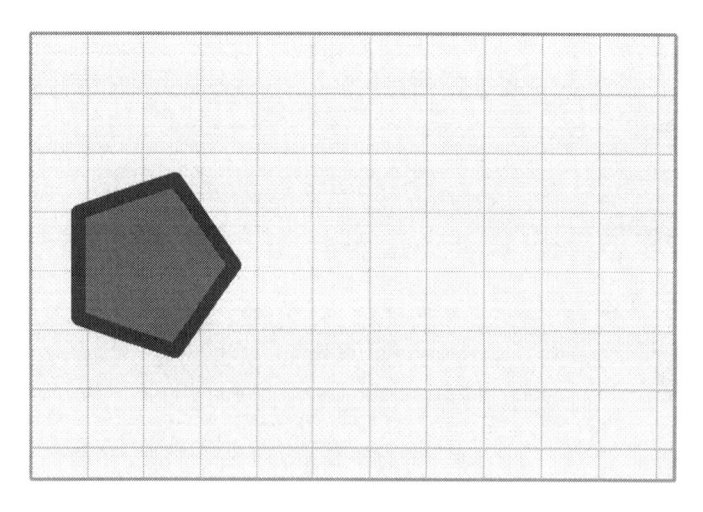

frame 1

You draw everything from the things in the foreground to things that appear in the middle to the things that make up the background. As you know well by now, every single detail is under your control. The `canvas` does nothing for you. It's really friendly like that.

Once you are happy with how the first frame looks like, you **clear** everything that is shown. What you have now is a new frame:

frame 2

In this new frame, which we will affectionately call **frame 2**, you re-draw everything you had in frame 1 but alter what you drew ever-so-slightly:

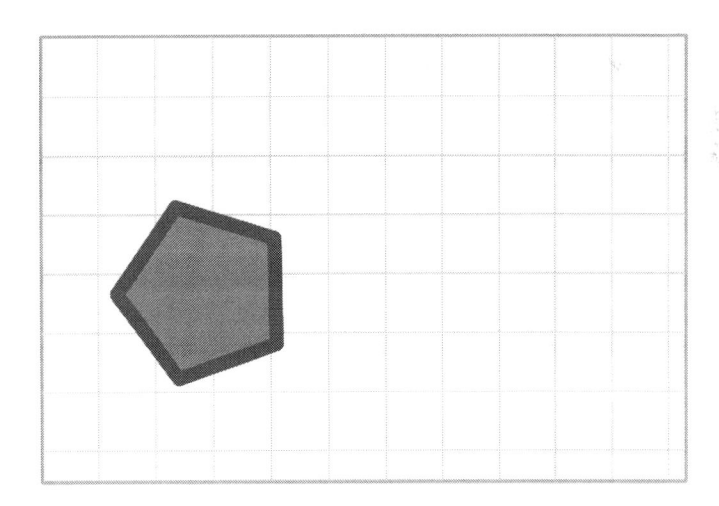

frame 2

In this example, between frame 1 and frame 2, our pentagon shape has rotated slightly and moved over and down a little bit. Everything else is pretty much the same. Now, if you compare frame 1 and frame 2 side by side, you'll be better able to see these two subtle changes:

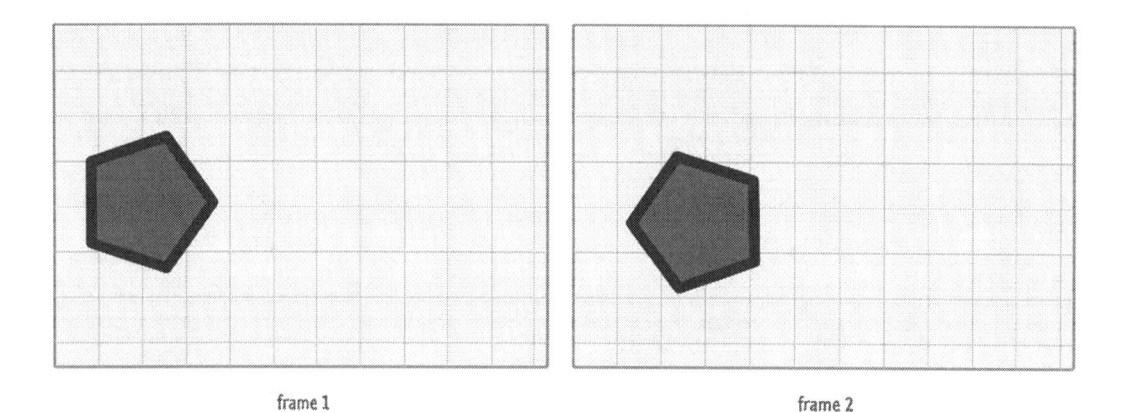

frame 1

frame 2

What you have just defined is an intermediate state. To create a smooth animation, you will need to define many MANY intermediate states. This means that you will need to repeat this **draw** and **clear** process over and over again for frame 3, frame 4, frame 5, and so on. In each frame, your pentagon shape is altered very slightly from the frame that preceded it. The following diagram shows the sequence of frames for this animation:

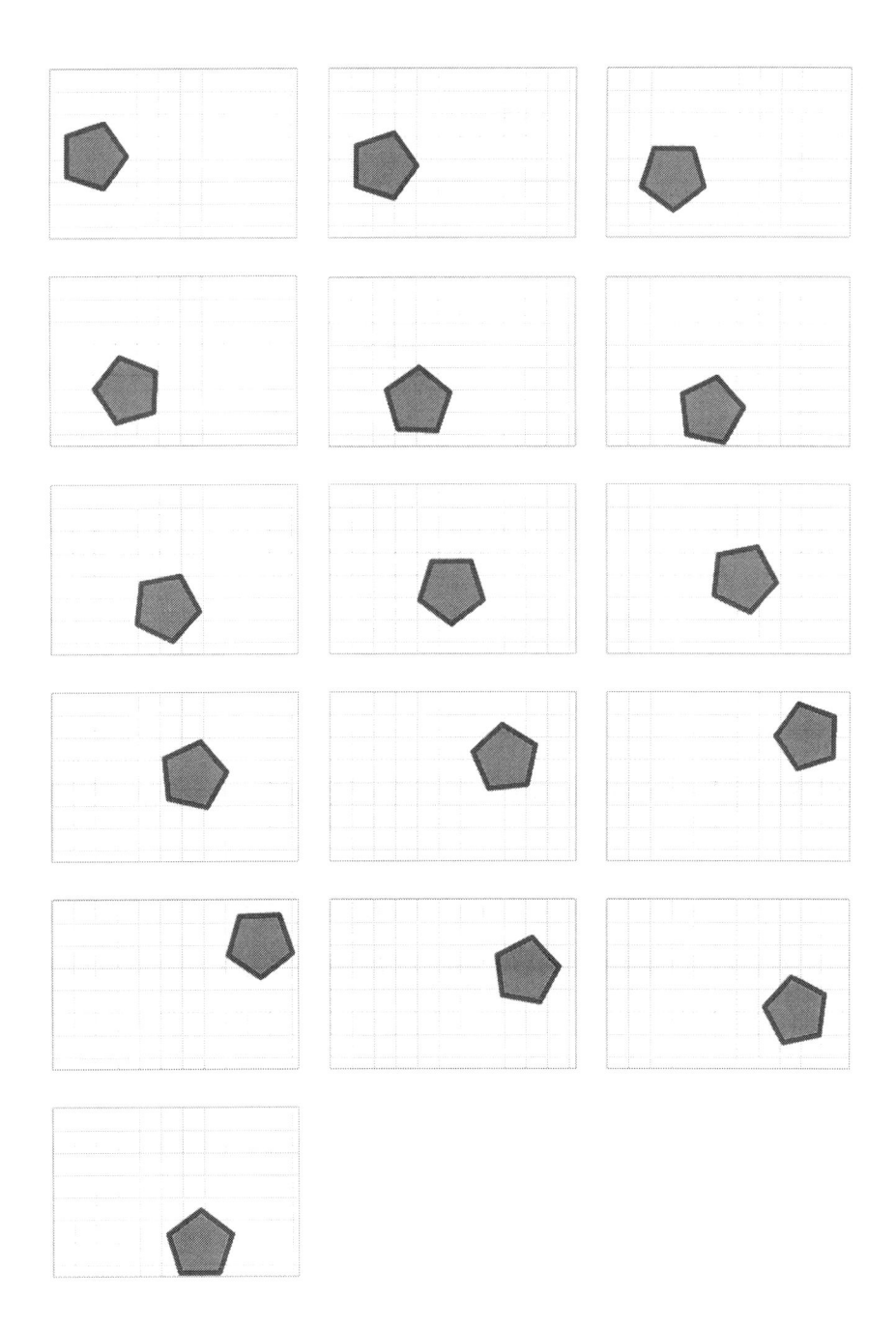

You will keep creating these intermediate frames until you hit your end state - which also signifies the end of this particular animation sequence. When all of these frames are played back-to-back really quickly, you have an animation. In the next few sections, we'll go even deeper and turn everything you've learned in this section into working code.

Implementation Time

In the previous section, you learned at a high-level what goes into drawing and animating something on your canvas. You basically have two main steps:

1. Draw

2. Clear

In this section, we'll create a simple circle slide animation and see how these **draw** and **clear** steps map to lines of sweet JavaScript code. Just make sure you have our usual starting point with a `canvas` element and an `id` value of **myCanvas** defined.

Drawing Our Circle

The first step is to draw the circle we would like to animate. Inside your `script` tag, add the following lines:

```
var mainCanvas = document.querySelector("#myCanvas");
var mainContext = mainCanvas.getContext("2d");

var canvasWidth = mainCanvas.width;
var canvasHeight = mainCanvas.height;

function drawCircle() {

}
drawCircle();
```

There is nothing exciting going on here. We are just writing some boilerplate code to more easily access the `canvas` element and its drawing context. While this is pretty boring, the exciting stuff is about to happen...

Inside this `drawCircle` function, add the following code that will actually draw our circle:

```
function drawCircle() {
  mainContext.clearRect(0, 0, canvasWidth, canvasHeight);

  // color in the background
  mainContext.fillStyle = "#F8F8F8";
  mainContext.fillRect(0, 0, canvasWidth, canvasHeight);

  // draw the circle
  mainContext.beginPath();

  var radius = 175;
  mainContext.arc(225, 225, radius, 0, Math.PI * 2, false);
  mainContext.closePath();

  mainContext.fillStyle = "#FFCC00";
  mainContext.fill();

  mainContext.lineWidth = 10;
  mainContext.strokeStyle = "#DCB001";
  mainContext.stroke();
}
```

If everything worked out fine, you will see our awesome circle that looks as follows when you preview in the browser:

So far, almost everything we've done has been a review of all the `canvas`-related things we've been learning together. I mention almost because there is something new that I want to call out. That is the `clearRect` method:

```
mainContext.clearRect(0, 0, canvasWidth, canvasHeight);
```

The clearRect method is responsible for the *clear* part of the two animation steps we need to implement.

This method takes the coordinates for the rectangular area you want to clear. Since we want to clear the entire area of our canvas, we define a rectangular area that starts at the top-left corner (0, 0) and has a size defined by the total width and height as specified by the `canvasWidth` and `canvasHeight` variables:

(0, 0)

canvasHeight

canvasWidth

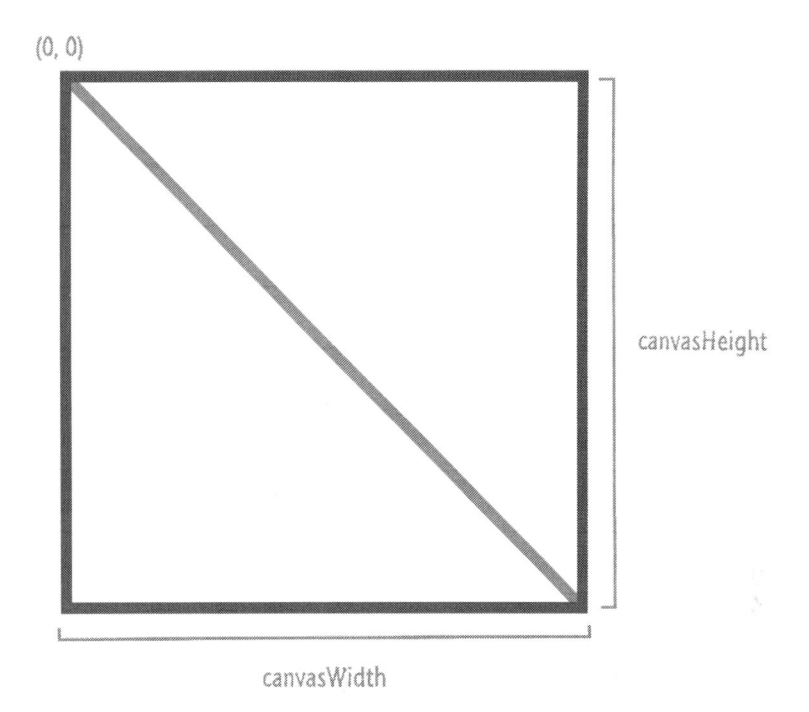

When that code runs, all of the pixels within that rectangular area are cleared out. After that line, all of the remaining code is just about getting our circle to appear. We've covered all of that code extensively in Chatper 8 where we learned how to draw circles, so let's skip over all of that and focus on something totally new in the next section.

Animating Your Circle

It's all well and awesome that you have a yellow circle that shows up, but what we really want to do is animate this circle by having it slide from left to right. More specifically, we want to animate our circle's x position value that controls where the circle is located horizontally. Doing this will require us to modify the x position value slightly every few milliseconds to create our animation's intermediate states.

The way we accomplish this is by using what is commonly known as an **animation loop**. An animation loop is a function that gets called very rapidly, and it is inside this function where you make the subtle changes **on each function call** that you'd like to see visualized. To help create these animation loops, you have a specialized function called `requestAnimationFrame` (you'll learn more about this in the next chapter!) that takes care of both calling a function and ensuring you call that function repeatedly.

The way `requestAnimationFrame` works is pretty cool. It calls your animation loop repeatedly (boring), but it times each call to coincide with when your browser is about to paint the screen (awesomesauce!). This allows you to only execute the code inside your animation loop when it actually leads to a screen update, and that level of optimization puts more traditional timer-based loops like `setTimeOut` and `setInterval` out in the dust.

Anyway, let's actually see the `requestAnimationFrame` in action! Go ahead and add the following highlighted line towards the bottom of your `drawCircle` function:

```
function drawCircle() {
  mainContext.clearRect(0, 0, canvasWidth, canvasHeight);

  // color in the background
  mainContext.fillStyle = "#F8F8F8";
  mainContext.fillRect(0, 0, canvasWidth, canvasHeight);

  // draw the circle
  mainContext.beginPath();

  mainContext.arc(225, 225, 175, 0, Math.PI * 2, false);
  mainContext.closePath();

  mainContext.fillStyle = "#FFCC00";
  mainContext.fill();

  mainContext.lineWidth = 10;
  mainContext.strokeStyle = "#DCB001";
```

```
    mainContext.stroke();


    requestAnimationFrame(drawCircle);
}
```

To reiterate what we talked about earlier, what we've just done is told our requestAnimationFrame function to call the drawCircle function every time your browser decides to redraw. The number of times your browser will decide to redraw will vary based on whatever else is going on in your page, but typically you redraw at around 60 times a second (or once every 16.67 milliseconds). Putting it all together, our drawCircle function is going to get called around 60 times a second as well.

Now, simply calling the requestAnimationFrame function isn't enough. We need to make some changes to how we draw our circle to ensure the horizontal position is changed slightly with each drawCircle call. That isn't too complicated, so to do this, make the following highlighted changes:

```
var xPos = -500;

function drawCircle() {
  mainContext.clearRect(0, 0, canvasWidth, canvasHeight);

  // color in the background
  mainContext.fillStyle = "#F8F8F8";
  mainContext.fillRect(0, 0, canvasWidth, canvasHeight);

  // draw the circle
  mainContext.beginPath();
  mainContext.arc(xPos, 225, 175, 0, Math.PI * 2, false);
  mainContext.closePath();
```

```
    mainContext.fillStyle = "#FFCC00";

    mainContext.fill();


    mainContext.lineWidth = 10;

    mainContext.strokeStyle = "#DCB001";

    mainContext.stroke();


    xPos += 5;


    if (xPos > 1000) {

        xPos = -500;

    }


    requestAnimationFrame(drawCircle);

}
```

If you preview your page right now, you should see a circle that happily slides from one side of the canvas to another. **What you've just done is successfully created a simple animation!** Now, before we wrap things up for the night (or daytime...if you are an early morning reader), let's look at how the lines of code we added leads to our circle getting all animated.

How the Animation Works

To help you better understand what is going on, let's walk through the code together to ensure everything makes sense. Starting at the top, the first thing we did is declare and initialize a global variable called **xPos**:

```
var xPos = -500;
```

This variable will store our circle's horizontal position, and we've given it an initial value of -500. This declaration by itself doesn't affect our circle's position, for that is actually set by calling the arc method:

```
mainContext.arc(xPos, 225, 175, 0, Math.PI * 2, false);
```

The arc method's first argument determines the horizontal position we draw our circle. That's why instead of providing a hard coded value, we pass in our xPos variable instead. If we stopped right here, all we would have accomplished is drawing our circle at a horizontal position of -500.

The key to this animation is not leaving xPos alone. We change the value of xPos each time drawCircle is called by incrementing it slightly. We do that with the following line:

```
xPos += 5;
```

Each time drawCircle is called, the value of xPos is increased by 5. This change combined with the arc method call from earlier draws our circle five pixels to the right each time. Eventually, the value of xPos gets large enough where you can actually see the circle when it gets drawn:

w00t!

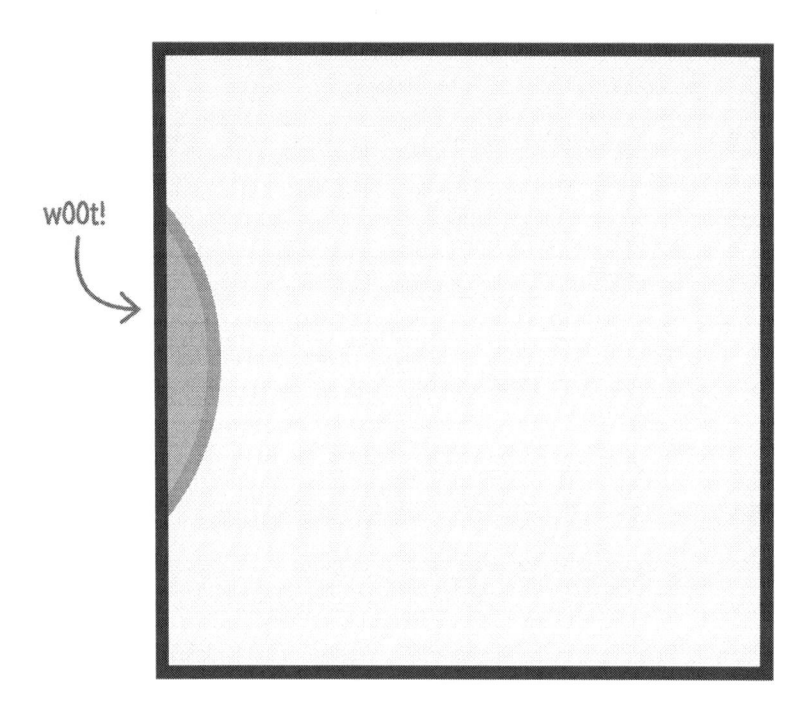

The value of xPos will keep growing unless we stop it. Otherwise, our circle will slide past just once and never return to its starting position. To ensure our circle doesn't disappear forever once it slides past, we reset the xPos variable once it hits a value of 1000. That is handled by the following code:

```
if (xPos > 1000) {
    xPos = -500;
}
```

When our xPos value gets reset to -500, it's almost as if the animation restarts. Our xPos value slowly increments by 5 with each drawCircle call, hits a value of 1000, and then starts all over again with a value of -500. Somewhere along the way, its value ensures the circle is visible when the arc method is called. Phew!

Conclusion

I love animation. It is what got me into web development in the first place. With that said, animating on the canvas is...um...interesting. It's like animating things in the 1990's where you have to handle all aspects of drawing, clearing the screen, re-drawing, and so on manually. In this chapter, you got a brief glimpse of all that. Giving you a longer glimpse goes beyond the scope of what we are going to do, but if you are interested, you should totally check out my book 100% dedicated to Web Animation called **Animation in HTML, CSS, and JavaScript**. You'll probably like it...maybe!

Chapter 16: Animating with requestAnimationFrame

When you are creating an animation, it goes without saying that you want your animation to run smoothly and fluidly when someone is viewing it. If you are using CSS Animations in the DOM world, then you have nothing to worry about. Your browser takes care of everything for you. If you are creating your animation using JavaScript just like we are, things are a bit different. Instead of the browser giving you some assistance, you are left on your own. It is up to you to make sure your animation runs smoothly while at the same time taking into account the various factors that could affect your animation's performance. Factors such as other things happening on the page. Factors such as your laptop / phone / tablet going into battery mode and halving its performance reduced. Factors such as another tab taking focus. You get the point.

Times have changed. Your prayers have been answered. You now have help in the form of the `requestAnimationFrame` function that allows you to create smooth and fluid animations in JavaScript without...you actually having to worry about making it smooth and fluid. Just add a few calls to `requestAnimationFrame` and your browser takes care of the rest. That's it.

In this chapter, we are going to learn all about this magical function and how we can use it to make our animations on the `canvas` run really awesomely.

Let's get started!

Meet requestAnimationFrame

Making your animations run smoothly depends on a lot of factors. It depends on what else is going in your page. It depends on what other animations might be running in parallel. It depends on whether the user is interacting with the page by clicking or typing. It depends on what browser you are using and when it decides to repaint or update what is shown on the screen.

Traditionally, you may have used a function like `setInterval` or its funnier cousin `setTimeout` to power your animation loop. The problem with these two functions is simple. They don't understand the subtleties of working with the browser and getting things to paint at the right time. They have no awareness of what is going on in the rest of the page. These qualities made them very inefficient when it came to powering animations because they often request a repaint/update that your browser simply isn't ready to do. You would often end up with skipped frames and other horrible side effects.

If `setInterval` and `setTimeOut` went out on a date, they would probably be heckled quite a bit. Despite how bad `setInterval` and `setTimeOut` were for working with animations, you had no real alternatives. You had to use them. This lack of better alternatives left animations created via JavaScript looking a little less polished when compared to animations created in CSS or via a dedicated runtime like Flash (you *do* remember Flash, right?!).

Fortunately, things changed. Given how important animations are for creating great looking applications and sites, the major browser vendors (starting with Mozilla) decided to address this problem in an elegant way. Instead of burdening you with having to deal with all of the issues related to creating a smooth animation in JavaScript using `setInterval` or `setTimeOut`, they created a function called `requestAnimationFrame` that handles all of those issues for you.

What makes `requestAnimationFrame` so awesome is that it doesn't force the browser to do a repaint that may never happen. Instead, it asks the browser nicely to call your animation loop when the browser decides it is time to redraw the screen. This results in no wasted work by your code on screen updates that never happen. Skipped frames are a thing of the past. Best of all, because `requestAnimationFrame` is designed for animations, your browser optimizes the performance to ensure your animations run smoothly depending on how much system resources you have available, whether you are running on battery or not, whether you switch away to a different tab, and so on.

Words haven't been invented in the English language to describe how awesome the `requestAnimationFrame` function is.

Using This Magical Function

We saw this function used in the previous chapter, but we are going to go into much greater detail here. The way you use `requestAnimationFrame` is very simple. Whenever you want to redraw your screen, simply call it along with the name of your animation loop function (aka a callback) that is responsible for drawing stuff to your screen:

```
requestAnimationFrame(callback);
```

The thing to note is that the `requestAnimationFrame` function isn't a loop. It isn't a timer. You need to call it every time you want to get the screen repainted. This means, unless you want your animation to stop, you need to call `requestionAnimationFrame` again through the same callback function that you specified. I know that sounds bizarre, but it looks as follows:

```
function animate() {

  // stuff for animating goes here

  requestAnimationFrame(animate);
}
animate();
```

The `animate` method is the callback function for our `requestAnimationFrame` call, and it will get called very rapidly once it starts running.

Vendor Prefixes Not Needed

At this point, `requestAnimationFrame` has extremely broad support among the browsers people use according to the caniuse statistics for it. There is no need to vendor prefix it any more, and the examples you'll see here won't have it prefixed either.

Your Frame Rate

So far, I've been extolling the virtues of `requestAnimationFrame` and how it can make your animations really smooth. The word **smooth** isn't really a good way to measure something. It won't hold up under scrutiny! The way we measure smoothness is by using a number you are probably very familiar with called the **frame rate**. You are probably already familiar with frames rates from watching movies or playing video games where you are told that the higher your frame rate, the better the result is. Guess what? That same holds for us in the HTML world also.

With `requestAnimationFrame`, your frame rate is typically around 60 frames per second (FPS). To repeat that differently, this means your `requestAnimationFrame` function and related code have the potential to refresh your screen 60 times every second. This number wasn't arbitrarily chosen. It is the upper limit on how quickly your laptop screen, computer monitor, phone display, etc. can physically update your screen.

> ### Your Frame Rate May Go Lower than 60 FPS
> If your animation loop is very complex and does a lot of work or your browser is swamped with other things, your frame rate will be lower than 60 frames per second. In general, your browser will do the right thing to ensure your animation is extremely smooth, but be prepared for some random slowdowns.

Now, there will be times when you may want to deliberately slow your animation down. You may not need your animation loop getting called 60 times every second. If you want to throttle your animation's speed, you can do something like the following:

```
var framesPerSecond = 10;

function animate() {
```

```
    setTimeout(function() {

        requestAnimationFrame(animate);


        // animating/drawing code goes here



    }, 1000 / framesPerSecond);
}
```

Notice that we are using setTimeout to delay when the next `requestAnimationFrame` call gets made. Yes, it is a bit ironic that we are using `setTimeOut` here despite me saying some terrible things about it earlier.

Stopping Your Animation Loop

Once your `requestAnimationFrame` loop starts running, rarely will you ever need to tell it to stop. If you do need to stop your animation loop from doing unnecessary work, you can do something like the following:

```
var running = true;

function animate() {
    if (running) {
        // do animation or drawing stuff


    }
    requestAnimationFrame(animate);
```

```
}
```

If your `running` variable were to ever be set to **false**, your animation loop will stop doing whatever work is being done. Your `animate` function will still get called by virtue of it being attached to your requestAnimationFrame. It just won't be doing any work since the `if (running)` check will return **false**.

Now, if you really REALLY need to stop your `requestAnimationFrame` from calling some poor function around 60 times a second, you do have `requestAnimationFrame`'s evil twin, `cancelAnimationFrame`. The best way to explain how it prevents `requestAnimationFrame` from working is by looking at a simple example:

```
// store your requestAnimatFrame request ID value
var requestId;

// setting up a click event listener
var bodyElement = document.querySelector("body");
bodyElement.addEventListener("click", stopAnimation, false);

function animate() {

    // doing some animation stuff

    // get the requestID as part of calling animate()
    requestId = requestAnimationFrame(animate);
}
animate();
```

```
function stopAnimation(e) {
    // use the requestID to cancel the requestAnimationFrame call
    cancelAnimationFrame(requestId);
}
```

This simple example should readily highlight how `cancelAnimationFrame` works. The thing that I didn't call out about `requestAnimationFrame` is that it returns an ID value whenever it gets called:

```
requestId = requestAnimationFrame(animate);
```

Normally, you don't care about this ID. The only time you really need to know this ID value is when wanting to use `cancelAnimationFrame`. The reason is that `cancelAnimationFrame` uses the ID value to identify the right `requestAnimationFrame` function to stop:

```
cancelRequestAnimationFrame(requestId);
```

That's all there is to the `cancelAnimationFrame` function. I should emphasize that you really don't need to go through all this trouble to cancel a `requestAnimationFrame` setup. The initial approach I outlined with the `running` variable is a good enough approach to use. With that said...if you really want to go the extra mile, you have a friend in `cancelAnimationFrame`!

Conclusion

All in all, this is pretty exciting. The `requestAnimationFrame` function brings to the table the same level of optimization your animations or transitions created in CSS have. Instead of your code telling the browser to redraw the screen and the browser (being the temperamental thing that it is) ignoring that request, the `requestAnimationFrame` politely asks the browser to call the animation loop when it is ready to redraw the screen. This cordial relationship results in really smooth animations. See! Being nice always pays off...especially if you are a JavaScript function!

Chapter 16: Animating Many Things

In the previous chapters, you learned all about drawing and animating something using the HTML canvas element. More specifically, you learned all about how to draw and animate **a single element**. Now, there is nothing wrong with that. Not every animation needs to have a lot going on, but you are definitely missing out on the whole canvas experience by not going a little crazy and animating a lot of things.

Take a look at the following example:

In this example, you have not one, not two, but a hundred blue circles happily moving around to create the final animation that you see. The static image isn't quite as cool as the live example you can see here: http://bit.ly/randomMovingCircles

Knowing how to create animations involving many thing is an important skill for you to learn, for a lot of really awesome visualizations revolve around making a lot of things animate in interesting ways. The way you are going to learn all of this is by deconstructing and breaking apart the animated blue circles example you see above.

Onwards!

Deconstructing the Example

Just like you can't break that which doesn't exist, you can't really have a deconstruction without an already-constructed example. Like I mentioned earlier, we are going to deconstruct the blue circles animation you see above. You can get the full HTML, CSS, and JavaScript that makes up this example by either going to the example link I posted in the previous page or by looking at the following:

```html
<!DOCTYPE html>
<html>

<head>
    <title>A Whole Lotta' Circles!</title>

    <style>
        body {
            margin: 0px;
            padding: 0px;
        }
        #myCanvas {
            border: 1px #CCC solid;
        }
```

```
        </style>

</head>

<body>
<div id="container">
    <canvas id="myCanvas" width="500" height="500"></canvas>
</div>

<script>

    var mainCanvas = document.getElementById("myCanvas");
    var mainContext = mainCanvas.getContext('2d');


    var circles = new Array();

    function Circle(radius, speed, width, xPos, yPos) {
        this.radius = radius;
        this.speed = speed;
        this.width = width;
        this.xPos = xPos;
        this.yPos = yPos;
        this.opacity = .05 + Math.random() * .5;

        this.counter = 0;
```

```
        var signHelper = Math.floor(Math.random() * 2);


        if (signHelper == 1) {
            this.sign = -1;
        } else {
            this.sign = 1;
        }
    }


Circle.prototype.update = function () {

    this.counter += this.sign * this.speed;

    mainContext.beginPath();
    mainContext.arc(this.xPos +
                    Math.cos(this.counter / 100) * this.radius,
                    this.yPos +
                    Math.sin(this.counter / 100) * this.radius,
                    this.width,
                    0,
                    Math.PI * 2,
                    false);

    mainContext.closePath();
```

```
        mainContext.fillStyle = 'rgba(185, 211, 238,' + this.opacity + ')';

        mainContext.fill();

};


function setupCircles() {

    for (var i = 0; i < 100; i++) {

        var randomX = Math.round(-200 + Math.random() * 700);

        var randomY = Math.round(-200 + Math.random() * 700);

        var speed = .2 + Math.random() * 3;

        var size = 5 + Math.random() * 100;


        var circle = new Circle(100, speed, size, randomX, randomY);

        circles.push(circle);

    }

    drawAndUpdate();

}

setupCircles();


function drawAndUpdate() {

    mainContext.clearRect(0, 0, 500, 500);


    for (var i = 0; i < circles.length; i++) {

        var myCircle = circles[i];

        myCircle.update();
```

```
        }
        requestAnimationFrame(drawAndUpdate);
    }
</script>
</body>


</html>
```

Take a few moments, read through the code, and try to understand what is going on. If you really want to get some Schrute Bucks, open this example (http://bit.ly/randomMovingCircles) in your favorite browser debugging tool, set some breakpoints, and step through the main sections line by line. That's how real ninjas try to understand what is going on.

Once you are done looking at the code and/or imagining a sweet life as a ninja or looking up what a Schrute Buck is, let's walk through all of this code together and understand what is going on.

Defining the Canvas

Let's start with the easy part - defining your `canvas` element that will display our animation. For this, you have to look at our HTML:

```
<div id="container">
    <canvas id="myCanvas" width="500" height="500">



    </canvas>
</div>
```

Our **canvas** element has an **id** value of **myCanvas**, and its **width** and **height** attributes are set to **500**. This results in your canvas being a square with each edge being 500 pixels. Remember, you can't set the width and height of your canvas in CSS. Doing so will result in everything inside your canvas getting all stretched and looking weird. You have to specify the width and height inline on the canvas element like I've done.

Now, despite the special treatment for width and height, this doesn't mean that other CSS styling-related stuff can't be attached to the canvas. In our style block, I have a style rule defined to give our canvas a dotted border:

```
#myCanvas {
    border: 1px #CCC solid;
}
```

At this point, if you were to take a snapshot of what this page would look like, here is what you would see:

What your canvas looks like right now!

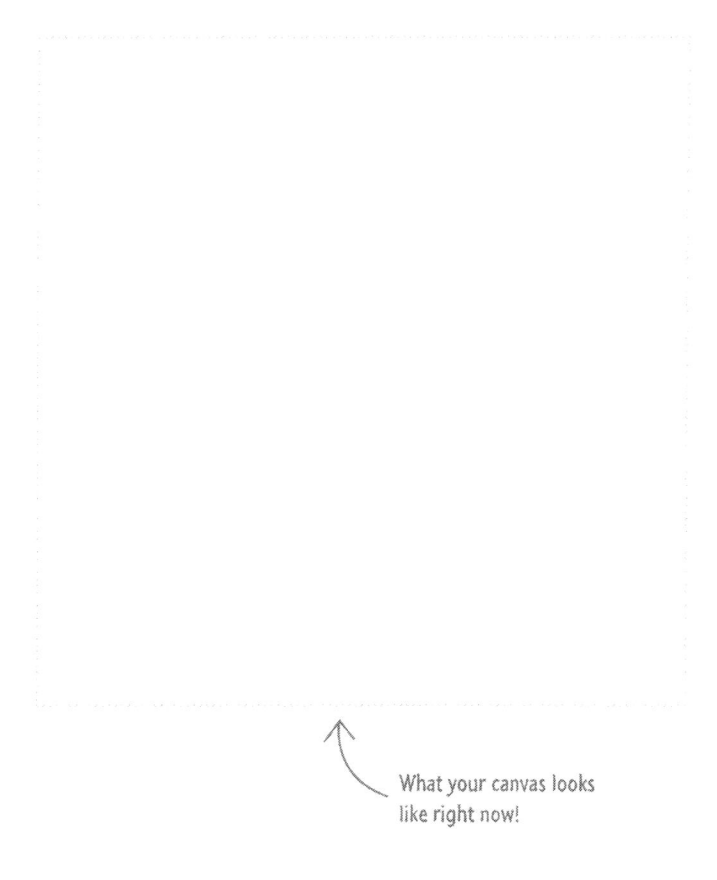

That's right. You would see nothing...except for the dotted border. The reason is that your canvas-based animation only knows one game, and that game is JavaScript. In the next few sections, we'll walk through the JavaScript and see how the lines of code result in some beautiful (totally hot!) blue circles animating around on the screen.

Overview of our Code

The bulk of what this animation does lives in JavaScript. Everything from drawing the circles to moving them around is handled entirely by our code which you can see below:

```javascript
var mainCanvas = document.getElementById("myCanvas");

var mainContext = mainCanvas.getContext('2d');
```

```javascript
var circles = [];

function Circle(radius, speed, width, xPos, yPos) {
    this.radius = radius;
    this.speed = speed;
    this.width = width;
    this.xPos = xPos;
    this.yPos = yPos;
    this.opacity = .05 + Math.random() * .5;

    this.counter = 0;

    var signHelper = Math.floor(Math.random() * 2);

    if (signHelper == 1) {
        this.sign = -1;
    } else {
        this.sign = 1;
    }
}

Circle.prototype.update = function () {

    this.counter += this.sign * this.speed;
```

```js
    mainContext.beginPath();
    mainContext.arc(this.xPos +
                Math.cos(this.counter / 100) * this.radius,
                this.yPos +
                Math.sin(this.counter / 100) * this.radius,
                this.width,
                0,
                Math.PI * 2,
                false);

    mainContext.closePath();

    mainContext.fillStyle = 'rgba(185, 211, 238,' + this.opacity + ')';
    mainContext.fill();
};


function setupCircles() {
    for (var i = 0; i < 100; i++) {
        var randomX = Math.round(-200 + Math.random() * 700);
        var randomY = Math.round(-200 + Math.random() * 700);
        var speed = .2 + Math.random() * 3;
        var size = 5 + Math.random() * 100;

        var circle = new Circle(100, speed, size, randomX, randomY);
        circles.push(circle);
```

```
    }
    drawAndUpdate();
}
setupCircles();


function draw() {
    mainContext.clearRect(0, 0, 500, 500);


    for (var i = 0; i < circles.length; i++) {
        var myCircle = circles[i];
        myCircle.update();
    }
    requestAnimationFrame(drawAndUpdate);
}
```

Before diving into the code, let me first describe what the code does in a very hand wavy fashion so that you will be better prepared for the details that you will see shortly.

Like I mentioned earlier, all of the JavaScript you see is responsible for drawing and animating the circles into the canvas. Now, you may be wondering if it really takes that much code to do something like this. After all, if you compare the amount of code here to the amount of code you had when animating a single element earlier...there is a lot of code here:

Lines of Code
(because somehow that is relevant...)

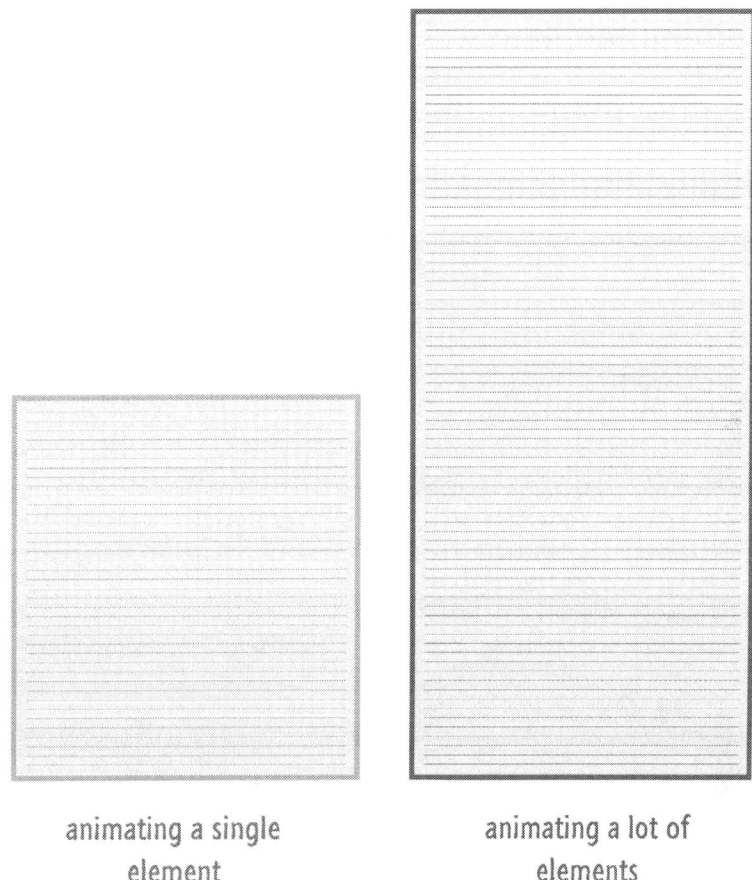

animating a single element

animating a lot of elements

The answer is "yes", and the reason for all of this extra code is because dealing with many elements requires a little more bookkeeping than what you saw when dealing with a single element.

What our code does can be broadly summarized in the following five steps:

i. Get a reference to our `canvas` element so that we can draw and animate into it.

ii. Create a `Circle` object whose purpose is to link the circle that you see to a circle that exists in memory that only your browser sees.

More specifically:

    a) Define a Circle class that helps store any details about its speed, size, initial position, etc.

    b) Add a function to our Circle "class" that is responsible for storing the circle's various properties and helping draw itself.

iii. Create a whole lot of Circle objects - each with their own unique set of properties such as initial position, size, movement speed, and so on.

iv. Update the position of each Circle as part of your `requestAnimationFrame` loop running.

v. Clear your entire canvas area to start all over again.

I am taking really broad brush strokes in describing what our code does and omitting important details. Don't worry! You'll see those details elaborated on shortly.

Referencing our Canvas Element

Let's go through our steps starting at the top. The first lines of our code allow us to gain access to our `canvas` element and its API via the context object:

```
var mainCanvas = document.getElementById("myCanvas");
var mainContext = mainCanvas.getContext('2d');
```

The first line allows us to access our `canvas` element by using `querySelector` and passing in our canvas's id value - myCanvas. You can also use the older `getElementById` function if you want to be uncool.

Our `canvas` element by itself isn't particularly interesting for what we are trying to do. What makes it interesting are the APIs it provides for drawing into it. You access that API by calling `getContext` on it and passing in the argument for the 2d API we want to use.

Declaring an Array to Store our Circles

The next variable we declare and initialize is our circles array:

```
var circles = [];
```

As its name implies, this array will eventually be used to store all of the individual `Circle` objects we create.

And with this, we are done with declaring the variables that we will be using through this animation. This part always seems a bit disjointed since these variables only make sense in the context they are eventually used in, so stay on your toes for when these variables make a guest appearance in the subsequent sections.

The Circle Object

With the basic variable declarations out of the way, the next thing we'll look at is the function that defines our `Circle` object. The `Circle` object is important because it helps keep track of every circle that ends up getting drawn on the canvas.

Remember, your `canvas` has no memory. It will simply draw whatever you tell it to draw. When you clear everything away to start a new frame, whatever was drawn before is completely lost. What we need is basically our own version of a retained mode graph that creates a virtual representation of what we are planning on drawing. We sort of saw this in Chapter 14 where we looked at how to structure your drawing code.

To borrow a graphic we saw in the DOM vs. Canvas chapter at the very beginning, we are creating a very lightweight way of combining the immediate mode-ness of the canvas with some of the advantages a retained mode system provides:

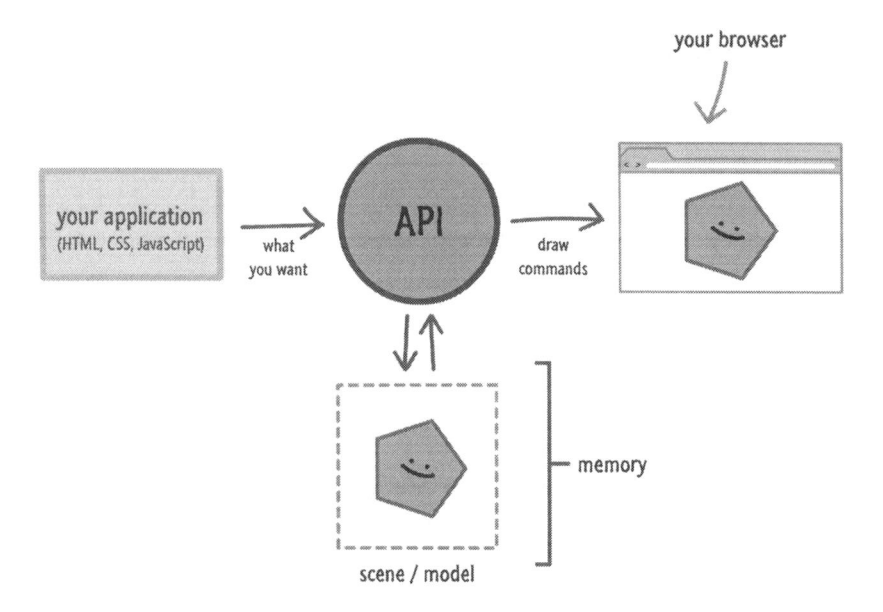

[Diagram: your application (HTML, CSS, JavaScript) → "what you want" → API → "draw commands" → your browser; API ↕ scene / model (memory)]

Our Circle object is an important part of this virtual representation since it contains all of the properties and method you need in order to draw and animate the circle on each frame.

It is defined entirely by the appropriately named `Circle` function:

```
function Circle(radius, speed, width, xPos, yPos) {

    this.radius = radius;

    this.speed = speed;

    this.width = width;

    this.xPos = xPos;

    this.yPos = yPos;

    this.opacity = .05 + Math.random() * .5;


    this.counter = 0;
```

```
    var signHelper = Math.floor(Math.random() * 2);


    if (signHelper == 1) {

        this.sign = -1;

    } else {

        this.sign = 1;

    }

}
```

This `Circle` function's primary job is to create little `Circle` objects that each contain the properties relevant to the circle that gets drawn on screen. As you can see, there really isn't much going on here except for a lot of properties that need to be declared and initialized on the `Circle` object itself.

To look at this in more detail, our `Circle` function takes five arguments. These arguments stand for the radius, speed, width, horizontal position, and vertical position - all important visual things that we will need when drawing our circle. These same five arguments are then made into properties unique to this object when you actually create it:

```
function Circle(radius, speed, width, xPos, yPos) {

    this.radius = radius;

    this.speed = speed;

    this.width = width;

    this.xPos = xPos;

    this.yPos = yPos;

    this.opacity = .05 + Math.random() * .5;
```

```
        this.counter = 0;


        var signHelper = Math.floor(Math.random() * 2);


        if (signHelper == 1) {
            this.sign = -1;
        } else {
            this.sign = 1;
        }
}
```

Besides these arguments, a few more object properties we set are for the `counter`, `opacity`, and `sign`. You'll see all of these properties used shortly...in the next section actually!

Creating our Circles

Finally! We get to see some action that ties together some of the random pieces of code you've seen so far. Jump on down a bit to the `setupCircles` function:

```
function setupCircles() {
    for (var i = 0; i < 100; i++) {
        var randomX = Math.round(-200 + Math.random() * 700);
        var randomY = Math.round(-200 + Math.random() * 700);
        var speed = .2 + Math.random() * 3;
```

```
            var size = 5 + Math.random() * 100;


            var circle = new Circle(100, speed, size, randomX, randomY);

            circles.push(circle);

        }

        drawAndUpdate();

    }
```

This code is responsible for creating each individual circle; giving each circle a random starting position, speed, and size; and calling the drawAndUpdate function that will take all of these circles and start animating them. That's a lot of things these handful of lines do!

Let's look at creating each circle first. The following highlighted lines are responsible for defining all of the arguments and actually creating a Circle object:

```
function setupCircles() {

    for (var i = 0; i < 100; i++) {

        var randomX = Math.round(-200 + Math.random() * 700);

        var randomY = Math.round(-200 + Math.random() * 700);

        var speed = .2 + Math.random() * 3;

        var size = 5 + Math.random() * 100;


        var circle = new Circle(100, speed, size, randomX, randomY);

        circles.push(circle);

    }

    drawAndUpdate();
```

```
}
```

Yeah, that's almost everything this function. The bulk of this code lives inside a for loop:

```
for (var i = 0; i < 100; i++) {

    .

    .

    .

}
```

Each time this loop gets called, a new `Circle` object is created. Given the range of this particular loop, we will be creating 100 circles because all of this code will get executed 100 times.

Next up are the various variables that define the arguments we will be passing in as part of creating our `Circle` object:

```
var randomX = Math.round(-200 + Math.random() * 700);
var randomY = Math.round(-200 + Math.random() * 700);
var speed = .2 + Math.random() * 3;
var size = 5 + Math.random() * 100;
```

The randomX and randomY variables help determine where on your canvas the circle's initial position will be:

```
var randomX = Math.round(-200 + Math.random() * 700);
```

```
var randomY = Math.round(-200 + Math.random() * 700);
```

Our canvas's size is a square of 500 pixels by 500 pixels, and we want to give 200 pixels extra all around to give our circles some ability to live outside the box - literally!

The next two lines define how fast our circle will move, its size, and its radius:

```
var speed = .2 + Math.random() * 3;
var size = 5 + Math.random() * 100;
```

Once you have all of these values, all that is really left is to create our Circle object. This is handled by the following line:

```
var circle = new Circle(100, speed, size, randomX, randomY);
```

The way you create an object is by calling the object's constructor/function and using the new keyword. That's exactly what we have done here, and as part of creating our objects, we pass in the arguments you spent the previous lines defining.

At the end of this, you have a brand new Circle object:

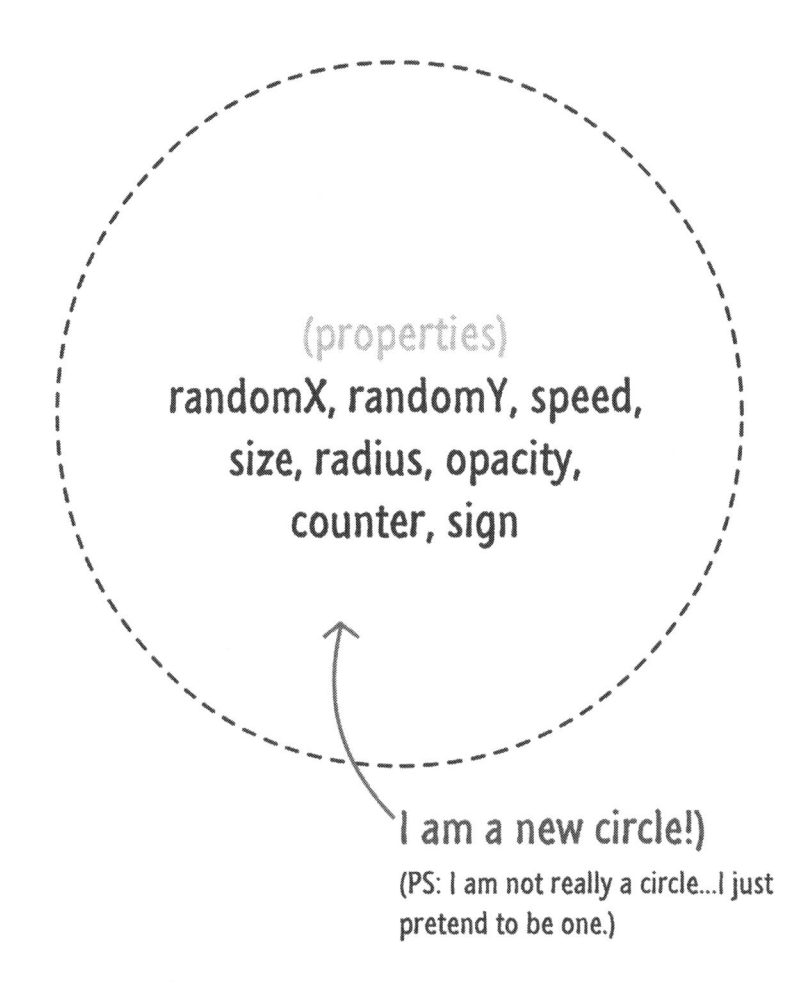

(properties)
randomX, randomY, speed, size, radius, opacity, counter, sign

I am a new circle!)
(PS: I am not really a circle...I just pretend to be one.)

Once our Circle object is created, it gets stored in our circle variable. Immediately after that, we add this circle to the circles array that we created much earlier:

```
circles.push(circle);
```

At the end of the loop, our `circles` array will contain a reference to every Circle object we have created:

circles

↑

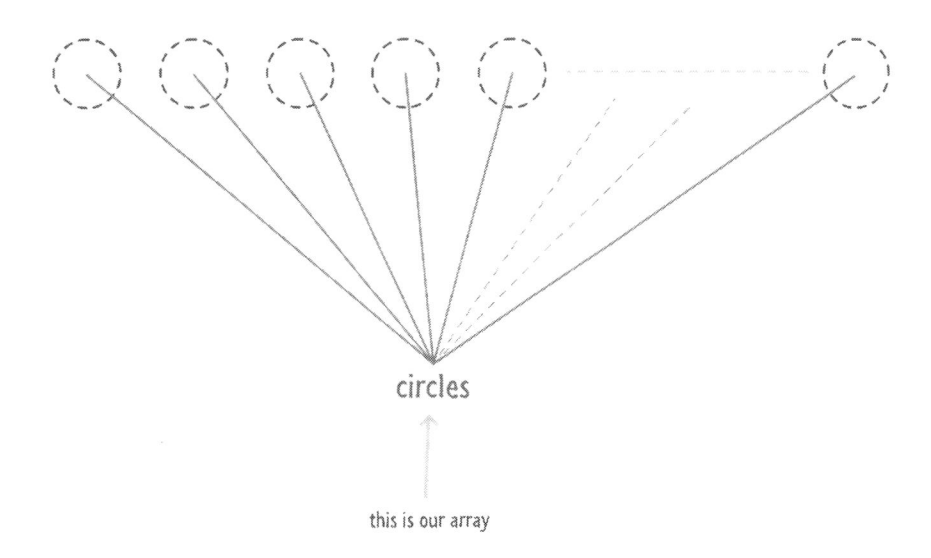

this is our array

This is important because this array and its contents are the only link between the circles we want and what you see drawn on the screen. This is the light-weight retained mode graph I was referring to actually coming to life.

The final thing we do after all of our circles have been created is call the drawAndUpdate function:

```
drawAndUpdate();
```

This function, as its name implies, is responsible for taking our circles array, drawing each circle onto the screen, and rapidly updating them to create the animation that you eventually see. We'll look at this function next.

Drawing and Updating the Circles

At this point, we just finished creating our Circle objects and storing them in our circles array. The next stage is to look at our drawAndUpdate function...a function that you just heard about:

```
function drawAndUpdate() {
```

```
    mainContext.clearRect(0, 0, 500, 500);


    for (var i = 0; i < circles.length; i++) {

        var myCircle = circles[i];
        myCircle.update();
    }


    requestAnimationFrame(drawAndUpdate);
}
```

The `drawAndUpdate` function seems pretty simple, but it is actually awesome...and dangerous. At a high level, it is responsible for taking these Circle objects and their properties and turning them into the lovable blue circles that you see on your screen.

More specifically, it does the following three things:

i. Clears your entire canvas drawing area to make room for a new frame.

ii. Goes through each `Circle` object in the circles array and calls the update function on it. (We'll look at the update function shortly, so don't be worried if you haven't heard of it yet.)

iii. Defines itself as your `requestAnimationFrame` callback to create our animation loop.

Let's look at how these three things are mapped to our code. The first thing I do is clear our canvas so that new things can be drawn:

```
mainContext.clearRect(0, 0, 500, 500);
```

Page | 216

In case you are wondering why, the reason is that there is no concept of moving something around the canvas like you may see when moving DOM elements around. You have to explicitly clear all of your contents before drawing new things. Otherwise, you'll just be drawing on top of existing content...and that will look pretty bad.

After you clear your canvas, everything is set to draw your circles in a slightly new location. That needs to be done on each circle, so we use a for loop and to take care of that:

```
for (var i = 0; i < circles.length; i++) {

    var myCircle = circles[i];

    myCircle.update();

}
```

This loop runs through every single element found in the circles array, and that element is our lovable Circle object. We just retrieve the Circle object and call the update function on it. Keep this function's memory under your hat, for we will look at in just a few moments.

The last thing our drawAndUpdate function does is ensure it calls itself:

```
requestAnimationFrame(drawAndUpdate);
```

To be less modest, this function hitches itself to the requestAnimationFrame bandwagon and ensures it gets called around 60 times every second...whether you like it or not.

Drawing and Updating the Circles (Part II)

We are almost nearing the end. The one last thing to mention about the drawAndUpdate function is that it probably doesn't live up to its hype. All it really did was clear your canvas, call the update function on every single circle, and then just call itself again. A highly trained cat could probably do that. If you were looking for closure, that function certainly wasn't going to provide it.

The big missing piece is really on how each circle gets drawn and displayed on the screen. That is handled by the mysterious update function that you saw mentioned earlier. This function looks as follows:

```
Circle.prototype.update = function () {

    this.counter += this.sign * this.speed;

    mainContext.beginPath();
    mainContext.arc(this.xPos +
                    Math.cos(this.counter / 100) * this.radius,
                    this.yPos +
                    Math.sin(this.counter / 100) * this.radius,
                    this.width,
                    0,
                    Math.PI * 2,
                    false);

    mainContext.closePath();

    mainContext.fillStyle = 'rgba(185, 211, 238,' + this.opacity + ')';
    mainContext.fill();
};
```

The first thing to note is that this function looks a little weird:

```
Circle.prototype.update = function () {
```

The reason is that this function is actually a prototype living on the Circle object. Discussing prototypes and why this function isn't just nested inside our constructor goes beyond the bounds of this chapter, but just know that every `Circle` object you create has the ability to call this `update` method. The properties and values your update method inherits and uses as part of its job are based on the particular `Circle` object that called it. That's all you need to know.

Inside this prototype, we start using the properties that you defined in the `Circle` function and populated with values in the `setupCircles` function. We start with the counter property:

```
this.counter += this.sign * this.speed;
```

The value of the `counter` property is being incremented by the product of the `speed` and the `sign` properties. You can see the role the `sign` property plays more clearly here. If the value of `sign` is negative, your `counter` variable is decreasing. If it is positive, your counter variable increases!

The most important takeaway is this: **each time your update function gets called and this code runs, your counter variable's value changes**. This value is what determines the position of your circle, so a smooth increase on decrease in this value will directly correlate to a smooth change in our circle's position. You'll see where next:

The next handful of lines help draw your circle:

```
mainContext.arc(this.xPos +
                Math.cos(this.counter / 100) * this.radius,
                this.yPos +
```

```
                Math.sin(this.counter / 100) * this.radius,

                this.width,

                0,

                Math.PI * 2,

                false);
```

The first and last line tell your context object to start drawing a path and to close the path you've drawn respectively. The real magic happens in the middle where the circle is being drawn. The main thing is to note how the `yPos`, `radius`, `counter`, and `width` properties play a role in making your circle work. Of these properties, your `counter` value is the one that changes each time the `update` function is called:

```
Circle.prototype.update = function () {

    this.counter += this.sign * this.speed;

    mainContext.beginPath();
    mainContext.arc(this.xPos +
                Math.cos(this.counter / 100) * this.radius,
                this.yPos +
                Math.sin(this.counter / 100) * this.radius,
                this.width,
                0,
                Math.PI * 2,
                false);
```

```
        mainContext.closePath();


        mainContext.fillStyle = 'rgba(185, 211, 238,' + this.opacity + ')';
        mainContext.fill();
};
```

Notice how the counter variable is prominently used in setting your circle's horizontal and vertical drawing locations. These are the magic lines that makes our animation work. Everything you've seen revolves around making these lines happy.

The last thing we are going to do, before calling it a night, is specify the color and opacity of the circle. This is accomplished by the following two lines:

```
mainContext.fillStyle = 'rgba(185, 211, 238,' + this.opacity + ')';
mainContext.fill();
```

The fillStyle property on our context object specifies the RGBa (red, green, blue, alpha) values that make our circle look as blue as it does. Once you have specified your colors, you actually apply it by calling the fill method on your context object. All of these things should be a review for you!

At the end of this, your drawAndUpdate function gets called all over again. In fact, your drawAndUpdate function gets called sixty times every second, and our update function gets called a hundred times with each drawAndUpdate call. That's a lot of work getting done!

Conclusion

At this point, we've looked at every single line of code that you have and visited and re-visited some important concepts that make this animation work. Animating many elements does require some extra work as you've seen. The bulk of our code, now that you've seen all of it, is in re-creating our retained mode graph that maps between all of the circles in memory to what actually gets shown on screen. Once you master that little detail, creating any kind of animation that involves many elements will become a breeze.

Chapter 16: Creating Sprite Animations

For billions of years, sprite sheets have been used to simplify how you can define 2d visuals for video games and (more recently) web sites. Sprites can be used for displaying just a single visual, but they can also be made up of many visuals that you sequentially play back to create an animation. You see sprite sheets all the time, and you probably never even notice.

Take a look at the following sprite sheet:

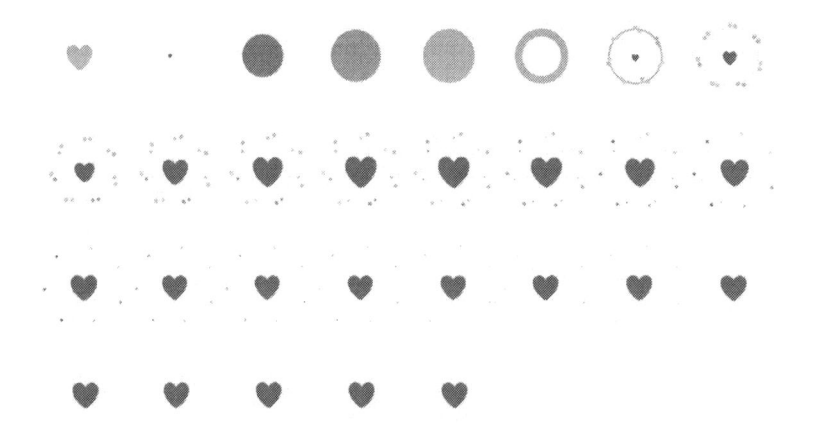

This sprite sheet is taken from Twitter's implementation of the heart icon:

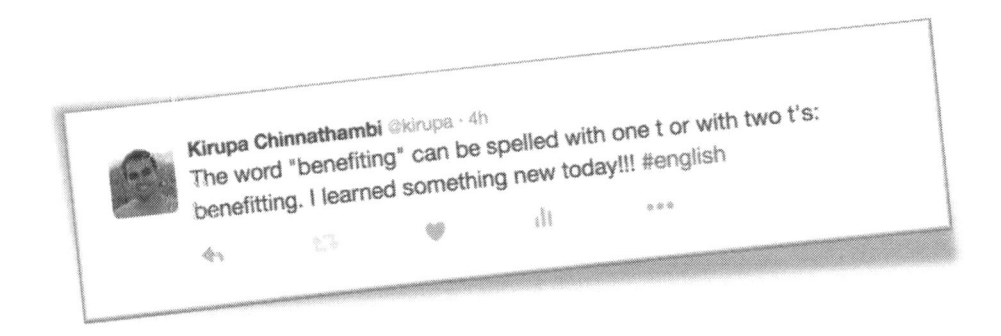

When you click on the heart icon to favorite a tweet, an animation plays. The animation you see when you click on the heart icon is made up of the same individual frames you saw in the sprite sheet earlier. Yes, seriously!

In this chapter, we are going to learn all about how to create an animation from a sprite sheet. The twist is that we will learn how to do that entirely inside the canvas. Also, we won't be re-creating the Twitter heart/favorite example. Instead, I have something equally exciting...and a whole lot less copyright infringing for us to work on instead.

Onwards!

The Sprite Sheet

Before you can animate sprites from a sprite sheet, you first need a sprite sheet. Don't start panicking just yet. If you don't have a sprite sheet, you can just use one that I have already created here: https://www.kirupa.com/stuff/sprites_blue.png (This is the same sprite sheet I will be using in our explanation and code, so I encourage you to use it if this is your first foray into creating animations from sprites.)

Now, if you are brave enough to want to create your own sprite sheet, then there are a variety of tools out there that can help you out with this. My favorite is Flash Professional's Generate Sprite Sheet functionality:

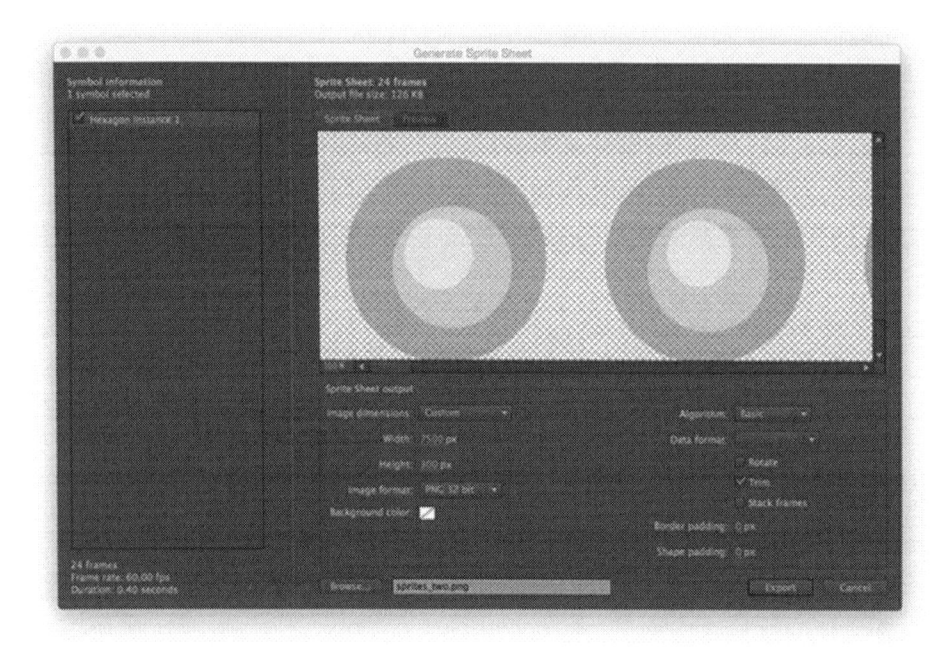

If you Google around, you'll find many other solutions that people rave about. Covering how to create a sprite sheet goes beyond the scope of this chapter, but whatever tool you use, just make your sprite sheet meets the following two criteria:

1. Each sprite in your sprite sheet is evenly sized.

2. The sprites you wish to animate are arranged on a single row. Some tools like to break up the sprites into a single column or a combination of rows and columns! We don't want that.

If all of this boggles your brain, just use the sprite sheet from the URL I provided earlier. You can always experiment with your own sprite sheet once you've learned all about how to use and manipulate them.

How All of This Works

Before we start looking at the implementation, let's first take a few steps back and learn more about how a series of sprites in a sprite sheet can end up creating an animation. Our sprite sheet looks as follows:

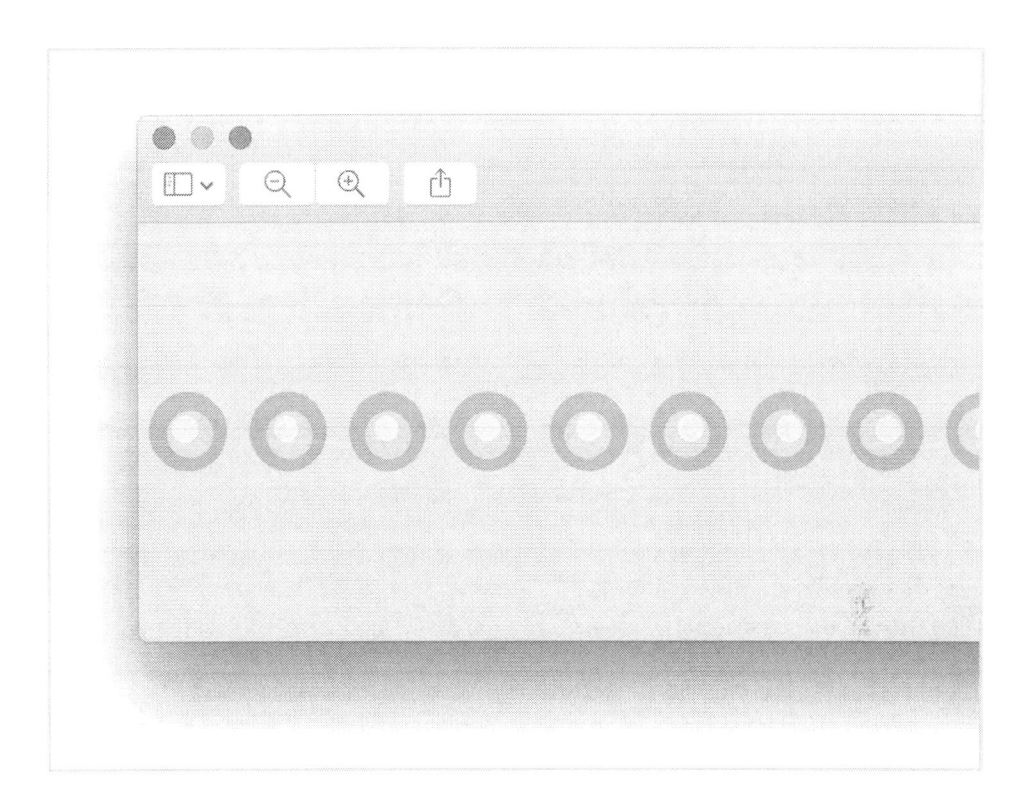

Displaying the full sheet would take up too much space, but there are a few more circles beyond what you see here. To generalize, I am going to replace our sprite sheet with just solid colored circles to explain what is going on. The secret magic sauce to a sprite animation is to display **just a single sprite at a time**:

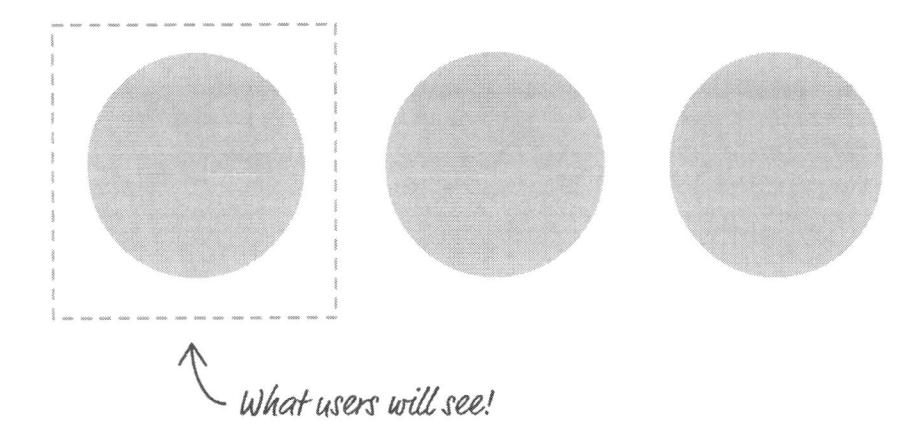

What users will see!

It doesn't matter how big or small your sprite sheet is. All users will ever see is just that one single sprite. To display the next sprite, we show the contents of our next sprite:

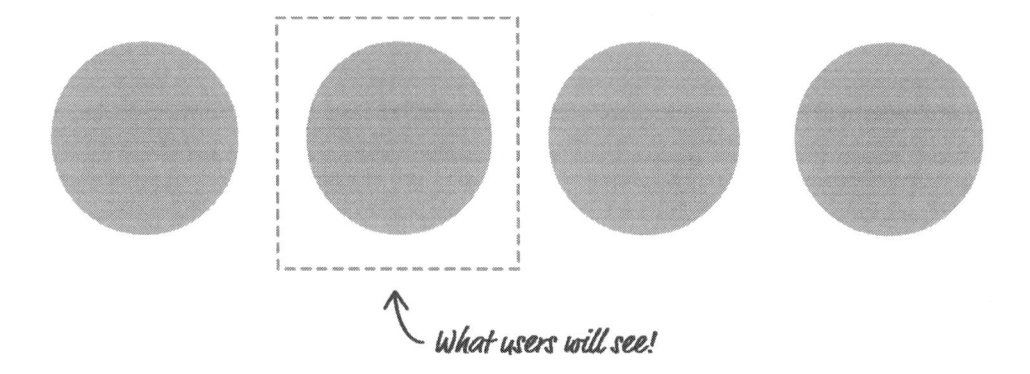

What users will see!

We keep going through our sprite sheet displaying each individual sprite. All of this is very sudden. Users will never see the transition from one sprite to another. All they will see is the end result of a sequence of images replacing each other. What you get is an animation in the most traditional sense. Really quickly replacing one picture with another is how hand-drawn animations and film strips basically work. What we are going to be doing isn't going to look a whole lot different than that!

It's Coding Time!

Now that we've seen an English version of how a sprite animation works, it's time to convert all of that into JavaScript. Our code is going to follow these four basic steps:

1. Load the sprite sheet. This is pretty straightforward.

2. Use `drawImage` to display just the first sprite from our sprite sheet. If you recall, the `drawImage` method allows you to optionally specify the exact co-ordinates and dimension of the image you want to display instead of displaying the whole thing.

3. Shift the `drawImage` co-ordinates to display the next sprite...and the next sprite...and so on.

4. Put all of the `drawImage` logic inside a `requestAnimationFrame` loop to create our animation.

We are going to add some code that does all four of these steps next! Make sure you have our usual HTML document setup with a `canvas` element whose `id` value is **myCanvas**. This is the same type of document we've been starting off from forever, but for your reference, the content look as follows:

```
<!DOCTYPE html>
<html>

<head>
  <title>Canvas Follow Mouse</title>
  <style>
    canvas {
      border: #333 10px solid;
    }

    body {
      padding: 50px;
    }
  </style>
</head>

<body>
  <canvas id="myCanvas" width="550px" height="350px"></canvas>

  <script>
```

Page | 229

```
        </script>

    </body>

</html>
```

Inside the **script** block, add the following code:

```
var canvas = document.querySelector("#myCanvas");
var context = canvas.getContext("2d");

var myImage = new Image();
myImage.src = "https://www.kirupa.com/stuff/sprites_blue.png";
myImage.addEventListener("load", loadImage, false);

function loadImage(e) {
    animate();
}

var shift = 0;
var frameWidth = 300;
var frameHeight = 300;
var totalFrames = 24;
```

```
var currentFrame = 0;

function animate() {
  context.clearRect(120, 25, 300, 300);

  //draw each frame + place them in the middle
  context.drawImage(myImage, shift, 0, frameWidth, frameHeight,
                    120, 25, frameWidth, frameHeight);

  shift += frameWidth + 1;

  /*
    Start at the beginning once you've reached the
    end of your sprite!
  */
  if (currentFrame == totalFrames) {
    shift = 0;
    currentFrame = 0;
  }

  currentFrame++;

  requestAnimationFrame(animate);
}
```

Once you've added your code, make sure everything works by previewing your document in your browser. If everything worked properly, you will see a blue circle (with a sweet circular design inside it) happily rotating. This is all a result of us animating the contents of the sprite sheet that you saw earlier. In the next section, we'll take apart this code and learn how everything works!

Loading the Image

Before we can even think about animating our sprite sheet, we first need to load the sprite sheet image into our `canvas`. That is handled by the following chunk of code:

```
var myImage = new Image();

myImage.src = "https://www.kirupa.com/stuff/sprites_blue.png";

myImage.addEventListener("load", loadImage, false);


function loadImage(e) {

   animate();

}
```

All of this should be familiar to you from Chapter 12 where we learned all about how to draw images on the `canvas`. We create a new `Image` object called `myImage`. We set the `src` property to the image we want to load, and then we listen for the load event to ensure we don't do anything until the image has fully made its way across the internet to your browser. Once our image has been loaded, we call the `animate` function via the `loadImage` event handler. The fun is about to start now!

It's Animation Time!

Before we get to the animate function, we have a few variables that we should look at first:

```
var shift = 0;

var frameWidth = 300;
```

```
var frameHeight = 300;

var totalFrames = 24;

var currentFrame = 0;
```

The variable names kinda hint at what they do, but for now, just know that they exist and pay attention to the default values assigned to them. We'll see all of these variables used really soon.

Now, we get to the `animate` function. This function is responsible for quickly cycling through each sprite in the sprite sheet to create the animation. A bulk of this responsibility lies in the following line:

```
context.drawImage(myImage, shift, 0, frameWidth, frameHeight,
                  120, 25, frameWidth, frameHeight);
```

This line handles which part of the sprite sheet to display, and it handles where to display it. Looking at this in greater detail, each sprite in our sprite sheet looks similar to this:

Each sprite is a square that is 300 pixels on each side. There are a bunch of sprites just like this arranged side-by-side, and what we are doing is taking just the first image and displaying it on the screen. To see how, let's look at our `drawImage` code with all of the variables replaced with their actual numerical values:

```
context.drawImage(myImage, 0, 0, 300, 300,
                  120, 25, 300, 300);
```

From our sprite sheet, we grab a 300px by 300px square starting at the (0, 0) mark. That is our first sprite and handled by the first line in our `drawImage` call. We place that grabbed sprite at its original size of 300px by 300px on our `canvas` at the (120, 25) mark. The end result looks a little bit like this:

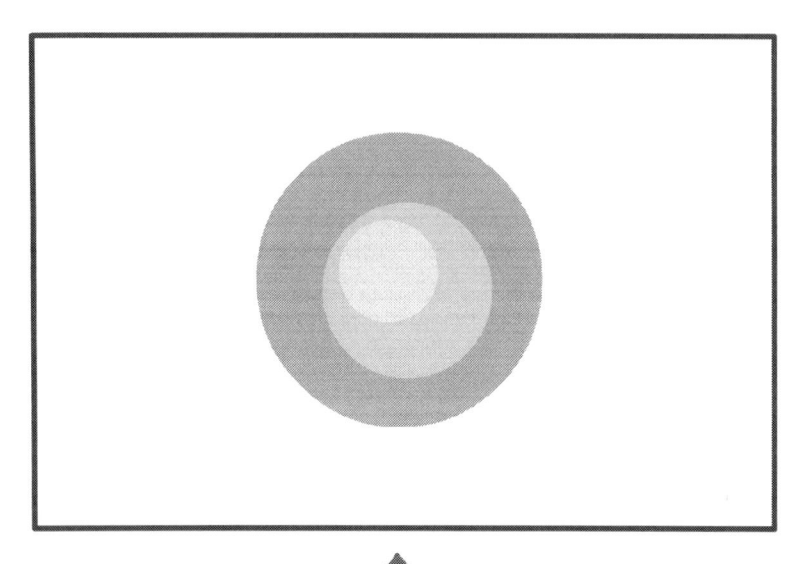

Our canvas...aka what people see!

Because of how `drawImage` works, we don't see any part of the rest of the sprite sheet. We only see the 300 by 300 pixel square we cut out from the sprite sheet and placed in our `canvas`.

To display the next sprite, we tell our `drawImage` method to grab the next sprite from our sprite sheet. Our `shift` variable is responsible for telling `drawImage` where to start looking for the next sprite, so what we need to do is simply adjust the value stored by the `shift` variable:

shift *is 301*

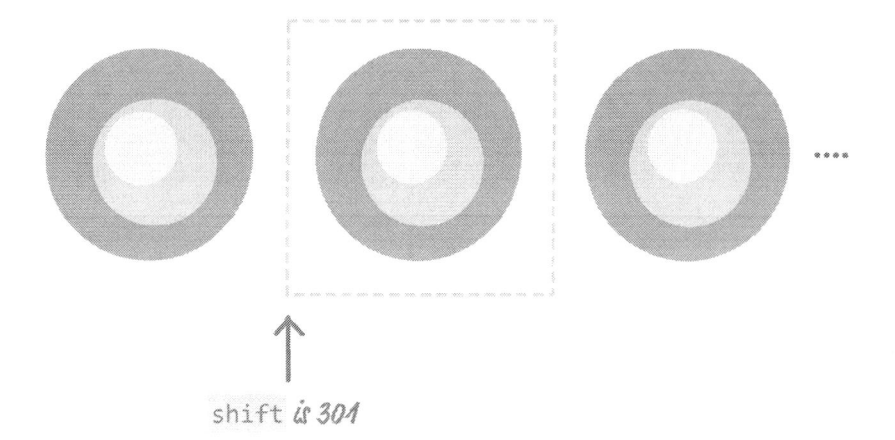

To move to our next frame, we increase our `shift` variable by 301. The number of pixels you need to shift to get to the next frame depends entirely on your sprite sheet. In our case, our sprite sheet has a 1 pixel gap between each sprite. That is why we increment our `shift` variable really awkwardly by both the `frameWidth` and a 1 value:

```
shift += frameWidth + 1;
```

Ignoring the rest of the code for a second, you can now see how our `drawImage` function works to create the animation. For the second frame, looking at our drawImage call with all of the variables replaced with their stored values, you'll see something that looks like the following:

```
context.drawImage(myImage, 301, 0, 300, 300,
                  120, 25, 300, 300);
```

This ensures that our next sprite is taken from the (301, 0) position at the same 300 by 300 pixel size. This taken sprite is then placed at the (120, 25) mark at the original 300 by 300 pixel size. To our users, this will look like a direct replacement of the earlier sprite with a new one that is slightly more rotated.

With every `requestAnimationFrame` call to the `animate` function, we shift over to the next frame in our sprite sheet. We do this shifting by increasing the value of the `shift` variable by 301 each frame. That's it! This automatically ensures `drawImage` is looking at the right part of our sprite sheet and displays the correct sprite. This is all done very rapidly, so what you end up seeing is each frame played back to create a smooth animation.

Ok, we are almost done here. The last thing we are going to look at is some of the code we skipped:

```
if (currentFrame == totalFrames) {
    shift = 0;
    currentFrame = 0;
}
```

The code we skipped is kinda important. We need a way to know when we have reached the end of our sprite sheet so that we can restart our animation from the beginning. The `currentFrame` variable acts as a counter, and the `totalFrames` variable specifies the number of frames in our sprite sheet. The way you can figure out how many frames you have is by simply counting the number of sprites you have. Some image tools may provide you with that information. If your particular sprite sheet doesn't come with that information, you'll have to manually count...like an animal :P

Anyway, we determine the end by constantly checking when the value of `currentFrame` is the same as totalFrames. When both of those variables are equal, it means that we've reached the end of our sprite sheet and it's time to reset everything:

```
if (currentFrame == totalFrames) {
    shift = 0;
    currentFrame = 0;
}
```

By setting the value of `shift` to 0, is we ensure our next `drawImage` call looks at the first frame in our sprite sheet. Setting `currentFrame` to 0 simply resets our counter.

If we are not at the last frame where `currentFrame` is equal to `totalFrames`, then we should go right on and increment the value of `currentFrame`:

```
currentFrame++;
```

And...that's exactly what we do! This ensures we keep an accurate tally of where in the sprite sheet we are, and that helps us pull the plug and reset everything back to the beginning when we've reached the end of our sprite sheet.

Conclusion

For displaying 2d visuals, sprite sheets are wildly popular. They are most commonly used in games, but as you saw here, you can also use sprite sheets to define normal (and boring) things. Now that you've seen how to implement an animation using a sprite sheet, it all seems pretty easy, right? All you do is just load your sprite sheet and use `drawImage` to display a frame of your sprite sheet at a time. The fun starts to happen when you have no control over the sprite sheets you have to work with. In those cases, your `drawImage` shifting logic might be more involved than just incrementing one variable by a fixed amount. Anyway, no need to worry about that now. When you get to that point, you'll know what to do. If not, just comment here or post on the forums, and I or somebody else will try to help you out :P

Chapter 18: Creating Motion Trails

Have you ever seen a comet or a meteor streaking across the sky? It looks something like this:

From looking at this picture (of the Hyakutake Comet) can you tell what direction the comet is moving in? You can! The comet's tail holds the answer. The trail of gas and dust just behind the comet seems to indicate that the comet is moving in a left-to-right direction. Ignoring for a moment that we are looking at a real thing, this idea of indicating motion by leaving behind a trail is a very common animation technique. There are many names for this, but all the cool kids call it **motion trails**.

In the following sections, we'll learn all about how motion trails work and the handful of lines of JavaScript you need to bring them to life.

Onwards!

The Basic Approach

The way motion trails work is pretty simple. Let's say that we have a circle that is moving from left to right:

Motion trails exaggerate the direction of movement by showing you where your object was just a few moments earlier. For this circle, you may see something like this:

Our motion trail!

How far back your motion trails go and what it looks like are all things under your control. In this case, our motion trail gets smaller and more faded the further away from the source that you go.

Thinking about motion trails is easy. Visualizing them is pretty easy. Implementing them is pretty easy as well...once you understand how exactly they work. The main thing to note is that your motion trails show **where your moving object has been in the past**. To look at that more precisely, take a look at the following diagram:

Time Elapsed

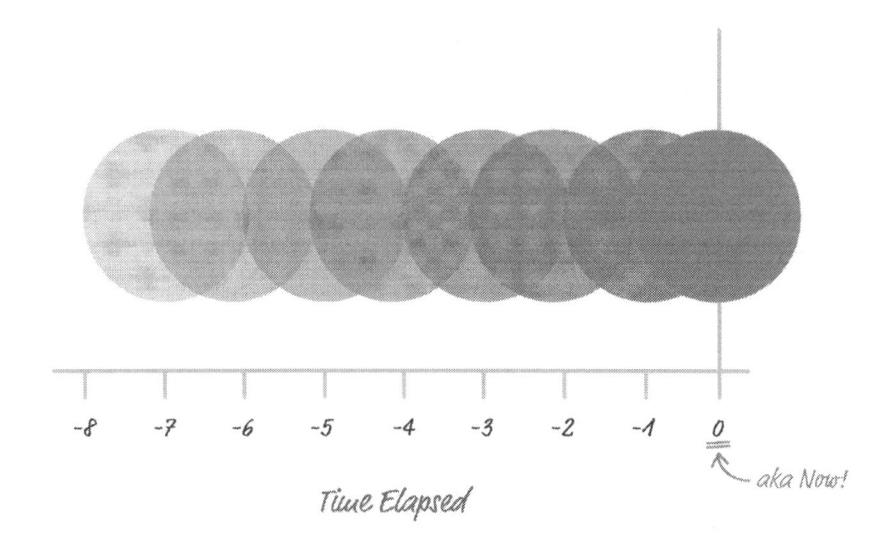

aka Now!

Looking at each part of our motion trail as a slice of time, you can see that at time 0, we have the **source object** we are moving. At each slice of time prior to that, we show where our source object was at that moment in the past. How can we implement such a thing? The answer lies in the array!

We can easily use an array to store where our source object was in the past:

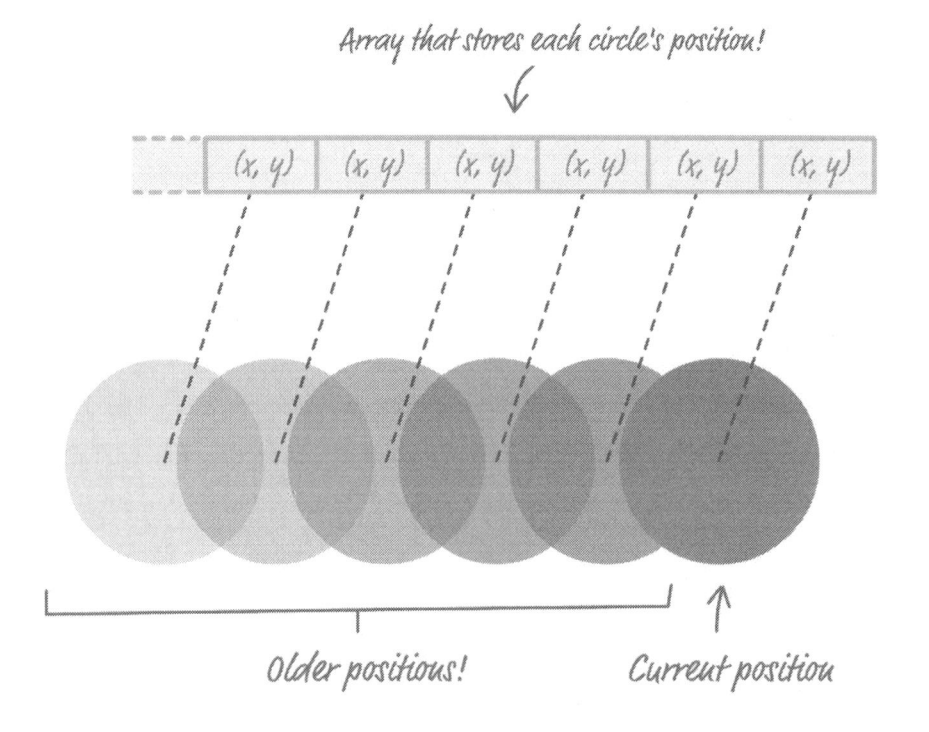

Array that stores each circle's position!

Older positions! *Current position*

Page | 240

The last item in the array will be our source object's current position. Every entry prior to that represents our source object's earlier positions. All of this may sound a bit confusing at first, so let's ignore motion trails for a moment and just focus on how we populate this array.

The way we populate this array is pretty simple. Every few moments, we store our source object's current position at the end of our array:

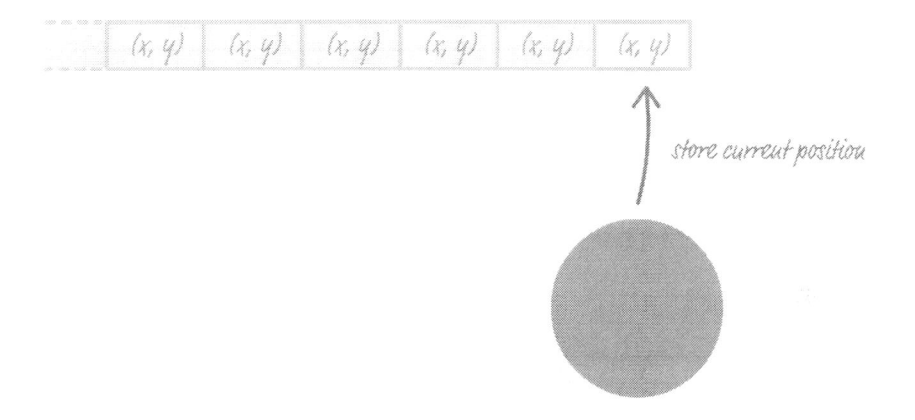

store current position

Over a period of time, our array is going to be filled with position values that map to where our source object was at the moment the array entry was populated. Our motion trail reads from this array to draw the historical snapshot of our source object:

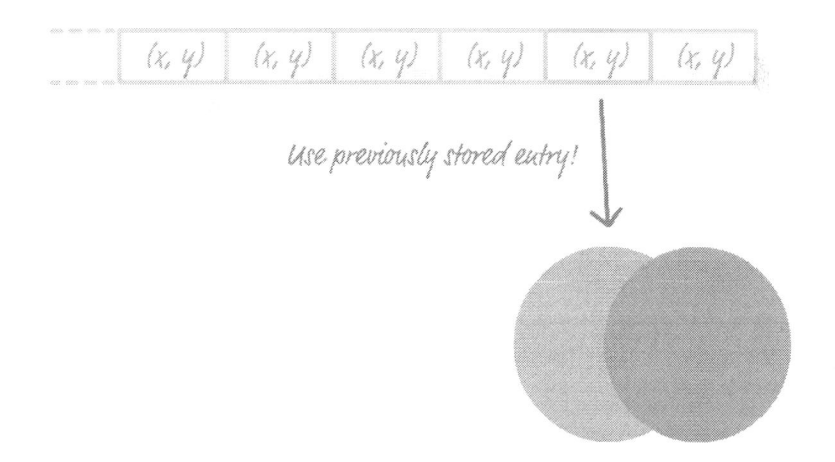

Use previously stored entry!

By re-drawing our source object and placing it at the points referenced by each entry in our array, we create our motion trail:

The last thing we are going to focus on is the array itself. Right now, I have given you the impression that our array has no fixed size. It just keeps growing with each new entry storing our source object's position. Unless you want a motion trail that is made up of every single place our source object has ever been, that isn't desirable. You want to restrict how big your array grows.

. There is nothing clever or complex about how we handle that. Let's say we want our motion trail to be made up of just seven elements. This means, we are going to limit our array's size by just seven elements as well:

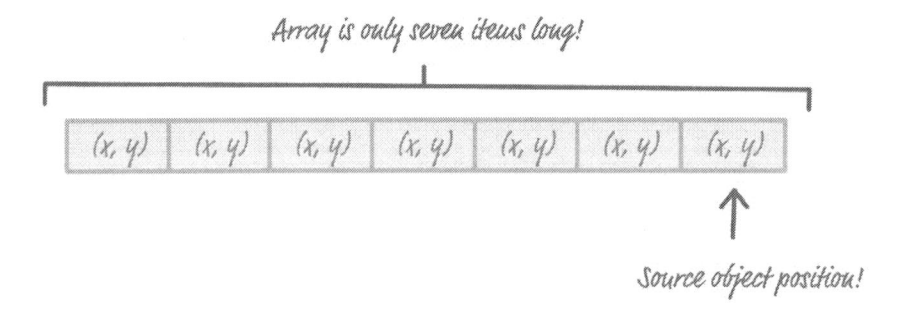

Array is only seven items long!

| (x, y) | (x, y) | (x, y) | (x, y) | (x, y) | (x, y) | (x, y) |

Source object position!

Each time we add a new entry to store our source object's position, we get rid of the oldest entry:

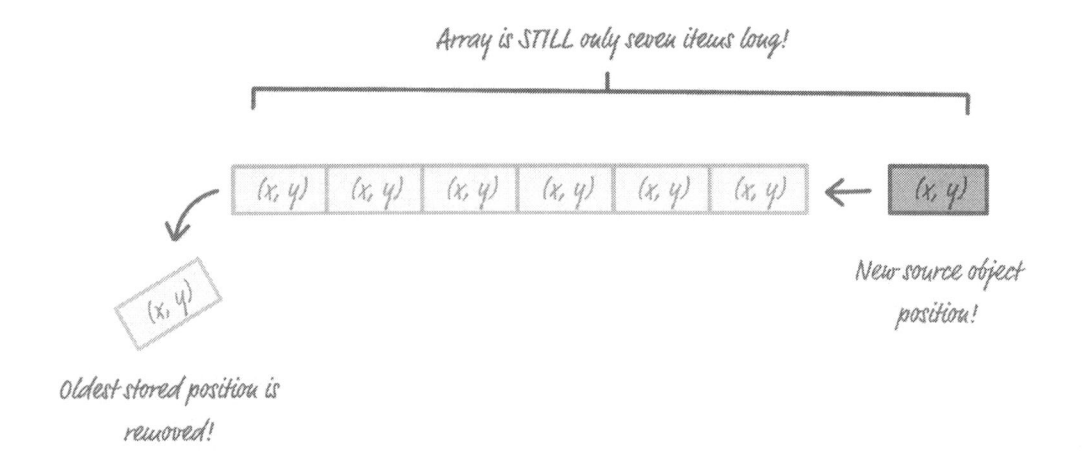

Array is STILL only seven items long!

| (x, y) | (x, y) | (x, y) | (x, y) | (x, y) | (x, y) | ← | (x, y) |

New source object position!

(x, y)

Oldest stored position is removed!

Page | 242

This allows us to maintain a constant size array of seven items where the last item is our source object's position and every preceding item shows where our source object was earlier. Using an array in this way isn't anything new. What we've just described is known as a **queue** or **a first-in first-out (FIFO)** system.

Phew! By now, you probably have a really good idea of how a motion trail works. It's time to turn all of these English-looking words into JavaScript our browser can understand.

Creating the Motion Trail

The task ahead of us is pretty straightforward - especially given what we looked at in the previous section. What we are going to do now is take an object that moves around the `canvas` and give it a motion trail. You can create your own starting point for this, but if you want to closely follow along, continue with our usual example where we have a `canvas` element with an `id` of **myCanvas**. Inside that HTML document, add the following into the `script` tag:

```javascript
var canvas = document.querySelector("#myCanvas");
var context = canvas.getContext("2d");


var xPos = -100;
var yPos = 170;


function update() {
  context.clearRect(0, 0, canvas.width, canvas.height);

  context.beginPath();
  context.arc(xPos, yPos, 50, 0, 2 * Math.PI, true);
  context.fillStyle = "#FF6A6A";
```

```
    context.fill();


    // update position

    if (xPos > 600) {

        xPos = -100;

    }

    xPos += 3;


    requestAnimationFrame(update);

}

update();
```

Once you've added this code, go ahead and preview what you have in your browser. If everything worked out fine, you should see a circle moving from left to right. Right now, this circle shows no motion trail. We are going to fix that right up in the next couple of sections.

Understanding How Things Get Drawn

The first thing to do is to get an idea of how things are getting drawn to the screen. In our example, we have the `update` function that is part of the `requestAnimationFrame` loop. Inside it, the following code is responsible for drawing our circle:

```
context.beginPath();
context.arc(xPos, yPos, 50, 0, 2 * Math.PI, true);
context.fillStyle = "#FF6A6A";
context.fill();
```

The xPos and yPos variables are responsible for figuring out where our circle is positioned. Just a few lines below our drawing code, we have the following:

```
// update position
if (xPos > 600) {
   xPos = -100;
}
xPos += 3;
```

This code is responsible for two things. The first is resetting the value of xPos if it gets larger than 600. The second is incrementing the value of xPos by 3 each time `requestAnimationFrame` calls our update function. In other words, around 60 times a second ideally.

You put all of this together, you can see why our circle moves the way it does. It starts off at -100, and makes its way right by 3 pixels each time our frame is updated. Once our xPos value gets larger than 600, the xPos value gets reset to -100 which causes our circle's position to be reset as well.

Storing our Source Object's Position

Now we get to the good stuff. This is the part where we specify how big our motion trail is going to be and create our array that stores the position of our source object. Above your update function, add the following code:

```
var motionTrailLength = 10;
var positions = [];


function storeLastPosition(xPos, yPos) {
   // push an item
```

```
    positions.push({

        x: xPos,

        y: yPos

    });


    //get rid of first item

    if (positions.length > motionTrailLength) {

        positions.shift();

    }

}
```

This `motionTrailLength` variable specifies how long our motion trail is going to be. The `positions` array stores the x and y values of our source object. The `storeLastPosition` function is responsible for ensuring our positions array is no longer than our motion trail's length. This is where the queue logic we looked at earlier comes into play.

Just adding this code isn't enough. We need to actually store our source object's position. For that, we go back to our `update` function and make a call to `storeLastPosition` just after we draw our circle. Go ahead and add the following highlighted line:

```
function update() {

    context.clearRect(0, 0, canvas.width, canvas.height);


    context.beginPath();

    context.arc(xPos, yPos, 50, 0, 2 * Math.PI, true);

    context.fillStyle = "#FF6A6A";
```

```
    context.fill();


    storeLastPosition(xPos, yPos);


    // update position
    if (xPos > 600) {
      xPos = -100;
    }
    xPos += 3;


    requestAnimationFrame(update);
}
```

This ensures that immediately after we draw our circle at its new position, we store that position in our `positions` array. There is a subtle detail I want you to pay attention to. Notice the order we are doing things in. We first draw our circle using the latest values from `xPos` and `yPos`. After the circle gets drawn, we store that position using the `storeLastPosition` function. Keep this in mind, for we will revisit this in a few moments.

Drawing the Motion Trail

We are now at the last and (possibly) most tricky step. It is time to draw our motion trail. What we are going to do is go through our `positions` array and draw a circle using the co-ordinates stored at each array entry.

Inside your `update` function, just below the `clearRect` call, add the following highlighted lines:

```
function update() {
```

```
context.clearRect(0, 0, canvas.width, canvas.height);

for (var i = 0; i < positions.length; i++) {
  context.beginPath();
  context.arc(positions[i].x, positions[i].y, 50, 0, 2 * Math.PI, true);
  context.fillStyle = "#FF6A6A";
  context.fill();
}

context.beginPath();
context.arc(xPos, yPos, 50, 0, 2 * Math.PI, true);
context.fillStyle = "#FF6A6A";
context.fill();

storeLastPosition(xPos, yPos);

// update position
if (xPos > 600) {
    xPos = -100;
}
xPos += 3;

requestAnimationFrame(update);
}
```

Preview what we have so far in the browser. If everything is running as expected, you'll see our circle sliding from left to right. You'll also see the motion trail. Now, this isn't too much of a reason to celebrate. The entire thing looks sorta like the following:

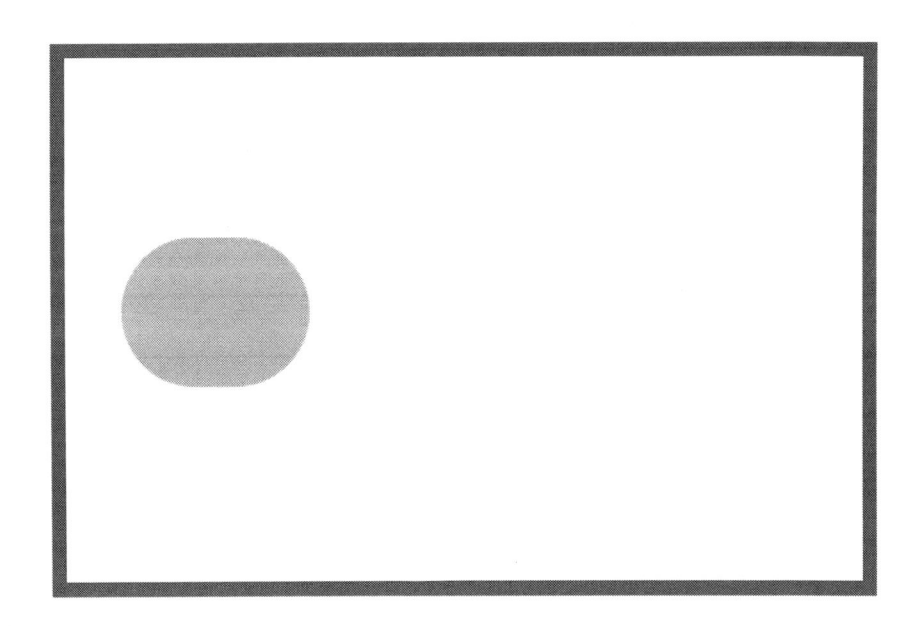

Our motion trail is literally a direct copy of our source object. The only difference is that each of our source object look-a-likes are positioned a few pixels in the past. You can see why by looking at the code you just added:

```
for (var i = 0; i < positions.length; i++) {
    context.beginPath();
    context.arc(positions[i].x, positions[i].y, 50, 0, 2 * Math.PI, true);
    context.fillStyle = "#FF6A6A";
    context.fill();
}
```

You can see that we simply copied the earlier drawing code for our source object, placed it all inside a **for** loop that goes through the **positions** array, and specified that the x/y position for our circle comes from values stored inside our **positions** array. As you just saw when you previewed in your browser, our code creates a motion trail in letter, but it doesn't quite create it in spirit! We don't want that.

Let's first adjust our motion trail by having the circles fade away the further away in the motion trail you go. We can do that easily by using some simple array length shenanigans and a RGBA color value. Modify our `for` loop by making the highlighted changes:

```
for (var i = 0; i < positions.length; i++) {

    var ratio = (i + 1) / positions.length;

    context.beginPath();

    context.arc(positions[i].x, positions[i].y, 50, 0, 2 * Math.PI, true);

    context.fillStyle = "rgba(204, 102, 153, " + ratio / 2 + ")";

    context.fill();

}
```

The changes we made allow your circles to fade away the further from the source object they are. The `ratio` variable stores a number between `1 / positions.length` (when `i` is equal to 0) and 1. This range is based on the result of dividing `i + 1` with the length of our `positions` array.

This `ratio` value is then used in the `fillStyle` property as part of specifying the alpha part for our RGBA color. For a more faded-out look, we are actually dividing the `ratio` value by two for an even smaller alpha value. If you preview your example now, you'll see our circle moving with a respectably faded-out motion trail following behind it! And with that, you are done creating a motion trail.

Tying Up Some Loose Ends

Now, before we call it a night, we talked earlier about the order in which we are doing things in. Right now, the order in our `update` function looks follows:

1. Draw the motion trail
2. Draw the source object
3. Store the source object's position

Why are we doing things in this deliberate manner? The reason has to do with something we've only casually touched upon in the past: **the canvas drawing order**. Just like painting in real life, drawing on the canvas works by layering pixels on top of older pixels. This is the painters model rendering approach we mentioned in Chapter 5.

In the life of our source object and motion trail, your source object is the shiny new thing. The end of your motion trail is where the oldest thing you are going to draw lives. We saw that with this earlier diagram:

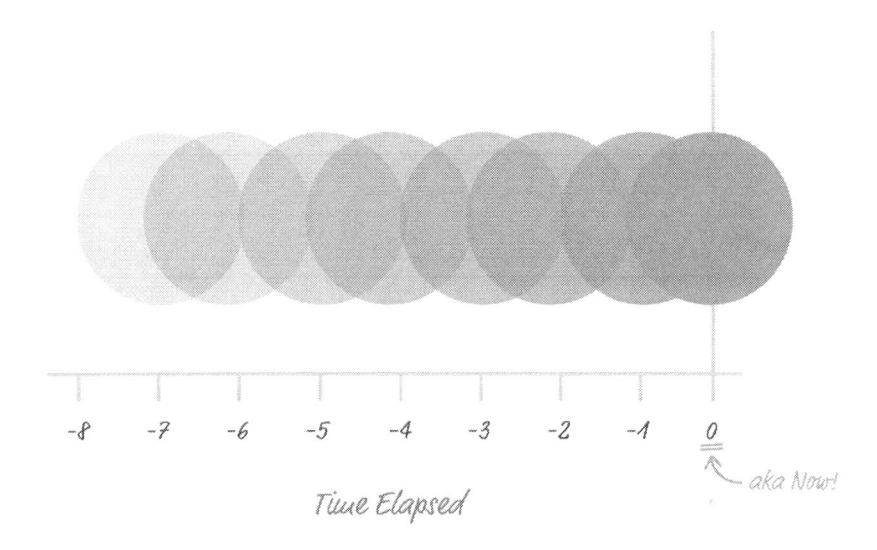

The way our code is arranged is to allow us to respect our `canvas`'s drawing order while still ensuring we draw our source object and motion trail properly. We draw our motion trail starting with the oldest item (start of the `positions` array) and gradually moving up in time until we get to the end of our `positions` array. This allows us to layer the items in our trail properly.

The grand finale is when our source object gets drawn independently from the riff-raff that is our motion trail. Because it is the last item to get drawn, it gets top placement on the `canvas` and is drawn over the most recent motion trail item. It is at this point, we store our source object's position for the next motion trail iteration. Like clockwork, everything on our `canvas` is cleared and things start back up from the beginning.

There is Plenty of Room for Improvement

Our motion trail implementation works, and it is the most literal translation of what we talked about towards the beginning. All of this doesn't mean that our solution can't be improved. For example, we have a lot of duplicated code between our code for drawing the source object and our code for drawing the motion trails themselves.

One optimization we can make is to move all of the drawing-related code into a drawCircle function that takes arguments for the position and ratio. Using that, our code looks a bit cleaner as shown in the following snippet:

```
function update() {

  context.clearRect(0, 0, canvas.width, canvas.height);


  for (var i = 0; i < positions.length; i++) {

    var ratio = (i + 1) / positions.length;

    drawCircle(positions[i].x, positions[i].y, ratio);

  }


  drawCircle(xPos, yPos, "source");


  storeLastPosition(xPos, yPos);


  // update position

  if (xPos > 600) {

    xPos = -100;
```

```
    }
    xPos += 3;

    requestAnimationFrame(update);
}
update();


function drawCircle(x, y, r) {

    if (r == "source") {

        r = 1;

    } else {

        r /= 4;

    }


    context.beginPath();

    context.arc(x, y, 50, 0, 2 * Math.PI, true);

    context.fillStyle = "rgba(204, 102, 153, " + r + ")";

    context.fill();

}
```

This code should contain no surprises...mostly. The only strange thing we are doing is passing in a value of **source** as opposed to a numerical ratio when our source object is being drawn. This ensures that our source object is always drawn with an opacity of 1. For all motion trail-related drawing, the usual ratio values are used.

> This is just one example of the sort of optimization you can make. You have a lot of runway when implementing motion trails, so go crazy!

Conclusion

Adding a motion trail is a really nice and fun way to make anything you are moving come to life. In this chapter, we applied a motion trail to a circle that was automatically moving from left-to-right. Nothing about what we've seen so far restricts you to such a narrow case, though. You can replicate this approach for all sorts of shapes and situations you may find yourself in. We'll look at a few such cases later!

Part III
Interactivity

Chapter 19: Working with the Mouse

When we talk about interactivity on the canvas, we can't go really far without talking about everyone's favorite pointing device...the mouse:

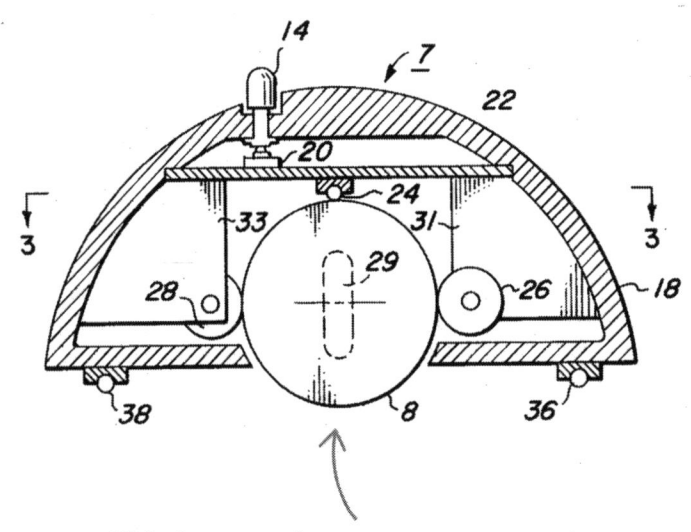

This is an early mouse prototype!

There are so many uses for the mouse on the canvas. You can use the mouse to draw, move things around, use it as part of a game, and more. I will warn you, though. This chapter is an introduction to the mechanics of working with the mouse. It's a bit boring, but you need to suffer through this in order to get to the much cooler things we'll look at directly after this. Think of this chapter as the bowl of vegetables you need to go through before getting dessert.

Onwards!

The Mouse and the Canvas

Often times, the canvas seems like its own mysterious beast. It is not until you run into areas like events that aren't specific to the canvas where you realize that all of this is just a small part of this larger JavaScript enclosure. For the next few sections, you are going to be learning general JavaScript 101 stuff about events, so feel free to skip or gloss over the material if you are intimately familiar with dealing with mouse events.

Meet the Events

Our canvas element works with all the mouse events that your browser exposes:

- click
- dblclick
- mouseover
- mouseout
- mouseenter
- mouseleave
- mousedown
- mouseup
- mousemove
- contextmenu
- mousewheel and DOMMouseScroll

What these events do should be somewhat easy to figure out given their name, so I won't bore you with details about that. Let's just move on to the next section where we learn how to listen to them.

Listening to and Handling Mouse Events

To listen for these events on your canvas element, use the addEventListener method and specify the event you are listening for and the event handler to call when that event is overheard:

```
var canvas = document.querySelector("#myCanvas");
var context = canvas.getContext("2d");


canvas.addEventListener("mousemove", doSomething, false);
```

That is pretty straightforward. In the highlighted line, we are listening for the **mousemove** event. When that event gets overheard, the `doSomething` function (aka the event handler) gets called. The last argument specifies whether we want our event to be captured in the bubbling phase or not. We won't focus on this argument. Instead, let's take another look at the event handler...

The event handler is responsible for reacting to an event once it is overheard. Basically, it's pretty important...and totally a big deal in the scene that is your code. Under the covers, an event handler is nothing more than a function with an argument for getting at what is known as the **event arguments**:

```
function doSomething(e) {
    // do something interesting



}
```

That detail is important. This event argument is the extremely awesome `MouseEvent` object that gives you access to a bunch of useful properties about the event that you just fired - properties that contains information such as the mouse's position, the button that was pressed, and more. We are going to devote the next few sections looking deeper into some of these useful properties.

The Global Mouse Position

The first `MouseEvent` properties we will look at are the `screenX` and `screenY` properties that return the distance your mouse cursor is from the top-left location of your primary monitor:

screenX / screenY diagram

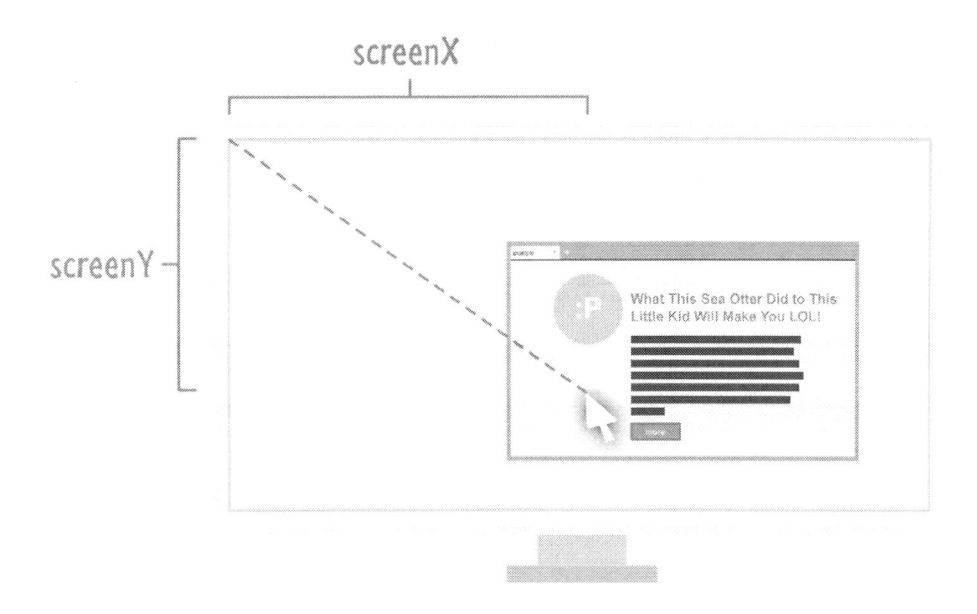

Here is a very simple example of the screenX and screenY properties at work:

```
canvas.addEventListener("mousemove", mouseMoving, false);

function mouseMoving(e) {
    console.log(e.screenX + " " + e.screenY);
}
```

It doesn't matter what other margin/padding/offset/layout craziness you may have going on in your page. The values returned are always going to be the distance between where your mouse is now and where the top-left corner of your primary monitor is.

The Mouse Position Inside the Browser

This is probably the part of the MouseEvent object that you will run into over and over again. The clientX and clientY properties return the x and y position of the mouse relative to your browser's (technically, the browser viewport's) top-left corner:

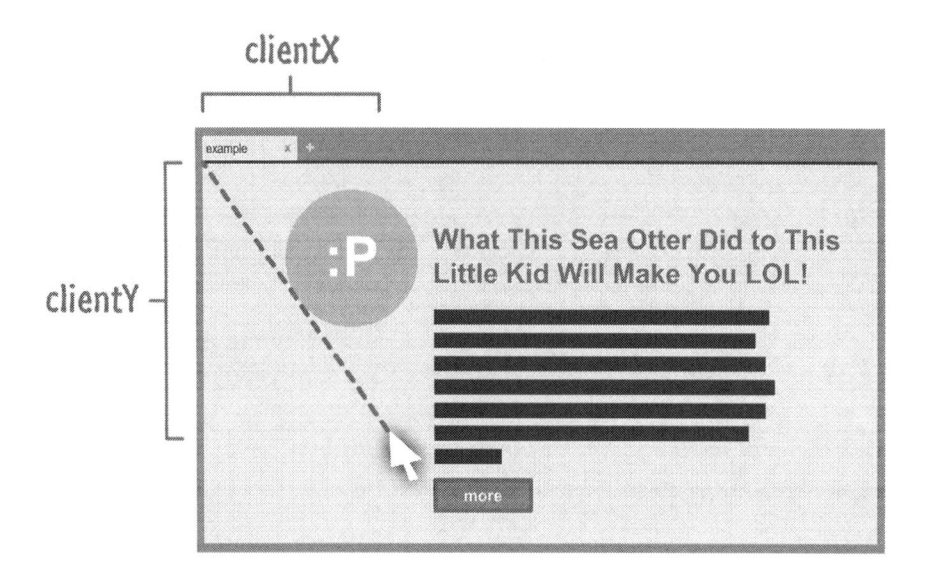

The code for this is nothing exciting:

```
var canvas = document.querySelector("#myCanvas");

canvas.addEventListener("mousemove", mouseMoving, false);


function mouseMoving(e) {
    console.log(e.clientX + " " + e.clientY);
}
```

We just call the `clientX` and `clientY` properties via the `MouseEvent` argument to see some sweet pixel values returned as a result. What these values don't advertise is that you often need to do a little extra bit of additional calculation to get the exact mouse position inside our `canvas`. That calculation isn't hard, and we will look at that in a few sections!

Detecting Which Button was Clicked

Your mice often have multiple buttons or ways to simulate multiple buttons. The most common button configuration involves a left button, a right button, and a middle button (often a click on your mouse wheel). To figure out which mouse button was pressed, you have the `button` property. This property returns a **0** if the left mouse button was pressed, a **1** if the middle button was pressed, and a **2** if the right mouse button was pressed:

The code for using the `button` property to check for which button was pressed looks exactly as you would expect:

```
canvas.addEventListener("mousedown", buttonPress, false);


function buttonPress(e) {

    if (e.button == 0) {

        console.log("Left mouse button pressed!");

    } else if (e.button == 1) {

        console.log("Middle mouse button pressed!");

    } else if (e.button == 2) {

        console.log("Right mouse button pressed!");

    } else {

        console.log("Things be crazy up in here!!!");

    }

}
```

In addition to the `button` property, you also have the `buttons` and `which` properties that sorta do similar things to help you figure out which button was pressed. I'm not going to talk too much about those two properties, but just know that they exist.

Getting the Exact Mouse Position Inside Your Canvas

Following up on a thread we left unexplored a few moments ago, the `clientX` and `clientY` properties don't give you the exact mouse position inside an element in many situations. Understanding the details of why is something that I cover in this article (http://bit.ly/kirupaMousePosition), but the gist of it is that the `clientX` and `clientY` properties don't account for your `canvas` element physically being pushed around by all of its ancestors. A margin or padding here and there can cause your positioning inside the `canvas` element to go out-of-sync. It's really quite sad. Why is this important? Who cares what the mouse position is inside the `canvas`?

Well, we care! So much of what you do with your mouse is have an element follow your mouse cursor around or move to the location of a mouse click. Knowing exactly where your mouse cursor is located turns out to be very important in those scenarios. Fortunately, getting the exact position is fairly straightforward. The solution is to pair up your `clientX` and `clientY` properties with the following code that takes into account all of the various position-related shenanigans that your `canvas` might be affected by:

```
// Helper function to get an element's exact position
function getPosition(el) {
    var xPos = 0;
    var yPos = 0;


    while (el) {
        if (el.tagName == "BODY") {
            // deal with browser quirks with body/window/document and page scroll
            var xScroll = el.scrollLeft || document.documentElement.scrollLeft;
            var yScroll = el.scrollTop || document.documentElement.scrollTop;

            xPos += (el.offsetLeft - xScroll + el.clientLeft);
```

```
      yPos += (el.offsetTop - yScroll + el.clientTop);
    } else {
      // for all other non-BODY elements
      xPos += (el.offsetLeft - el.scrollLeft + el.clientLeft);
      yPos += (el.offsetTop - el.scrollTop + el.clientTop);
    }

    el = el.offsetParent;
  }
  return {
    x: xPos,
    y: yPos
  };
}
```

Here is an example of this code in action inside our canvas element:

```
var canvas = document.querySelector("#myCanvas");
var context = canvas.getContext("2d");
var canvasPosition = getPosition(canvas);


canvas.addEventListener("mousemove", doSomething, false);


// take into account page scrolls and resizes
```

```
window.addEventListener("scroll", updatePosition, false);
window.addEventListener("resize", updatePosition, false);

function updatePosition() {
    canvasPosition = getPosition(canvas);
}

function doSomething(e) {
    // get the exact mouse X and Y coordinates
    var mouseX = e.clientX - canvasPosition.x;
    var mouseY = e.clientY - canvasPosition.y;

    // print it to the console
    console.log("The mouse position is: " + mouseX + ", " + mouseY);
}
```

The `canvasPosition` variable stores the object returned by the `getPosition` function, and the `mouseX` and `mouseY` variables store the exact position once you combine `canvasPosition`'s result with the `clientX` and `clientY` value:

```
var mouseX = e.clientX - canvasPosition.x;
var mouseY = e.clientY - canvasPosition.y;
```

For completeness, we even listen to the **window** **resize** and **scroll** events to update the value stored by `canvasPosition`:

```
// take into account page scrolls and resizes

window.addEventListener("scroll", updatePosition, false);

window.addEventListener("resize", updatePosition, false);


function updatePosition() {

  canvasPosition = getPosition(canvas);

}
```

We do this to ensure that our mouse position values remain accurate even if users scroll the page or resize the browser window. All of the code you see here might be going away in the future, though. There is a scheme underway to add an `offsetX` and `offsetY` property to the `MouseEvent` object that automatically takes care of all this.

Conclusion

In this chapter, we just covered the basics of working with the mouse. If there is anything you take out of this, the section on getting the correct mouse position is the one you should keep in mind. It isn't obvious that your `clientX` and `clientY` properties aren't entirely adequate for getting your mouse position, and the solution for that isn't very obvious either. Now that you know about this issue, though, you can safely avoid it without running into any sort of problems! You'll get plenty of practice with all of that in the several examples that you are about to see.

Chapter 20: Follow the Mouse Cursor

In the previous chapter, we looked at some boring things about working with the mouse in our code. In this chapter, we will start to apply some of the things we learned by creating a simple "mouse follow" example. It is an example where we have a small circle inside our canvas:

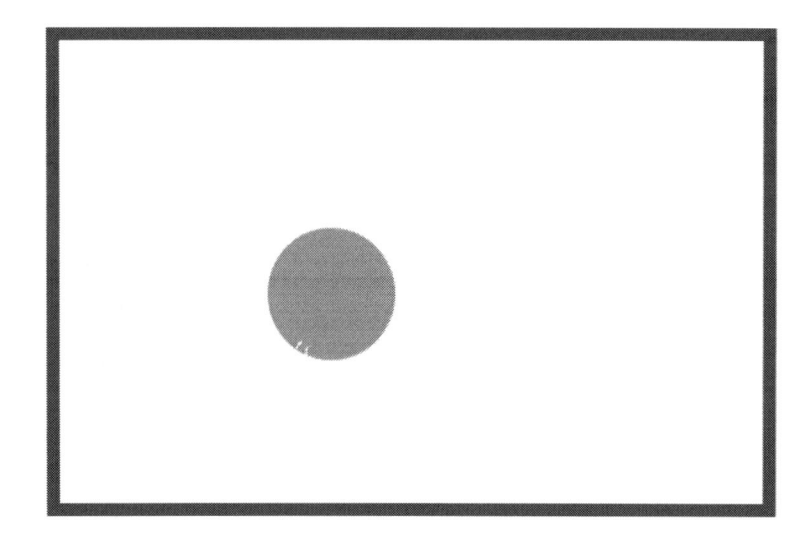

As we move our mouse around the `canvas`, the circle gets redrawn at the position our mouse cursor is in. In the following sections, you'll learn all about how to make something like this work...and then some!

Onwards!

The Basic Approach

Before we get to the code, let's talk using English how we are going to make the circle follow our mouse. First, we all know that we need to draw **something**, and that **something** will be a circle in our case:

Circle not drawn to scale.

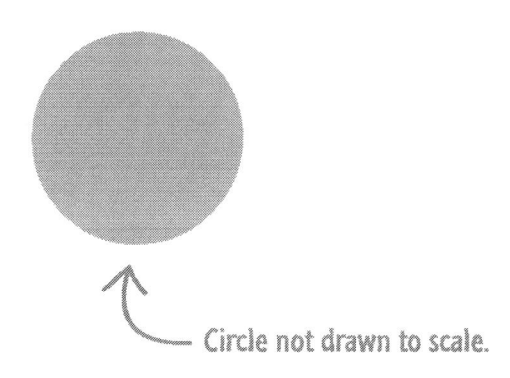

Second, our circle is not going to be loitering around a single location inside our `canvas`. Our circle's position will change based on where exactly our mouse cursor is at any given time. This means that we need to redraw our circle each time the mouse position changes:

You put these two things together, you have the example that you see. Now, as you may have imagined going into this section, this example isn't a particularly hard one to wrap your head around. That doesn't mean there is nothing exciting going on behind the scenes, though. When we look at the JavaScript in the next few sections, we'll touch upon some things that you may not have realized were relevant for this example.

Getting Started

You probably know the drill by now, but the first thing we need is an HTML page with a `canvas` element with an `id` value of **myCanvas** ready to run. If you don't already have a page ready, then put the following into a blank HTML page:

```html
<!DOCTYPE html>
<html>

<head>
  <title>Canvas Follow Mouse</title>
  <style>
    canvas {
      border: #333 10px solid;
    }

    body {
      padding: 50px;
    }
  </style>
</head>

<body>
  <canvas id="myCanvas" width="550px" height="350px"></canvas>

  <script>
    var canvas = document.querySelector("#myCanvas");
    var context = canvas.getContext("2d");

  </script>

</body>

</html>
```

If you preview this page in your browser, you'll notice that there really isn't much going on here. There is a `canvas` element, and this element has the `id` value of **myCanvas**. As a timesaver, I provide you with the two lines of code needed to access the `canvas` element and its rendering context.

Drawing the Circle

The first thing we are going to do is draw our circle. Inside your `script` tag, add the following code after where we have the line with the `context` variable:

```
function update() {
    context.beginPath();
    context.arc(100, 100, 50, 0, 2 * Math.PI, true);
    context.fillStyle = "#FF6A6A";
    context.fill();
}
update();
```

All we are doing here is defining a function called **update** that contains the code for drawing our circle. Note that we not only define the **update** function, we also invoke it as well right afterwards. This means that if you test your page in the browser, you will see something that looks as follows:

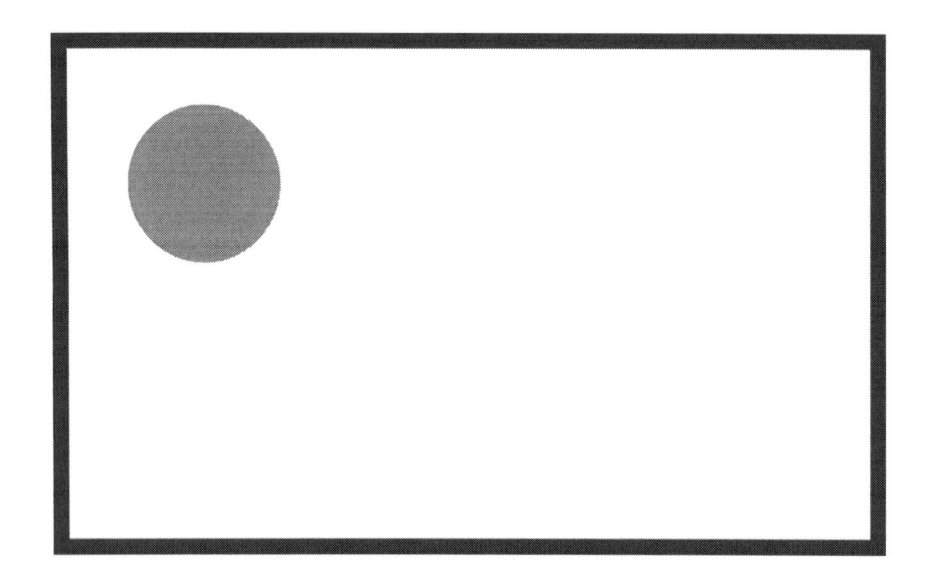

Our circle has a radius of 50 pixels and is positioned at the (100, 100) mark. For now, we are going to keep the position of the circle fixed. That won't last for long as you'll see shortly once we get the mouse position!

Getting the Mouse Position

The next step is where the magic happens. We are going to add the code that deals with the mouse. There are two parts to this code. The first part is listening for the mouse movement on the `canvas` element and storing that mouse position somewhere accessible. That is easy. The second part is ensuring our mouse position takes into account the position of our `canvas` element. That is less easy, but one we looked at in the previous chapter. We'll tackle both of these parts in the next two sections.

Listening for the Mouse Event

Let's look at the code for the first part...um...first. Go ahead and add the following code just above your `update` function:

```
var mouseX = 0;
```

If you preview this page in your browser, you'll notice that there really isn't much going on here. There is a canvas element, and this element has the id value of myCanvas. As a timesaver, I provide you with the two lines of code needed to access the canvas element and its rendering context.

Drawing the Circle

The first thing we are going to do is draw our circle. Inside your script tag, add the following code after where we have the line with the context variable:

```
function update() {
    context.beginPath();
    context.arc(100, 100, 50, 0, 2 * Math.PI, true);
    context.fillStyle = "#FF6A6A";
    context.fill();
}
update();
```

All we are doing here is defining a function called update that contains the code for drawing our circle. Note that we not only define the update function, we also invoke it as well right afterwards. This means that if you test your page in the browser, you will see something that looks as follows:

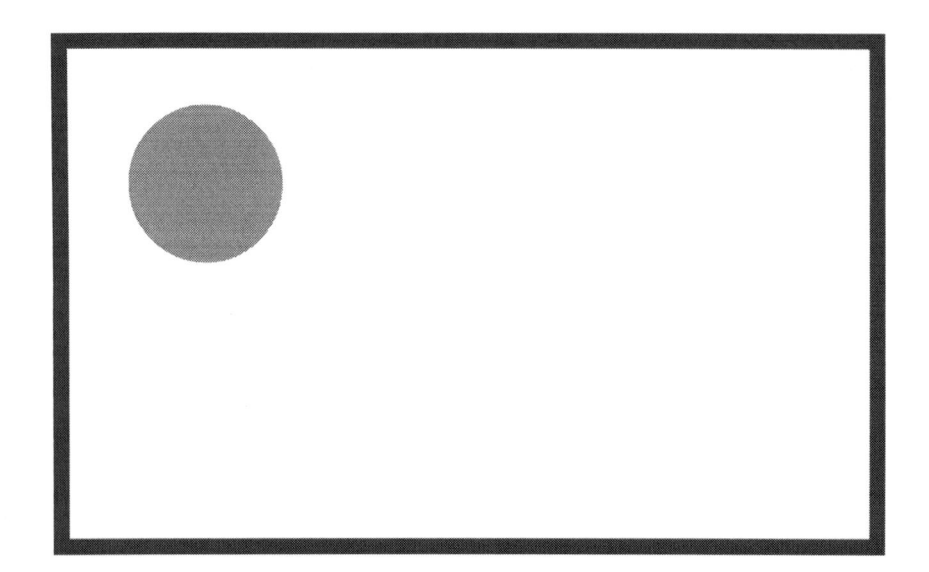

Our circle has a radius of 50 pixels and is positioned at the (100, 100) mark. For now, we are going to keep the position of the circle fixed. That won't last for long as you'll see shortly once we get the mouse position!

Getting the Mouse Position

The next step is where the magic happens. We are going to add the code that deals with the mouse. There are two parts to this code. The first part is listening for the mouse movement on the `canvas` element and storing that mouse position somewhere accessible. That is easy. The second part is ensuring our mouse position takes into account the position of our `canvas` element. That is less easy, but one we looked at in the previous chapter. We'll tackle both of these parts in the next two sections.

Listening for the Mouse Event

Let's look at the code for the first part...um...first. Go ahead and add the following code just above your `update` function:

```
var mouseX = 0;
```

```
var mouseY = 0;


canvas.addEventListener("mousemove", setMousePosition, false);


function setMousePosition(e) {

  mouseX = e.clientX;

  mouseY = e.clientY;

}
```

What this code does is pretty straightforward. We are listening for the **mousemove** event on our canvas element, and when that event is overheard, we call the setMousePosition event handler function thingaroo:

```
function setMousePosition(e) {

  mouseX = e.clientX;

  mouseY = e.clientY;

}
```

All the setMousePosition function does is assign the current horizontal and vertical mouse position to the mouseX and mouseY properties. It does that by relying on the clientX and clientY properties that the MouseEvent-based event argument object provides.

Getting the Exact Mouse Position

The mouse position stored by the mouseX and mouseY properties currently only store the position from the **top-left corner of our browser window**. They don't take into account where the canvas element is located on the page, so the mouse position values we have right now are going to be inaccurate. That is not cool.

To fix that, we have the `getPosition` function that we saw earlier:

```
function getPosition(el) {
  var xPos = 0;
  var yPos = 0;

  while (el) {
    if (el.tagName == "BODY") {
      // deal with browser quirks with body/window/document and page scroll
      var xScroll = el.scrollLeft || document.documentElement.scrollLeft;
      var yScroll = el.scrollTop || document.documentElement.scrollTop;

      xPos += (el.offsetLeft - xScroll + el.clientLeft);
      yPos += (el.offsetTop - yScroll + el.clientTop);
    } else {
      // for all other non-BODY elements
      xPos += (el.offsetLeft - el.scrollLeft + el.clientLeft);
      yPos += (el.offsetTop - el.scrollTop + el.clientTop);
    }

    el = el.offsetParent;
  }
  return {
```

```
        x: xPos,

        y: yPos

    };

}
```

Add this function towards the bottom of your code below the update function. You can put this function towards the top if you want, but I generally prefer helper functions like this to be towards the bottom of our code...and out of sight!

Anyway, the way you use this function is by passing in the element whose position you are interested in. This function then returns an object containing the x and y position of the element. We will use this function to figure out where our canvas element is on the page and then adjust our mouseX and mouseY values accordingly.

To use the getPosition function and fix the mouseX and mouseY values, make the following additions and modifications that I've highlighted:

```
var canvasPos = getPosition(canvas);

var mouseX = 0;

var mouseY = 0;


canvas.addEventListener("mousemove", setMousePosition, false);


function setMousePosition(e) {

    mouseX = e.clientX - canvasPos.x;

    mouseY = e.clientY - canvasPos.y;

}
```

The `canvasPos` variable now stores the position returned by our `getPosition` function. In the `setMousePosition` event handler, we use the returned x and y values from `canvasPos` to adjust the value stored by the `mouseX` and `mouseY` variables. Phew!

Moving the Circle

In the previous section, we got the mouse code all setup with the `mouseX` and `mouseY` variables storing our mouse's current position inside the `canvas`. All that remains is to hook these values up with our drawing code inside the `update` function to have our circle's position reflect the mouse position.

First, we are going to turn our boring update function into the target of a `requestAnimationFrame` callback. This will ensure this function gets sync'ed up with our browser's drawing rate (around 60 times a second). This is a very simple modification. Go ahead and add the following highlighted line towards the bottom of the `update` function:

```
function update() {
    context.beginPath();
    context.arc(100, 100, 50, 0, 2 * Math.PI, true);
    context.fillStyle = "#FF6A6A";
    context.fill();

    requestAnimationFrame(update);
}
update();
```

What we are going to do next is pretty epic. We need to update our circle drawing code to use the `mouseX` and `mouseY` values instead of using the fixed (100, 100) position that we specified initially. Make the following highlighted change to the `context.arc()` call:

```
function update() {

  context.beginPath();

  context.arc(mouseX, mouseY, 50, 0, 2 * Math.PI, true);

  context.fillStyle = "#FF6A6A";

  context.fill();


  requestAnimationFrame(update);
}
update();
```

Once you have made this change, save your HTML document and preview it in your browser. When you move your mouse around the canvas, notice what happens. Our friendly little circle will now follow your mouse cursor around, and you'll see something that looks a bit like this:

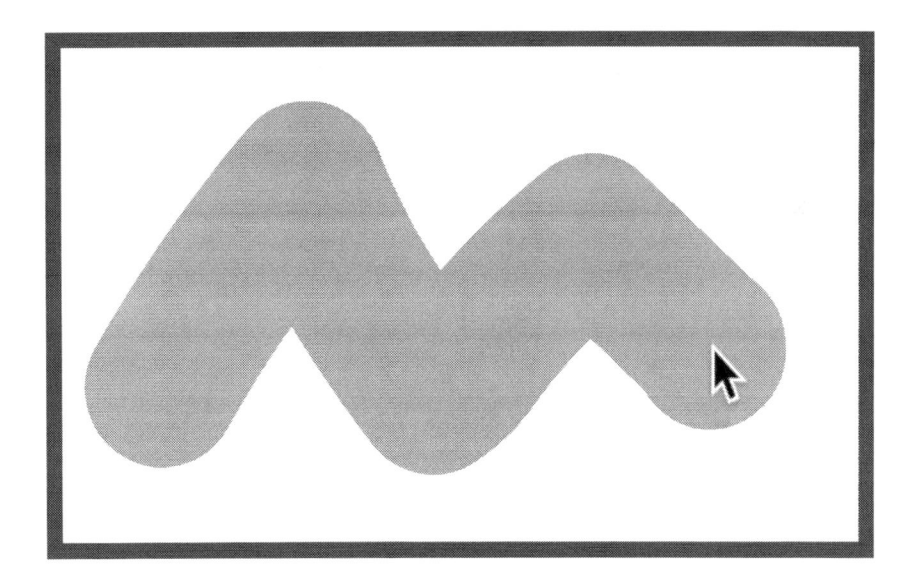

Your circle is following the mouse position (rock on!), but your circle's earlier positions aren't being cleared out (sigh!). While this creates a cool finger painting effect, that isn't quite what we were going for. The fix is to clear out everything in the `canvas` before drawing our circle at its new position, and that is much more simple than it sounds.

To make this fix, go ahead and add the following highlighted line of code towards the top of the `update` function:

```
function update() {

    context.clearRect(0, 0, canvas.width, canvas.height);


    context.beginPath();

    context.arc(mouseX, mouseY, 50, 0, 2 * Math.PI, true);

    context.fillStyle = "#FF6A6A";

    context.fill();


    requestAnimationFrame(update);
}
```

The line we added contains a call to the `clearRect` method, and this method is responsible for clearing all pixels from a `canvas` region. The way we use it is by passing in the dimensions of the region we want to clear, and what we do is pass in the full dimensions of our `canvas` to get everything cleared out:

```
context.clearRect(0, 0, canvas.width, canvas.height);
```

This ensures that our circle is being drawn onto a blank surface with no traces of earlier draw operations remaining. If you preview your page in your browser at this point, our example should work perfectly.

Why use requestAnimationFrame?

You may have noticed that all of our drawing-related code is inside the **update** function that is looped by the `requestAnimationFrame` function. There is no animation going on here. We are just moving our mouse cursor around, and we want to update our circle's position only when the mouse cursor positions. Given all that, why wasn't all of our drawing code inside the **mousemove** event handler instead? That would look something like the following:

```
canvas.addEventListener("mousemove", setMousePosition, false);

function setMousePosition(e) {
  mouseX = e.clientX - canvasPos.x;
  mouseY = e.clientY - canvasPos.y;

  context.clearRect(0, 0, canvas.width, canvas.height);

  context.beginPath();
  context.arc(mouseX, mouseY, 50, 0, 2 * Math.PI, true);
  context.fillStyle = "#FF6A6A";
  context.fill();
}
```

If you were to make this change (and get rid of the **update** function completely), our example will still work. Our example may even work just as well as our `requestAnimationFrame` approach.

The reason has to do with us helping our browser not do unnecessary work and doing the "right" thing since our **end goal** is to draw something to the screen. When it comes to drawing things onto the screen, we want to be in-sync with when the browser is ready to paint the pixels. The **mousemove** event has no idea when the browser is ready to draw to the screen, so our event handler will unnecessarily try to force your browser to paint the screen. The only way to avoid that is to do what we did and use the `requestAnimationFrame` function.

We separated the code for updating our mouse position from the code for actually drawing to the screen. This ensures that we only draw our new circle when the browser is ready. When the circle is about to be drawn, we ensure that the mouse position at that time is as accurate as possible. Win. Win. Win. (Yes, it's a rare triple win situation!)

Conclusion

This all started out as a very simple effect. We just have a circle that follows the mouse around. How complicated could that be? Famous last words in the world of JavaScript!

Chapter 20: Mouse Follow with Ease

In the previous chapter, we had a circle follow the mouse cursor around and learned all about how to make that example work. In this page, we are going to continue our look at having something follow the mouse cursor, but there is going to be a twist. The twist is that we are going to throw an ease into the mix. Instead of having our shape follow the mouse cursor very closely, we are going to have our shape slowly animate to where our mouse cursor is. To be more precise, our shape is going to decelerate towards our mouse cursor without any hurry.

Oh, and our shape this time around is going to be a square:

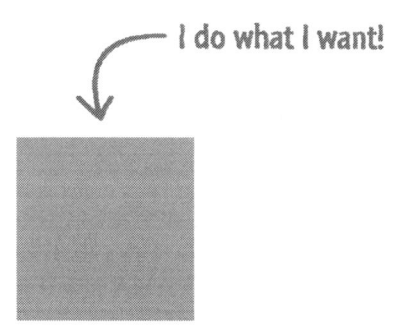

In the next few sections, we'll take a look at how this example works. This isn't going to be a full on chapter where you build this effect from scratch. A bulk of this code is almost identical to the Follow Mouse Cursor chapter from earlier, so I don't want to bore you with a rehash of what you've already seen. Instead, I am going to show you the full code, and we'll just look at the highlights that are worth remembering for the future.

Onwards!

Here's the Code

Using our usual HTML document with a `canvas` element whose `id` value is **myCanvas**, the full code inside the `script` tag for making this example work looks as follows:

```
var canvas = document.querySelector("#myCanvas");

var context = canvas.getContext("2d");


var canvasPos = getPosition(canvas);

var mouseX = 0;

var mouseY = 0;

var sqSize = 100;

var xPos = 0;

var yPos = 0;

var dX = 0;

var dY = 0;


canvas.addEventListener("mousemove", setMousePosition, false);


function setMousePosition(e) {

  mouseX = e.clientX - canvasPos.x;

  mouseY = e.clientY - canvasPos.y;

}


function animate() {

  dX = mouseX - xPos;

  dY = mouseY - yPos;


  xPos += (dX / 10);
```

```
  yPos += (dY / 10);


  context.clearRect(0, 0, canvas.width, canvas.height);


  context.fillStyle = "#00CCFF";
  context.fillRect(xPos - sqSize / 2,
                   yPos - sqSize / 2,
                   sqSize,
                   sqSize);


  requestAnimationFrame(animate);
}
animate();


// deal with the page getting resized or scrolled
window.addEventListener("scroll", updatePosition, false);
window.addEventListener("resize", updatePosition, false);


function updatePosition() {
  canvasPos = getPosition(canvas);
}


// Helper function to get an element's exact position
function getPosition(el) {
  var xPos = 0;
```

```
  var yPos = 0;


  while (el) {
    if (el.tagName == "BODY") {
      // deal with browser quirks with body/window/document and page scroll
      var xScroll = el.scrollLeft || document.documentElement.scrollLeft;
      var yScroll = el.scrollTop || document.documentElement.scrollTop;


      xPos += (el.offsetLeft - xScroll + el.clientLeft);
      yPos += (el.offsetTop - yScroll + el.clientTop);
    } else {
      // for all other non-BODY elements
      xPos += (el.offsetLeft - el.scrollLeft + el.clientLeft);
      yPos += (el.offsetTop - el.scrollTop + el.clientTop);
    }


    el = el.offsetParent;
  }
  return {
    x: xPos,
    y: yPos
  };
}
```

In the following sections, we are going to be taking parts of this code and looking at in greater detail. Before we do that, to make the most of our time together, you should take a few minutes and walk through the code by yourself and try to see how what you see maps to the mouse follow example you saw a few moments earlier. Once you have given the code a good glance through, we'll look at the interesting parts together...starting...now!

How the Easing (Deceleration) Works

The first thing we are going to look at is how the square decelerates its way towards the mouse cursor. The way we accomplish this is by forcing our square to take incremental steps towards where the mouse cursor is. That probably makes no sense, so let's walk through what I mean by that.

At the very beginning, you have a situation that looks as follows:

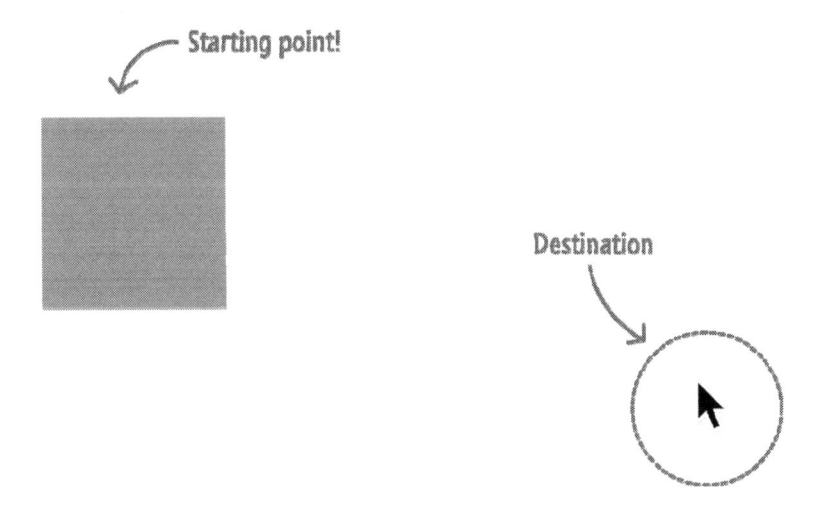

Your mouse cursor is somewhere. Your square is somewhere else. The goal is for our square to get to where the mouse cursor is:

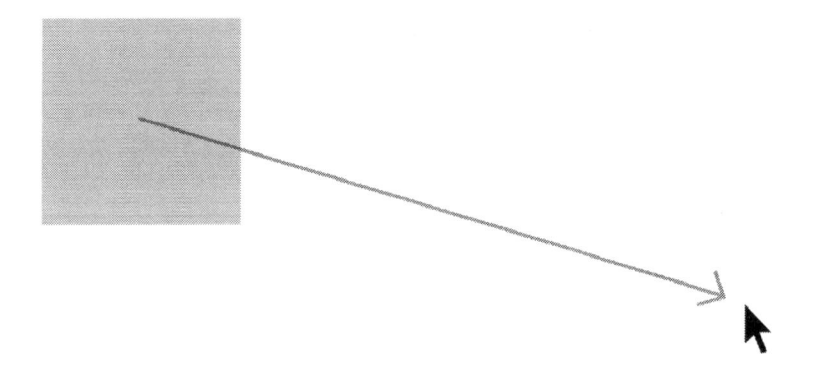

Looking at where the square needs to go in the form a straight line makes sense for us, but we have to break that down further to have our code understand this as well. The way to do this is to figure out how far the square needs to travel both horizontally as well as vertically. Because we know the location of the mouse cursor and the location of the square, this is an easy subtraction. To designate the remaining distance, I use the common dX and dY naming scheme as you can see in the following visualization:

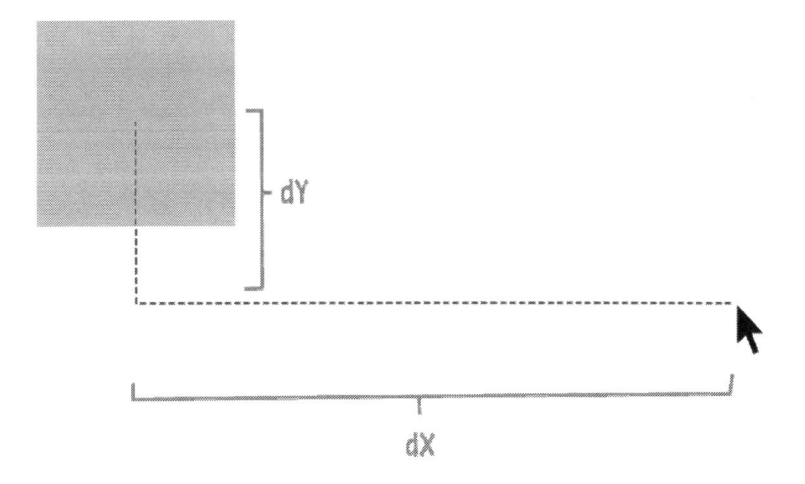

Once we've figured out how far the square needs to travel horizontally and vertically, the rest of the work becomes a bit more straightforward. All that remains is to animate the square to the destination.

As animations go, what we are trying to do here is well defined. Each time our code runs to update the square's position, we need to move a bit *closer* to the destination. Visually, *closer* means that the square and the mouse cursor are at the same place. From a mathematical point of view, *closer* means that the values for **dX** and **dY** keep getting smaller and smaller.

Now, the code for turning all of the text and diagrams we just saw looks as follows:

```
canvas.addEventListener("mousemove", setMousePosition, false);

function setMousePosition(e) {
  mouseX = e.clientX - canvasPos.x;
  mouseY = e.clientY - canvasPos.y;
}

function animate() {
  dX = mouseX - xPos;
  dY = mouseY - yPos;

  xPos += (dX / 10);
  yPos += (dY / 10);

  .
  .
  // removed drawing code for now
  .
  .

  requestAnimationFrame(animate);
}
animate();
```

The mouse event handling stuff is pretty simple, so let's skip all of that and jump directly to the `animate` function where we see our dX and dY variables. These variables, as we saw from earlier, store the difference between our square's current position and where the mouse cursor is:

```
dX = mouseX - xPos;
dY = mouseY - yPos;
```

Storing the difference is one part of what we need to do. The other part is moving our circle closer to the destination. That's where the xPos and yPos variables come in. These variables are ultimately what you will use to specify the location we draw our square, but right now their goal is to take the dX and dY values and store a position that is closer horizontally and vertically to where the mouse cursor is.

We accomplish that by incrementing their values by dX and dY and using a step value to slow things down a bit:

```
xPos += (dX / 10);
yPos += (dY / 10);
```

These two lines of code are responsible for the deceleration that you see, and the number that determines the rate of deceleration is the **10**. This number determines the number of "steps" your code will take your square to reach the destination:

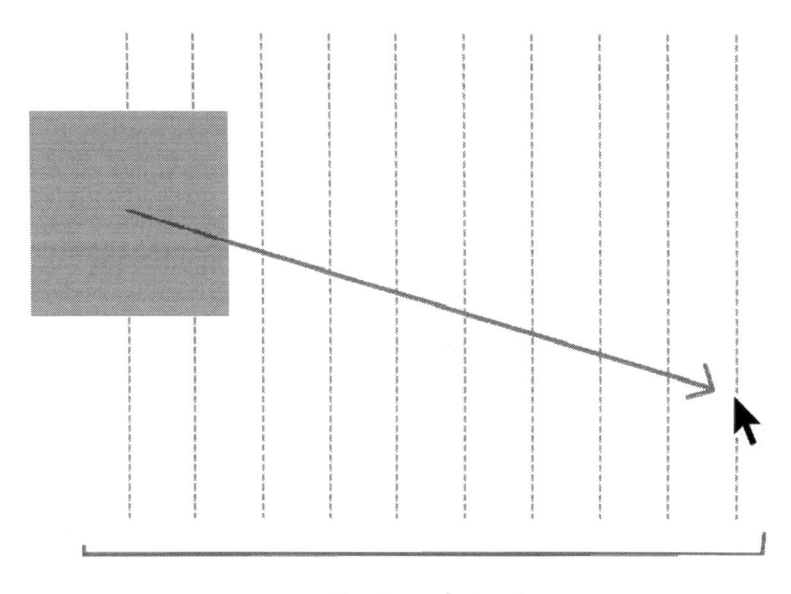

Number of steps!

The more steps you have, the longer it will take your square to reach the mouse cursor position. The fewer steps you have, the less time it will take your square to reach the mouse cursor position. If you are insanely curious and specify a step value of 1, our square will perfectly follow our mouse cursor with no delay at all. It will mimic our earlier mouse follow example perfectly.

Ok. Now that we have an idea of how the square's position is calculated, let's look at where all of these calculations happen. Because we want to smoothly visualize our square's position changing, all of this code lives inside the `animate` function that is also the target of a `requestAnimationFrame` callback:

```
function animate() {
    dX = mouseX - xPos;
    dY = mouseY - yPos;


    xPos += (dX / 10);
    yPos += (dY / 10);
```

```
    .

    .

    .

    requestAnimationFrame(animate);
}
animate();
```

This means that each time the code we looked at runs (~60 times a second), the values for dX, dY, xPos, and yPos are rapidly changing to reflect our square's new position. These rapidly changing values are visualized by us drawing the square using some of these values. Speaking of drawing...

Drawing the Square

Inside the `animate` function, we don't just have the code for updating the various position variables. We also have the code for drawing our square:

```
context.clearRect(0, 0, canvas.width, canvas.height);


context.fillStyle = "#99CC00";
context.fillRect(xPos - sqSize / 2,
                 yPos - sqSize / 2,
                 sqSize,
                 sqSize);
```

The square is drawn using the `fillRect` method that you've seen in the Drawing Rectangles (and Squares) chapter.

There are several closely related things to call out here. First, to reiterate what you saw earlier, notice that the xPos and yPos variables are what we use to specify the x and y position we want to draw our square. Second, notice that the xPos and yPos variables are adjusted by subtracting half of the square's size (sqSize). Why are we doing this?

Let me answer that indirectly by showing you the following diagram:

When our square reaches its destination, which of the two variations would you like? There is a good chance you'd pick the second one where the mouse cursor is centered nicely inside the square itself.

We need to write some code to ensure we get the second variation, and that code simply involves shifting our square's position by 50% of its width and height:

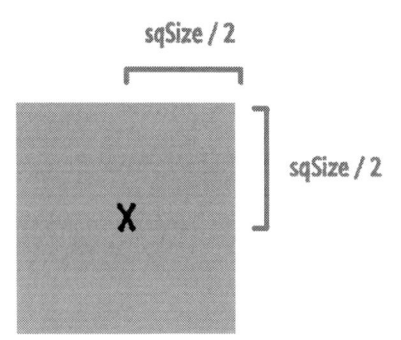

Remember, you should use this offset technique only when necessary. Some shapes, like the circle, start from the center and don't require you to do extra work to calculate the center position. This is yet another reason why circles are a superior breed of shape when compared to the rectangular square :P

Dealing with Window Scrolls and Resizes

The last thing to look at is some code that I provided for ensuring everything is positioned properly even if the page containing the canvas element is scrolled or resized:

```
window.addEventListener("scroll", updatePosition, false);

window.addEventListener("resize", updatePosition, false);


function updatePosition() {

    canvasPos = getPosition(canvas);

}
```

As I've lamented many times so far, getting the exact position of the mouse is tricky. That's why we offload all of that trickiness and use the handy getPosition function. Now, all that work doesn't matter if the user repositions the canvas element by scrolling the page or resizing the browser window. Fortunately, dealing with this is pretty easy thanks to the **scroll** and **resize** events that you can listen for and update the position of canvasPos when those events are overheard. All of the code that relies on the new position will adapt and work beautifully!

Conclusion

This example wasn't anything groundbreaking since the bulk of what we did was covered in the previous Follow Mouse Cursor chapter. Instead, this deconstruction focused on some of the subtle details that you may run into when dealing with the mouse - getting the center point of a shape, dealing with page scrolls/resizes, truly taking advantage of our requestAnimation frame function by throwing easing into the mix, and other shenanigans.

Chapter 21: Working With the Keyboard

We spend a lot of time in various applications tapping away at our keyboards. In case you are wondering what a keyboard looks like, below is a sweet one [2]from I think about a hundred years ago:

This is a keyboard!

Anyway, our computers (more specifically, the applications that run on them) just know how to deal with our board of plastic depressible keys. You never really think about it. Sometimes, depending on what you are doing, you will have to think about them. In fact, you'll have to deal with them and make them work properly.

By the end of this chapter, you will learn all about how to listen to the keyboard events, what each of those events do, and see a handful of examples that highlight some handy tricks that may come in...um...handy.

Onwards!

---

[2] http://commons.wikimedia.org/wiki/File:Atari_XEGS_keyboard.jpg

Meet the Keyboard Events

To work with keyboards in a HTML document, there are three events that you will need to familiarize yourself with. Those events are:

- keydown
- keypress
- keyup

Given what these events are called, you probably already have a vague idea of what each event does. The **keydown** event is fired when you press down on a key on your keyboard. The **keyup** event is fired when you release a key that you just pressed. Both of these events work on any key that you interact with.

The keypress event is a special bird. At first glance, it seems like this event is fired when you press down on any key. Despite what the name claims, the keypress event is fired only when you press down on a key that displays a character (letter, number, etc.). What this means is somewhat confusing, but it makes sense in its own twisted way.

If you press and release a character key such as the letter y, you will see the **keydown, keypress,** and **keyup** events fired in order. The keydown and keyup events fire because the y key is simply a key to them. The **keypress** event is fired because the y key is a character key. If you press and release a key that doesn't display anything on the screen (such as the spacebar, arrow key, function keys, etc.), all you will see are the **keydown** and **keyup** events fired.

This difference is subtle but very important when you want to ensure your key presses are actually overheard by your application.

Using These Events

The way you listen to the **keydown, keypress**, and **keyup** events is similar to any other event you may want to listen and react to. You call `addEventListener` on the element that will be dealing with these events, specify the event you want to listen for, specify the event handling function that gets called when the event is overheard, and a true/false value indicating whether you want this event to bubble.

Here is an example of me listening to our three keyboard events on `window`:

```
window.addEventListener("keydown", dealWithKeyboard, false);
window.addEventListener("keypress", dealWithKeyboard, false);
window.addEventListener("keyup", dealWithKeyboard, false);


function dealWithKeyboard(e) {
    // gets called when any of the keyboard events are overheard
}
```

If any of these events are overheard, the `dealWithKeyboard` event handler gets called. In fact, this event handler will get called three times if you happen to press down on a character key. This is all pretty straightforward, so let's kick everything up a few notches and go beyond the basics in the next few sections.

The Keyboard Event Properties

When an event handler that reacts to a keyboard event is called, a `KeyboardEvent` argument is passed in. Let's revisit our `dealWithKeyboard` event handler that you saw earlier. In that event handler, the keyboard event is represented by the `e` argument that is passed in:

```
function dealWithKeyboard(e) {
    // gets called when any of the keyboard events are overheard
}
```

This argument contains a handful of properties:

- keyCode
  Every key you press on your keyboard has a number associated with it. This read-only property returns that number.

- charCode
  This property only exists on event arguments returned by the keypress event, and it contains the ASCII code for whatever character key you pressed.

- ctrlKey, altKey, shiftKey
  These three properties return a true if the Ctrl key, Alt key, or Shift key are pressed.

- metaKey
  The metaKey property is similar to the ctrlKey, altKey, and shiftKey properties in that it returns a **true** if the Meta key is pressed. The Meta key is the Windows key on Windows keyboards and the Command key on Apple keyboards.

The KeyboardEvent contains a few other properties, but the ones you see above are the most interesting ones. With these properties, you can check for which key was pressed and react accordingly. In the next couple of sections, you'll see some examples of this.

Some Examples

Now that you've seen the horribly boring basics of how to work with Keyboard events, let's look at some examples that clarify (or potentially confuse!) everything you've seen so far.

Checking that a Particular Key Was Pressed

The following example shows how to use the **keyCode** property to check if a particular key was pressed:

```
window.addEventListener("keydown", checkKeyPressed, false);
```

```
function checkKeyPressed(e) {
    if (e.keyCode == "65") {
        alert("The 'a' key is pressed.");
    }
}
```

The particular key we check is the **a** key. Internally, this key is mapped to the **keyCode** value of 65. You can find a handy list of all key and character codes when you scroll down the following link: bit.ly/kirupaKeyCodes Please do not memorize every single code from that table. There are far more interesting things to memorize instead.

Some things to note. The **charCode** and **keyCode** values for a particular key are not the same. Also, the **charCode** is only returned if the event that triggered your event handler was **keypress**. In our example, the **keydown** event would not contain anything useful for the **charCode** property.

If you wanted to check the **charCode** and use the **keypress** event, here is what the above example would look like:

```
window.addEventListener("keypress", checkKeyPressed, false);

function checkKeyPressed(e) {
    if (e.charCode == "97") {
        alert("The 'a' key is pressed.");
    }
}
```

The charCode for the a key is 97. Again, refer to the table of key and character codes I listed earlier for such details.

Doing Something When the Arrow Keys are Pressed

You see this most often in games where pressing the arrow keys does something interesting. The following snippet of code shows how that is done:

```
window.addEventListener("keydown", moveSomething, false);

function moveSomething(e) {
    switch(e.keyCode) {
        case 37:
            // left key pressed
            break;
        case 38:
            // up key pressed
            break;
        case 39:
            // right key pressed
            break;
        case 40:
            // down key pressed
            break;
    }
}
```

TheAgain, this should be pretty straightforward as well. The only potentially weird thing is the `switch` statement, for you don't see it very often compared to your usual `if` and `else` statements.

Detecting Multiple Key Presses

Now, this is going to be epic! An interesting case revolves around detecting when you need to react to multiple key presses. Below is an example of how to do that:

```
window.addEventListener("keydown", moveSomething, false);


window.addEventListener("keydown", keysPressed, false);
window.addEventListener("keyup", keysReleased, false);


var keys = [];


function keysPressed(e) {
    // store an entry for every key pressed
    keys[e.keyCode] = true;


    // Ctrl + Shift + 5
    if (keys[17] && keys[16] && keys[53]) {
        // do something
    }


    // Ctrl + f
    if (keys[17] && keys[70]) {
        // do something
```

```
            // prevent default browser behavior
            e.preventDefault();
    }
}


function keysReleased(e) {
    // mark keys that were released
    keys[e.keyCode] = false;
}
```

Going into great detail about this will require another chapter by itself, but let's just look at how this works.

First, we have a `keys` array that stores every single key that you press:

```
var keys = [];
```

As keys get pressed, the `keysPressed` event handler gets called:

```
function keysPressed(e) {
    // store an entry for every key pressed
    keys[e.keyCode] = true;
}
```

Notice how these two event handlers work with each other. As keys get pressed, an entry gets created for them in the keys array with a value of **true**. When keys get released, those same keys are marked with a value of **false**. The existence of the keys you press in the array is superficial. It is the values they store that is actually important.

As long as nothing interrupts your event handlers from getting called properly such as an alert window, you will get a one-to-one mapping between keys pressed and keys released as viewed through the lens of the keys array. With all of this said, the checks for seeing which combination of keys have been pressed is handled in the `keysPressed` event handler. The following highlighted lines show how this works:

```
function keysPressed(e) {
    // store an entry for every key pressed
    keys[e.keyCode] = true;

    // Ctrl + Shift + 5
    if (keys[17] && keys[16] && keys[53]) {
        // do something
    }

    // Ctrl + f
    if (keys[17] && keys[70]) {
        // do something

        // prevent default browser behavior
        e.preventDefault();
    }
}
```

There are two things you need to keep in mind. The order of your checks matter. Ensure the checks are arranged in decreasing order of the number of keys that are pressed. Second, some key combinations result in your browser doing something. To avoid your browser from doing its own thing, use the `preventDefault` method like I show when checking to see if Ctrl + F is being used:

```
function keysPressed(e) {
    // store an entry for every key pressed
    keys[e.keyCode] = true;

    // Ctrl + Shift + 5
    if (keys[17] && keys[16] && keys[53]) {
        // do something
    }

    // Ctrl + f
    if (keys[17] && keys[70]) {
        // do something

        // prevent default browser behavior
        e.preventDefault();
    }
}
```

The preventDefault method prevents your browser from reacting to it by showing the Find dialog for Ctrl + f. You put all of this together, and you have a basic blueprint for how to check for multiple key presses easily.

Conclusion

The keyboard is pretty important when it comes to a boatload of `canvas` scenarios. In the DOM world, your browser, the various text-related controls/elements, and everything in-between just handle it as you would expect by default. In the `canvas` world, things are obviously more difficult. Outside of getting basic event handling support, everything else you have to figure out on your own. That's OK. You won't be entirely on your own. We'll look at some common situations together in the next few chapters.

Chapter 22: Using the Arrow Keys to Move Things Around

On the `canvas`, one of the most common things you'll do with the keyboard is use the arrow keys to move something around. In this chapter, you will learn all about how to listen for key presses and move something around the screen as a reaction to whichever key was pressed. Of course, since nothing is ever as straightforward as it seems, we'll touch upon a bunch of other relevant topics along the way.

Onwards!

The Basic Approach

By now, you've probably seen how to work with the keyboard and the approach we use for having something we draw follow the mouse cursor around. The way we move things using the keyboard combines a little bit of what you've seen in those two chapters. If you haven't already seen what is in those two chapters, don't worry. You aren't missing that much, and we'll review the interesting parts again over here :P

Starting at the very top, we have something we've drawn on our `canvas`:

That *something* for our example is a triangle. This triangle is made up of three points that are represented by a horizontal and vertical number:

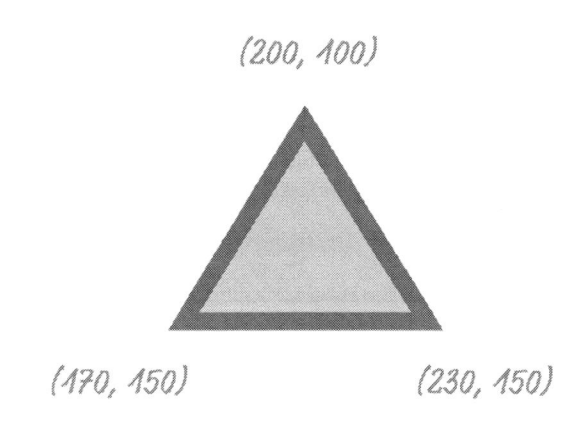

(200, 100)

(170, 150)   *(230, 150)*

These numbers are the only things that ensure our triangle looks they way it does. More importantly, for what we are trying to do, these numbers are the only things that help specify where our triangle is actually positioned.

At this point, our task should be getting a bit clearer. Because we can adjust where the triangle appears by just fiddling around with a couple of numbers, our job is to figure out how to have each arrow key press be responsible for that fiddling. What we are going to do in the next couple of sections is put all of these English words together into some totally rad JavaScript that works...more or less!

Displaying Our Triangle

Let's start easy by first drawing our triangle. The way we are going to do that is by defining a function called **drawTriangle** that draws a triangle at a fixed position in our **canvas**.

Using our usual example where we have a **canvas** element defined with an **id** value of **myCanvas**, ensure the contents of your **script** tag look as follows:

```
var canvas = document.querySelector("#myCanvas");
var context = canvas.getContext("2d");


function drawTriangle() {
  // the triangle
  context.beginPath();
  context.moveTo(200, 100);
  context.lineTo(170, 150);
  context.lineTo(230, 150);
  context.closePath();


  // the outline
  context.lineWidth = 10;
  context.strokeStyle = "rgba(102, 102, 102, 1)";
  context.stroke();


  // the fill color
  context.fillStyle = "rgba(255, 204, 0, 1)";
  context.fill();
```

```
    }
    drawTriangle();
```

Once you have added this code to your document, go ahead and preview your document in your browser. If everything worked out properly, you'll see a yellow triangle displayed. There is nothing exciting going on with this code that you haven't seen before, but there is one thing I want to call out. Notice that our triangle is defined by the following X and Y values:

```
context.moveTo(200, 100);
context.lineTo(170, 150);
context.lineTo(230, 150);
```

It is these values that we'll eventually end up adjusting to accommodate our arrow key presses.

Dealing With the Keyboard

With our triangle drawn, our next job is to deal with the keyboard. This involves the following steps:

1. Listening for the events your keyboard fires
2. Inside the event handler, accessing the `KeyboardEvent`'s `keyCode` property.
3. Handling the cases when the left, right, up, and down arrow keys are pressed.

There are several ways of doing this, but we are going to use a familiar (but less-than-ideal approach). Go ahead and add the following lines of code just above where you defined your `drawTriangle` function:

```
window.addEventListener("keydown", moveSomething, false);

function moveSomething(e) {
```

```
    switch(e.keyCode) {
        case 37:
            // left key pressed
            break;
        case 38:
            // up key pressed
            break;
        case 39:
            // right key pressed
            break;
        case 40:
            // down key pressed
            break;
    }
}
```

With the code we have just added, we first listen for a key press by listening for the **keydown** event. When that event gets overheard, we call the `moveSomething` event handler that deals with each arrow key press. It does this dealing by matching the `keyCode` property with the appropriate key value each arrow key is known by.

Adjusting the Position

It is time to tie together the triangle we've drawn with the code we just added for dealing with the arrow keys. What we are going to do is define two counter variables called `deltaX` and `deltaY`. What these variables will do is keep a count of how far to move our triangle as a result of arrow key presses. This may sound a bit confusing right now, but hang on tight!

First, let's go ahead and define our `deltaX` and `deltaY` variables and put them to use inside our `moveSomething` function. Add the following highlighted lines to your code:

```
var deltaX = 0;

var deltaY = 0;


function moveSomething(e) {

    switch(e.keyCode) {

        case 37:

            deltaX -= 2;

            break;

        case 38:

            deltaY -= 2;

            break;

        case 39:

            deltaX += 2;

            break;

        case 40:

            deltaY += 2;

            break;

    }

}
```

Depending on which arrow key was pressed, either the `deltaX` or `deltaY` variable will be increased or decreased. These variables changing in isolation has no effect on our triangles. We need to modify our `drawTriangle` function to actually use the `deltaX` and `deltaY` variables. Guess what we are going to do next?

Go ahead and make the following highlighted changes to the `drawTriangle` function:

```
function drawTriangle() {

    context.clearRect(0, 0, canvas.width, canvas.height);

    // the triangle

    context.beginPath();

    context.moveTo(200 + deltaX, 100 + deltaY);

    context.lineTo(170 + deltaX, 150 + deltaY);

    context.lineTo(230 + deltaX, 150 + deltaY);

    context.closePath();


    // the outline

    context.lineWidth = 10;

    context.strokeStyle = "rgba(102, 102, 102, 1)";

    context.stroke();


    // the fill color

    context.fillStyle = "rgba(255, 204, 0, 1)";

    context.fill();

}
```

The code changes should be pretty straightforward to make sense of. The call to `clearRect` ensures we clear our canvas before attempting to re-draw our triangle. The additions to the `context.moveTo` and `context.lineTo` methods take the `deltaX` and `deltaY` values into account. This ensures our triangle is always drawn with an offset that is determined by the number of times you pressed each arrow key. Putting that last sentence into human terms, this means you can move your triangle around using the keyboard.

At this point, if you preview your page now, our example still won't work. The reason is because there is one more thing you need to do. We need to call drawTriangle each time a key is pressed to actually draw our triangle in the new position. To make this happen, go back to the moveSomething function and add a call to drawTriangle towards the bottom:

```
function moveSomething(e) {
    switch(e.keyCode) {
        case 37:
            deltaX -= 2;
            break;
        case 38:
            deltaY -= 2;
            break;
        case 39:
            deltaX += 2;
            break;
        case 40:
            deltaY += 2;
            break;
    }

    drawTriangle();
}
```

If you preview your page in your browser this time around, give your canvas element focus by clicking on it, and then use your arrow keys. If everything worked out properly, you'll see our triangle moving around the screen!

Preventing Default Keyboard Behavior

When relying on the keyboard, the thing you need to keep in mind is that everything from your browser to your operating system is listening to the keyboard as well. Strange and unexpected things happen when your keyboard is used. In our case, the arrow keys are used to scroll your page up and down (and occasionally left and right). Even if users have their focus on the `canvas`, tapping the arrow keys will cause your entire page to scroll if your content gets large enough to display scrollbars. You don't want that.

The way you fix this is very simple. In your `moveSomething` function (aka the event handler), simply add a call to `preventDefault` as highlighted:

```
function moveSomething(e) {
    switch(e.keyCode) {
        case 37:
            deltaX -= 2;
            break;
        case 38:
            deltaY -= 2;
            break;
        case 39:
            deltaX += 2;
            break;
        case 40:
            deltaY += 2;
            break;
    }
    e.preventDefault();

    drawTriangle();
```

```
}
```

The preventDefault method prevents your browser from reacting to any keyboard events as long as your page has focus. This ensures that you can do all sorts of keyboard-ey things inside your canvas without worrying about your key presses accidentally triggering normal (yet unwanted) browser behavior. The downside is that some **wanted** browser behavior using the keyboard will also be disabled. For example, if you expect visitors copy and paste content, if they use the keyboard shortcuts, they will be out of luck. The way to work around that is to put your `preventDefault` call inside each of the four arrow key case blocks instead. For what we are doing, any keyboard access outside of the arrow keys isn't very important.

Improved Keyhandling Logic

When talking about our current logic for dealing with the keyboard events, I mentioned that we are using a less-than-ideal solution. To see why, go back to your example and *press and hold* the Up and Right arrow keys at the same time. What you would expect to see is your triangle moving diagonally. What you actually see is your triangle moving in only one direction - either right or up. That isn't what we want!

The reason for this bizarre behavior is because we are using a `switch` statement to figure out which arrow key was pressed. There is nothing wrong with this general approach, for `switch` statements are far less verbose than `if/else-if` statements for checking which condition happens to equate to true. For many general cases, this is fine. How often are people going to hold down multiple keys at the same time? As it turns out, for the interactive/game-ey things that we are doing, pressing multiple keys will be a common occurrence. Pressing the Up and Right arrows on the keyboard at the same time is the equivalent of pushing a joystick diagonally. Don't tell me you've never done that before!

The solution is to change how we check for which key was pressed. Replace your existing `addEventListener` call and `moveSomething` function with the following instead:

```
var deltaX = 0;
```

```
var deltaY = 0;

window.addEventListener("keydown", keysPressed, false);
window.addEventListener("keyup", keysReleased, false);

var keys = [];

function keysPressed(e) {
    // store an entry for every key pressed
    keys[e.keyCode] = true;

    // left
    if (keys[37]) {
        deltaX -= 2;
    }

    // right
    if (keys[39]) {
        deltaX += 2;
    }

    // down
    if (keys[38]) {
```

```
        deltaY -= 2;

    }



    // up

    if (keys[40]) {

        deltaY += 2;

    }



    e.preventDefault();



    drawTriangle();

}



function keysReleased(e) {

    // mark keys that were released

    keys[e.keyCode] = false;

}
```

This code change looks pretty massive, but it's not that bad. What we've done is simply take our existing code and combine it with the Detecting Multiple Key Presses code you saw earlier. This change ensures that we can press multiple keys and get the desired behavior that we want. You can see that if you test your page out again and try pressing multiple arrow keys. Win!

Why we aren't using requestAnimationFrame

Earlier, when having a circle follow our mouse cursor around, we gave `requestAnimationFrame` the responsibility of drawing (and re-drawing) our circle. We didn't have our draw code be part of the **mousemove** event handler that fires each time your mouse cursor moves. That is in stark contrast to what we did here where our `moveSomething` (and `keysPressed`) event handlers are directly responsible for calling our `drawTriangle` function. Why did we do two different things in what looks like an identical situation?

The reason has to do with how chatty some events are with respect to your frame rate. The goal is to do work to update our screen at a rate that is consistent with our frame rate - ideally 60 times a second. Your **mousemove** event fires waaaaaaay too rapidly. Forcing things to get drawn with each **mousemove** fire would lead to a lot of unnecessary work with only a fraction of that work actually showing up on screen. That is why we defer drawing our circle in the **mousemove** case to `requestAnimationFrame` and its insane ability to stay in sync with the frame rate. Our **keydown** event (kinda like all keyboard events) is not very chatty at all. Having our keydown event handler (`moveSomething`) be responsible for drawing and shifting our triangle by two pixels is totally an OK call.

With all of this said, we will look at an example later where we will use `requestAnimationFrame` to **smoothly** move things using our keyboard!

Conclusion

Even in a world filled with devices where you touch and tap to do things, the keyboard is still very useful. Our goal was to move something around depending on which of the arrow keys was pressed. On the surface, this seemed like a very simple goal. As you saw in the many sections that followed our introduction, getting the basic functionality up and running was easy. Getting the functionality right turned out to be a bit more complicated.

In this chapter, we uncovered some of the biggest quirks involved with using the keyboard. Note that I didn't say that we covered **all of the quirks**. That honor is spread across a few more chapter we'll look at in the future where we touch upon some other keyboard and canvas-related shenanigans.

Chapter 23: Conclusion

In the past three hundred-ish pages, we covered a lot of ground! We started at the very beginning by learning about the differences between the canvas and the DOM, barreled through a ton of drawing-related topics afterwards, and slowly eased-out by learning about animation and interactivity. At this point, we've covered almost all there is to cover about what you can do on the `canvas`.

This doesn't mean we've learned all there is to learn. The material we looked at is only a fraction of the vast amount of things you can create using the `canvas`:

We just learned the basic building blocks. Putting these blocks together into interesting arrangements and structures is where your creativity and ingenuity comes in. This book isn't going to help with that, and that is deliberate. Where you go next is entirely domain specific. Are you interested in building games? Are you interested in creating visualizations? Is your goal to create a faster DOM entirely in the canvas? Depending on your answer on where you want to go next, there is a vast amount of material out there for you. The basics you learned in this book will have prepared you for whatever lies ahead.

Some Parting Words

I hope you really liked this book and found it informative...and maybe even sorta kinda funny at times! Before we part ways, I have a favor to ask you: If you have a few moments, please write a review on Amazon.com about your experiences. Even a short two-word review helps a lot in getting people to notice this book.

Also, to echo what I mentioned at the beginning, if you need any technical assistance, please post on the Forums: http://forum.kirupa.com. If you would like to contact me, please feel free to! I love hearing from readers like yourself. You can send e-mail to kirupa@kirupa.com, tweet to @kirupa, or message me on Facebook (facebook.com/kirupa). Don't be surprised if you see a response within 30 seconds of you sending me a message haha!

Until next time!

Cheers,

Kirupa

Kirupa ☺

Made in the USA
Lexington, KY
19 August 2016